Crescent City Girls

Crescent City Girls

The Lives of Young Black Women
in Segregated New Orleans

LaKisha Michelle Simmons

The University of North Carolina
Chapel Hill

893452563

This book was sponsored by the postdoctoral fellows program at the
Center for the Study of the American South, University of North
Carolina at Chapel Hill, and by the Julian Park Fund, College of Arts
and Sciences, University at Buffalo.

Set in Minion
by codeMantra, Inc.
Manufactured in the United States of America

The paper in this book meets the guidelines for permanence and
durability of the Committee on Production Guidelines for Book Longevity
of the Council on Library Resources.

The University of North Carolina Press has been a member
of the Green Press Initiative since 2003.

Cover illustration: The sophomore class of 1931 at McDonogh #35 High School in New Orleans
as pictured in *The Roneagle*, the school's yearbook (Courtesy of the Cherrie Family Collection)

Library of Congress Cataloging-in-Publication Data
Simmons, LaKisha Michelle.
Crescent City girls : the lives of young Black women in segregated
New Orleans / LaKisha Michelle Simmons.
pages cm. — (Gender and American culture)
Includes bibliographical references and index.
ISBN 978-1-4696-2280-4 (pbk : alk. paper) — ISBN 978-1-4696-2281-1 (ebook)
1. African American women—Louisiana—New Orleans—History—20th century.
2. African Americans—Louisiana—New Orleans—History—20th century.
3. Women—Louisiana—New Orleans—History—20th century. 4. African American
women—Louisiana—New Orleans—Social conditions—20th century.
5. African Americans—Louisiana—New Orleans—Social conditions—20th century.
6. Women—Louisiana—New Orleans—Social conditions—20th century.
7. Racism—Louisiana—New Orleans—History—20th century. 8. New Orleans (La.)—
Social conditions—20th century. 9. New Orleans (La.)—Race relations. I. Title.
F379.N59N447 2015
305.48'896073076335—dc23
2015003751

THIS BOOK WAS DIGITALLY PRINTED.

FOR

Jason, Idris, and Layla Young,
who make my every day rich and full of love.

AND FOR

the named and unnamed New Orleans women
in these pages.

Contents

Illustrations

Acknowledgments

I have looked forward to writing my acknowledgments since the day I began this book. Now that it is time, I find that I have so many people to thank, and for so much, that I have lost my words. What I have to say here can never be enough.

Much of what I know about New Orleans I have learned from Lolita Villavasso Cherrie. Her love of history and the archive sustained me whenever I went to New Orleans. She has supported me through research, writing, and difficult moments in my personal life. She has become a close friend and made New Orleans one of my homes. The very best of this research is influenced by her; my mistakes are all my own. Lolita also gave me the beautiful photograph for the cover of this book: it features Onelia Bazenac, Onelia Sayas, Marie Boyer, Edwina Boyer, Alphonsine Watts, Mildred Fauria, and Dorothy Jolissant from McDonogh #35's sophomore class of 1931. This book is written for them. I would like to thank Marie Boyer Brown, who, at ninety-three years old, remembered the names of every single one of her classmates in a 2007 oral history conducted by Lolita and myself. Mrs. Brown was a phenomenal woman.

I would like to thank all the extraordinary women who let me into their lives by agreeing to do an oral history. They have inspired me to be a better and stronger person; I will always be trying to live up to their examples. For their help in thinking through issues specific to New Orleans, I thank Catherine Michna; Leslie Harris; Jari Honora, my research assistant whom I met years ago when he was deep in the archive as a fourteen-year-old; and Clyde Woods, who was a mentor to so many. He is truly missed.

The archives and archivists I have worked with over the years also deserve mention: the Amistad Research Center at Tulane (especially Christopher Harter), the Hogan Jazz Archive at Tulane, the Newcomb Archive at Tulane, the Historic New Orleans Collection (especially Eric Seiferth), the New Orleans Public Library (especially Irene Wainwright and Greg Osborn), Xavier University Special Collections (especially Lester Sullivan, who is missed), the Special Collections Research Center at the University of Chicago Library, the John Hope Franklin Research Center (especially Karen

Jean Hunt) at Duke University, University of New Orleans Special Collections, the Hoover Institute, the Archdiocese of New Orleans (especially Lee Leumas), Susan Stauffer from Union Metal Corporation, Vickie Wilson at Johnson Publishing Company, and the Schomburg Center for Research in Black Culture.

As I have written this book, I have had the good fortune to work with a number of wonderful colleagues at Davidson College, at the University of North Carolina at Chapel Hill, and in the history and transnational studies departments at the University at Buffalo, SUNY. I would especially like to thank those who have mentored me or read large parts of the manuscript: Sally McMillen, Michael Meng, Hilton Kelly, Anderson Blanton, Marcie Ferris, Bill Ferris, Lisa Woolfork, Brian Balogh, Victoria Wolcott, Susan Cahn, Gwynn Thomas, Lillian Williams, Camilo Trumper, Dalia Muller, Carl Nightingale, Y. G. Lulat, and Keith Griffler. Deborah Pierce-Tate, Karen Reinard, and Beth Schonert provided day-to-day support, going above and beyond their job descriptions. I would also like to thank the wonderful group of friends who have had much cake together: Carole Emberton, Theresa Runstedtler, Theresa McCarthy, Cynthia Wu, Alyssa Mt. Pleasant, and Christine Varnado. For making Buffalo a place to call home, I thank the Wajed and Drayton families for their friendship.

I also thank Michele Mitchell and Hannah Rosen—their intellectual influence and guidance are on every page of this final product. I could not have finished this without them. Penny Von Eschen, Mary Kelley, and Jonathan Metzl are appreciated for their guidance and comments on this project. Penny, Kevin Gaines, and Maceo Gaines have become dear friends—I am thankful for all of their intellectual support, fellowship, and delicious food (most recently, two platefuls of breakfast scramble to help Layla grow!). The faculty and my fellow graduate students at the University of Michigan made graduate school intellectually exciting and rigorous—I miss that time and space. I would especially like to thank Tiffany McClain, Isabela Quintana, Monica Kim, Ying Zhang, Diana Mankowski, Alice Weinreb, and Emily Klancher, brilliant women who have sustained me with sisterhood and friendship. Sara Babcox First, Sherri Harper Charleston, Alice Weinreb, and Cookie Woolner read large parts of this book. Tamar Carroll and I have gone through the writing and editing process at the University of North Carolina Press together, and I am thankful that she is now living so near. And Michigan friends Melynda Price, Tandiwe Aebi-Moyo, Angela Parker, Alex Lovit, Dan Livesay, Clay Howard, Allison Abra, Isabel de Rezende, Nicol Partida, and Sara McClean, thank you for giving me support both professionally and personally.

The book has benefited from long discussions with Marisa Fuentes and Nathan Connolly. Rhonda Williams and Thadious Davis gave of their time to travel to Buffalo and comment on the entire manuscript. Their detailed comments, along with the anonymous reader reports from UNC Press, made this book much stronger. Chuck Grench from UNC Press has guided this project smoothly along its path.

Research for this book has been supported by the Mellon Postdoctoral Fellowship (Davidson College), the Center for the Study of the American South (UNC), the Baldy Center for Law and Social Policy (University at Buffalo), Rackham Graduate School (Michigan), the John Hope Franklin Research Center (Duke University), the Institute for Research on Women and Gender (Michigan), and the SUNY Faculty Diversity Program.

Finally, I thank my family: William Simmons, Michael Young, Patricia Whitt, Robby Whitt, "Memaw" Story, Roxanne Pittman, Arthur Perkins, Marta and D'Anthony Batiste, Alicia and Kenny Dalton, and the entire Dalton, Kohler, Pittman, Simmons, Story, West, and Young families. My sisters are my best friends: Brianna and Alicia. Solomon and Martha have taught me about enduring love and the mysteries of the past and hopeful futures. My mother, Cynthia Pittman, was my first teacher, nurturing my love of reading as a child. Now she is doing the same for her grandchildren. I could not have had the courage to start this project, or the time to finish, without her help. And Jason Young, my love for you spans centuries and galaxies. I am so glad to have taken that walk with you across that bridge between Indiana and Kentucky.

Crescent City Girls

Introduction

Growing Up within the Double Bind,
1930–1954

After a long fight to save his life, African American Willie McGee died in the electric chair in Mississippi in 1951, six years after he allegedly raped a white woman in Laurel. In this case, the justice system worked only as a lynch mob. On the occasion of McGee's death, the black newspaper in New Orleans, the *Louisiana Weekly*, opined, "There have been many 'Willie McGees' who have paid the supreme price, and whom the world has never heard about. Sometimes they get a trial and sometimes they don't. The dual system of justice only demands the life of a Negro for the crime of rape. How the God of white supremacy is satisfied doesn't really matter."[1] McGee's story hit close to home in New Orleans. The case was argued in circuit court in the city, and the *Louisiana Weekly* paid close attention to every development.

It may seem strange to begin a book about black girlhood in segregated New Orleans with a story about a man officially lynched by the American justice system 140 miles north of the city. Yet the *Louisiana Weekly*'s editorial, "What to Do about It!," offered another critique of southern justice, not only bemoaning McGee's death but also denouncing the other side of segregation's "dual system of justice"—black women and girls' inability to protect their bodies from the attack of white men. "Thousands of Negro women and children have been raped by white men," reported the *Weekly*; "seldom is the death penalty exacted." The author then told the story of a thirteen-year-old black girl raped by a white truck driver in New Orleans in 1949. The truck driver was found guilty only of carnal knowledge of a minor, not of rape, and therefore sentenced to one year in prison. There are many silences in this story. Historians know very little about the black girl who remained nameless in the *Louisiana Weekly* or countless others like her who experienced the violence of Jim Crow from the other side of white supremacy's "dual system of justice." *Crescent City Girls: The Lives of Young Black Women in Segregated New Orleans* asks, What was it like to grow up black and female in the

American South during legalized segregation—a period of state-sponsored racism and white supremacy?

I chose to begin this introduction with the *Louisiana Weekly*'s editorial on Willie McGee's death because it is a variation on a familiar theme of racialized violence in the segregated South—the (extralegal or legal) lynching of black men and boys for supposed trespasses over the color line. White attacks on black men who allegedly engaged in sex with white women served to prove white supremacist logic for segregation: white supremacists argued that black men were not qualified for full citizenship on the basis of their improper sexuality. Their narratives of sexually dangerous black men also worked to generate fear in white citizens that racial mixing would dilute white society.[2] Both unofficial and official lynching of black men functioned as a spectacle of violence during the Jim Crow years. White supremacists terrorized blacks publicly to instill fear.

Historians of Jim Crow have focused on the unequal justice system and the lynching of black men to explore the meanings of violence during segregation and to illuminate the links between sexuality, race, and segregation.[3] The taboo around color line crossing—sex between black men and white women—becomes a trope in this narrative.[4] For example, one historian explains the overlapping historiography of race and sex in this way: "The history of racial categories is often a history of sexuality as well, for it is partly as a result of the taboos against boundary crossing that such categories are invented."[5] Of course, the history of racial categories and sexuality in this formulation is conceptualized primarily through illicit sex between white women and black men, without taking into account the permissible— or, rather, tacitly tolerated—sex between white men and black women.

Historians of African American life have carefully demonstrated the ways in which black men encountered the violence of segregation and Jim Crow culture—through lynching, police brutality, economic terrorism, and a vastly unequal justice system.[6] Yet racial violence against black women has been little understood. Historian Jacquelyn Dowd Hall has noted that "most studies of racial violence have paid little attention to the particular suffering of [black] women" and includes her own early work in that group.[7] Along a similar line, Hazel Carby has argued that "the institutionalized rape of black women has never been as powerful a symbol of black oppression as the spectacle of lynching."[8] Historian Danielle McGuire has begun the important work of challenging histories of the Jim Crow South by documenting the rape of black women. McGuire pays particular attention to the ways such violence fueled the civil rights movement.[9] This renewed discussion of the violence of Jim Crow sheds light onto the relationship between racial violence and sexual violence. It is time to look at the question of the Jim Crow South anew. The recent focus on sexual violence by historians provides the opportunity to consider the wider connection to black women's sexuality and sense of self during the period. I am interested in understanding how the sexualized violence of Jim Crow affected black girls' coming-of-age. This is especially important given more recent revelations that a white employer may have sexually assaulted Rosa Parks—a major protagonist in McGuire's work—when she was just a teenager.[10]

During segregation, much of the violence against black girls remained in the shadows. Unlike lynching or even white economic intimidation of black male workers and business owners, violence against black women and girls was rarely intended as a public spectacle; indeed, much of the violence enacted on black women and girls required silences. White male violence against black girls had the power to collapse racial meanings because white men were supposed to be upright, controlled, thoughtful citizens. Therefore, source material often reveals the history of racial violence toward black men while telling incomplete stories about black women and girls' experience with racial violence. Indeed, the *Louisiana Weekly*'s editorial on Willie McGee serves as an example of this. Although we know many aspects of McGee's story, we know very little about the experiences of the nameless thirteen-year-old who was raped by a white man.

This book works to unveil the gendered violence of segregation from 1930 to 1954. In so doing, I begin to open up a place for the articulation of black girls' experience with the emotional and physical violence of Jim Crow. Among historians, and even in the general public, there is an incomplete understanding of how racial violence functioned in the Jim Crow South. Some gendered experiences of Jim Crow coming-of-age cannot be fully expressed or even conceptualized. For example, Ambassador Andrew Young reinforced this history when, just after Coretta Scott King's death, he spoke of her experience growing up with racism in the rural South. Young said that King had endured an extraordinarily "bitter experience of racism and segregation" during her childhood in Alabama because she witnessed the burning of her father's businesses by "Klan types." In Young's account, Coretta Scott King experienced racism primarily through the violence that happened *to her father.* Her own "bitter experiences" of growing up a girl during the Jim Crow era were unspoken; even in the moment of her memorial, there was no language to describe her coming-of-age during segregation. Harl Douglass, an educator and scholar of children, wrote in 1940,

"The American people have gone far to disinherit the Negro boy" economically. "Negro girls fare better than boys," he argued, "but they too constitute an important group among those which go to give us the American youth problem."[11] The idea that the racism of the United States had disinherited boys more so than girls speaks to the invisibility of black girls' experiences during the Jim Crow years.

Within the Double Bind

In segregated southern cities, the Jim Crow state partially dictated black youths' lives. Black girls encountered "For Whites Only" signs that dotted the urban landscape of segregated streetcars, schools, pools, lakes, zoos, and parks. They also faced the racist narratives of black femininity so common and deeply rooted in the larger Jim Crow South. For example, in 1895 Representative A. C. Tompkins of Kentucky argued against age of consent laws on the grounds that it was impossible for white men to rape black women. He declared, "We see at once what a terrible weapon for evil the elevating of the age of consent would be when placed in the hands of a lecherous, sensual negro woman, who for the sake of black mail or revenge would not hesitate to bring criminal action even though she had been a prostitute since her *eleventh year!*"[12] Such sentiments, whether articulated through politics, local law enforcement, or cultural productions and images, partly shaped black girls' coming-of-age during Jim Crow.

At the same time that black girls faced the restraints of legalized segregation and the violence of white supremacy, they also negotiated middle-class African Americans' notions of what a proper girl should be: pure and respectable. Public discourses in the African American community—by sociological experts, pastors, clubwomen, newspaper editors, activists, and schoolteachers—demanded that girls defend their chastity and honor against the encroachments of white men.

Often, respectability corresponded with class status, but it also transcended customary notions of class partly because of the "quickening of class stratification within African American communities."[13] Respectability represented an ideal for the proper behavior of the middle class and the "aspiring" or "striving" class of black men and women—people who attempted to reach middle-class status, not necessarily through higher incomes and "better" jobs but through an adoption of a specific set of mores.[14] Civil rights activist Lolis Elie described black New Orleans class distinctions in just this way. In his neighborhood he remembered the black middle class at the top, the "blues people" who represented the poor, and those of the striving class in the middle whose mothers woke early, readied their children for school, worked tirelessly caring for white homes and white children, and then "returned to their own houses and their own children where they again cooked, cleaned, served and loved and grew flowers and prayed. Three days of work in one."[15] For both the middle class and striving class, the ideology of respectability dictated how young women interacted with the city, what they wore, how they carried themselves, and, in turn, how they understood themselves. The emphasis on traditional notions of virtue and dignity in the black middle-class and striving-class communities reminded young black women that their acceptance and belonging within the middle-class black community, and their value in the fight for racial justice, hinged on their respectability.

The ways in which black girls negotiated these two poles—racialized violence in the Jim Crow South and the social constraints imposed by the black community—make up the central focus of *Crescent City Girls*. This book examines black girls' lives, subjectivities, and expressions of self within the double bind of white supremacy and respectability from 1930 to 1954 in New Orleans. White supremacy and the restrictions imposed by respectability are not analogous—certainly, the constraints of racism, racial violence, and segregation affected black girls' worlds more than all else. However, both white supremacy and ideologies of respectability were strictures influencing young women's personhood and subjectivity. They were the two lenses through which girls came to understand themselves and their place in the world.

Although I do not invoke the term "subjectivity" at all points throughout the book, the concept frames my study. Subjectivity is the making of the self and can be best understood "as a verb as opposed to a noun" because it is "a process, as opposed to an identity or a stable thing."[16] Subjectivity is historically specific. Based on "positionality" and "standpoint," the self comes into being at intersections, at "the spaces of dynamic encounter."[17] Many different, often contradictory experiences constituted black girls' subjectivities during Jim Crow. Some of these experiences were linguistic, such as being called a monkey on the street. Others were experiences of the body, such as being sexually accosted by a white man while riding a streetcar. Some experiences were spatial—for instance, knowing that one could not play at a whites-only city park a few blocks from one's home. Others were cultural, such as entering a Catholic church on a Sunday morning. Still others were familial and emotional, such as a young girl's relationship to her mother, who tried to protect her daughters from physical assaults by white men. Therefore, black girls' subjectivities were never completely stable or fixed because they encountered a multitude of conflicting experiences and because youths' worlds were always changing. Reconstructing black girls' subjectivity can never be a completed project. But doing so even in part provides a glimpse into their inner worlds, emotions, and psychic structures.

By conceptualizing black girls' coming-of-age through their subjective experiences, this work builds on studies in African American gender history. This area of study has established the groundwork for thinking about the "inner lives" of black women. In 1989 historian Darlene Clark Hine asked what noneconomic motives had driven black women to join the Great Migration, escape the confines of the South, and move to the Midwest, North, or West. She began by looking for the "hidden motivation" in black women's migratory patterns and theorized that the greatest factor was their desire to possess rights to their own bodies, fleeing from both interracial sexual violence and domestic abuse. That struggle for reproductive freedom and bodily autonomy, she argued, was difficult to recover because black women hid their inner struggles from racist, judgmental eyes, creating a "culture of dissemblance." By choosing the word "dissemblance," Hine emphasized "the behavior and attitudes of Black women that created the appearance of openness and disclosure but actually shielded the truth of their inner lives and selves from their oppressors."[18] The culture of dissemblance created a veil of secrecy and silence around black women and girls' daily struggles and also around their sense of inner self. This secrecy is often reflected in the archive, creating yet another layer of silence.

Still, Hine's work opened up a space for new scholarship on black women's history by highlighting black women's struggles with violence; over the past decade, scholars have begun to fill the lacunae on the racial history of sexual violence.[19] In addition to confronting issues of sexual violence, this book is also interested in black girls' "inner lives"—a phrase Hine used in the title of her 1989 essay. By choosing the term, she asked scholars of black women to think closely about subjective experience and psychic worlds. In other words, scholars of African American gender history need to work to fill in the silences left by editorials such as the *Louisiana Weekly's* "What to Do about It!" I read the culture of dissemblance as an affective culture; it was the method by which black women dealt with their emotions and shielded themselves from further psychic harm. Dissemblance, Hine argued, was a "self-imposed invisibility" that gave black women the "psychic space" for "mental and physical survival in a hostile world."[20] This psychic space was just as important for black girls' survival as it was for black women. Turning to the construction of black girls' subjectivities is one way to begin to investigate psychic worlds and articulate a story rarely told.

Black Girls' Coming-of-Age

Black adolescent girls—which I broadly define as girls and young women between the ages of nine to twenty—are at the center of this study. In 1930 there were over 12,000 black girls in New Orleans in this age group, forming 2.6 percent of the total population.[21] These young women, who grew up in the Jim Crow South, came to understand themselves in a world segregated by color; later, they became women with notions of race, gender, place, and justice informed by the childhood experiences delineated in these pages. I believe this period of adolescence is crucial to the formation of girls' subjectivity.

The categories of girl, child, and adolescent have their own complex histories. Feminist scholars interested in the burgeoning field of girls' studies (as well as childhood studies) have begun to trace out a genealogy of girlhood.[22] Ideas about "feminine adolescence" took shape at the turn of the century through the work of G. Stanley Hall and Sigmund Freud and a few years later by Havelock Ellis, Margaret Mead, and others.[23] They hypothesized that adolescence was a period of transition and change. For young women, this was imagined as a phase between childhood and the eventuality of womanhood. The process of adolescence was understood as somatic (going through puberty and becoming sexual subjects), psychological (developing mentally, emotionally, and cognitively), and cultural (being part of a group of youth with a specific culture). By the 1920s and 1930s, scientists, scholars, and doctors of childhood development emphasized adolescence as a signature diagnostic moment.[24] Unhealthy and unstable sexual and social psyches revealed themselves during adolescence. African American writers and scholars often judged the health and future of the race by studying black adolescent sexual and social behavior.[25] Although many of these scholars cited Hall and Freud, they most often employed the term "youth," as did the black newspapers. During the 1930s and 1940s, the African American press investigated the "youth problem"; black New Orleans, like other cities, believed it was combating a rise in religious apathy, delinquency, truancy, and alcoholism among its young people.[26]

By the early 1950s, the idea of female adolescence as a transitional period linking girlhood and womanhood became firmly established in American popular culture and scientific thought. Marking less a specific age and more a period of life, adolescence was thought to affect each girl differently in length and timing, but every girl transitioned through adolescence all the same. In *Personality Development in Adolescent Girls*, originally published in 1951, the authors defined adolescence and "late adolescence" as the moments of development just before puberty, during puberty, and several years past menarche when girls were *almost* fully sexually mature.[27] For these authors, this most often occurred in the "second decade" of life, from ages ten to twenty. They noted, "Every girl in the second decade of life is undergoing much the same process of maturation as other girls, as she grows and develops, slowly or rapidly matures into an adult woman and faces the inescapable life tasks presented by our culture to adolescent females."[28] Even so, the authors of the study believed that girls of certain "ethnic-cultural" groups learned "traditional beliefs" unfit for modern living. These girls, according to the authors of the study, "exhibit what at first appears to be indications of actual or incipient pathology."[29] White scholars such as these often linked black girlhood with a failure to develop properly.

By laying out this genealogy of adolescence, I want to point to the curious intersections between girlhood, race, and subjectivity. According to experts and reformers of the time of this study, black girls' coming-of-age marked a period when they were *supposed* to learn how to become a full, gendered person and to discover how to inhabit a particular identity. Following this logic, this project asks how girls came to understand themselves as black women. Studying girlhood allows me to turn to this crucial moment in the formation of subjectivity. How were girls taught to behave? How were black girls, in the Jim Crow order, expected to understand themselves, and how, in turn, did they comprehend themselves? The importance of such questions is reflected in gender theorist Jack Halberstam's discussion of girls' coming-of-age: "Female adolescence represents the crisis of coming of age as a girl in a male-dominated society. If adolescence for boys represents a rite of passage (much celebrated in Western literature in the form of *bildungsroman*), and an ascension to some version (however attenuated) of social power, for girls adolescence is a lesson in restraint, punishment, and repression. It is in the context of female adolescence that the tomboy instincts of millions of girls are remolded into compliant forms of femininity."[30]

For black girls coming of age during Jim Crow, the "crisis" of growing up took place in the context of a white supremacist society. As such, for black girls, the racialized context informed each lesson "in restraint, punishment, and repression." Punishment and repression existed in the very real forms of racial violence—not solely linguistic violence, such as jeers and taunts on the streets, but also sexual and physical violence perpetrated by white men who believed they had unmitigated access to young black bodies. For black girls, lessons in restraint, silence, and dissemblance were also basic lessons in physical and psychic survival. Further, learning "compliant" femininity meant something particular for black girls—it connoted what *black women* "ought to be and to do."[31] At best, white New Orleanians believed black adolescent girls ought to remain in their place—subservient and obedient to the Jim Crow order. At worst, white New Orleanians believed black adolescent girls ought to be available, physically and sexually, to the demands of whites. Meanwhile, black New Orleanians had grander expectations for their daughters. They aspired to keep their children safe and protected; they wanted their young women to remain pure and nice. Middle-class black New Orleanians, and those who aspired to middle-class status, wanted their daughters to obtain an education, becoming part of a black professional class.

The Sources of Childhood: Toward a Methodology of "Disciplined Imagination"

Historians of childhood and youth continually draw analogies to ethnic and minority studies in order to describe the archival challenges of the field. In the inaugural edition of the *Journal of the History of Childhood and Youth*, for example, Joseph Hawes and Ray Hiner describe childhood history as a "subaltern field" akin to African American history or gay and lesbian history.[32] Peter Stearns goes a step further, suggesting that finding children's voices in the archives represents a "virtually unprecedented problem of getting information."[33] It is clear from these comparisons and in the conversations surrounding methodology in the field that there is a considerable archival challenge for historians of children. If an analogy between minority histories and childhood histories exists, then researchers of minority children face an even more daunting task. Are children of color doubly invisible in the archives?

Comparisons of ethnic studies and childhood studies appear to work as a rhetorical strategy, emphasizing the difficulty of finding sources on children's lives (especially sources authored by children). At the same time, the comparisons also bring to bear the ways in which historians of childhood and youth have gained insight from historical fields that have had to think broadly and carefully about the archive. Nonetheless, when the analogies between ethnic studies and childhood studies are made, children of color are erased from the conversation. Children—in these conversations—are conceptualized as white children.

Despite archival challenges, pursuing this history, for me, has been a political project. If historians assume that certain stories are impossible to tell because of a lack of sources, then some lives remain outside the bounds of scholarly importance. These people are usually the most marginalized in a given society—left without a voice and a history. I believe, however, there is an importance in telling stories built from fractured and incomplete pieces. *Crescent City Girls* makes use of a wide range of sources. While all of these sources are flawed—each in their own way—they each contribute to a larger story. I have built this story from oral histories, the black and white press, social workers' reports, social scientists' documents, delinquency home records, police reports, school records, girls' fiction writing, autobiographies, photography, and interviews with girls in New Orleans. At crucial moments in the text, these sources allow me to tell the stories of individual girls: some from poor working-class families, others caught in the Jim Crow judicial system, and others from middle-class, "respectable" families. At times, this collection of stories and voices comes together as a cohort biography of ordinary girls living in an extraordinary time, of girls who did not intend to make history. The nature of this archive has shaped my methodological choices.

By employing what Paula Fass has called "disciplined imagination," this book demonstrates a methodology for social history that gets at the emotional inner worlds that historians often assume are inaccessible in the archive.[34] Linking methods from social history (such as having an interest in the everyday, examining collections of a variety of source materials, engaging in systematic research, and studying a single location) and from cultural studies (such as deconstructing sources, paying careful attention to narrative constructions, studying individual subjectivities, and purposefully looking for gaps, silences, and inconsistencies), *Crescent City Girls* argues that discovering information about the inner lives of marginalized and sometimes invisible citizens is indeed possible.

For this project, the "disciplined" piece of disciplined imagination required systemic research into all of New Orleans' numerous archives and investigation into archives throughout the country that hold information on the city. In the archives I became a miner, looking for any usable and even seemingly unusable scrap. The "imagination" part of the puzzle required new ways of looking at and using sources and scraps that might otherwise be discarded by historians. To this end, I interpret my sources and explore black girls' Jim Crow lives through three interrelated analytic categories: geography, sexuality, and affect. The three analytic categories work to structure the book and represent my methodological choices. This means that I interpret the source material through the lenses of cultural geography, the history of sexuality, and affect studies. Merging approaches from these fields, I have been able to open up a wider world of possible materials and information and a new way of thinking about traditional sources.

Geography

Crescent City Girls is as much a story about New Orleans as it is about girlhood. The first theme, geography, is central to the narrative. My interest in space began deep in the archives. Sources continued to point to the importance of the spatial world, particularly oral histories that emphasized the geographies of local neighborhoods and their relationship to black girls' varying experiences of segregation and definitions of self. One interviewee, for example, noted that black New Orleanians "were very neighborhood-conscious, and unless you had relatives who were living in another section of the city, you were not likely to cross Canal Street, which was considered the boundary for downtown and uptown."[35] The field of cultural geography helped me better understand the Jim Crow city that came to life in the recollections of interviewees. Cultural geography expanded my readings of other source material as well, including maps, buildings, and photographs.

Reading these sources in tandem, I found that the physical placement of buildings revealed black youths' relationship to power in the city. How did black girls travel to and from these spaces? How did they interact with the geographies inside and outside of the buildings? Approaching the question of space in this way brings into view lived experiences of segregation through a street-by-street and neighborhood analysis. Understanding racialized geographies teaches us to note what space is "occupied by the colonized, the enslaved, the incarcerated, the disposable."[36] In segregated New Orleans, that means looking to neighborhoods and analyzing the occupants' access to safety, protection, sanitation, and livable conditions. Racialized geographies also point clearly to the politics of "racial-sexual domination" on which these neighborhoods were built.[37] The nature of segregated space differed in each area of New Orleans; black girls were aware of this as they crisscrossed the city streets. As children

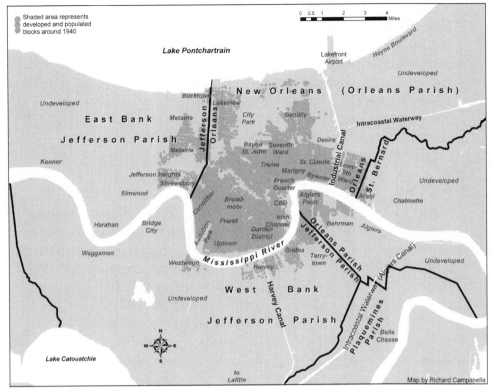

FIGURE I.1. New Orleans, ca. 1940 (map by Richard Campanella)

navigated the city, their subjectivities shifted with the changing nature of power and space. Many historians conceptualize segregation on a larger scale through analyses of, for instance, state politics, legal statutes, or the justice system. My analysis, however, maps the culture of segregation at a microlevel because this is how many children experienced segregation in their daily lives.

Cultural geography also helped me reexamine notions of "place" in segregated spaces. Doing so unveiled gendered violence in new and important ways; I saw more clearly what spaces were dangerous for black girls, where they commonly experienced sexual harassment, and where they might find safety. This focus on the meanings of space challenges scholars of the American South whose theorizations of "place" during segregation center primarily on social performance. For example, Neil McMillen argues that "place" has always implied "behavioral" rather than spatial relationships for southern whites. Whites, he maintains, were less interested in the question of proximity to blacks than they were in social hierarchies and etiquette. From this he concludes that "place" did not have spatial meaning; other scholars have since followed his insight.[38] However, by focusing on geography it becomes clear that social performances of place occur in space soaked in meanings of power, particularly when these performances take place in an urban center. Even more, proximity itself is a spatial relationship; thus, when blacks and whites are near one another in social space, relationships of power expressed through spatial economies are still at work. For example, how might a young black women working as a waitress think about "proximity" and "place" when white male customers sexually harass her?

Notions of place were also determined by geographies of exclusion; this is clear when we examine the standpoint of black youth rather than that of upper-class white southerners who were more interested in hierarchy than in thinking about relationships of proximity. Black children's encounters in public spaces such as parks and in private spaces such as stores taught them lessons in exclusion and rejection. Exclusion and rejection and, in turn, acceptance and safety were ways in which black girls began to understand themselves in connection to the racialized world around them. These encounters occurred because of and on the raced body. As Thadious Davis explores in *Southscapes*, the body is a "geographic construct" that functions as a "spatial parameter or boundary."[39] Experiences of exclusion, then, were also intimately embodied and embodying experiences. Based on their particular experiences with geographies of exclusion, black girls' relationship to and conceptualization of the city's landscape was markedly different from that of black and white boys or white girls and contributed significantly to their notions of self.

In linking space and subjectivity in this way, *Crescent City Girls* rethinks southern cities during the Jim Crow era. To date, work on childhood and segregation, including Jennifer Ritterhouse's *Growing Up Jim Crow* and Susan Cahn's *Southern Reckonings*, have focused on large regions of the South (both rural and urban), considerable swaths of time, and both black and white children.[40] By centering on black girls living in a single city, this work challenges these two scholars' notions of and assumptions about the Jim Crow city. Ritterhouse traces the spatial aspect of "racial etiquette" to the plantation South without investigating the changed nature of space in the modern southern city. Meanwhile, Cahn's sources and methodology do not give her access to the differences between rural and urban space or between large southern cities and smaller towns. The methodological focus on urban space in *Crescent City Girls* demonstrates how in southern cities, at Jim Crow's very center, there was a regulation of geography that relied on gendered and sexed notions of spatial power.

In this context, the specific history and place of New Orleans becomes important. New Orleans, Louisiana, is a compelling site for studying the geography of the double bind. By the start of the twentieth century, New Orleans had become a vibrant southern urban center shaped by de jure segregation. By 1930, black New Orleanians faced the violence of white supremacy in their daily lives, not only through segregation laws but also through a particularly brutal police department.

In addition, New Orleans' historically strong black middle class provides another entrée into the double bind. The city, home to two black colleges, helped to train and educate the black middle class. And black Creoles of the city had acquired some small amount of wealth, land, and prestige. Referred to as *gens de couleur libres* (free people of color) prior to the Civil War, and Creoles after, this class of New Orleanians traced their roots to France, Spain, and Africa as well as to Haiti and Cuba.[41] Thus, the politics of respectability in black New Orleans was also deeply entrenched in complex negotiations of ethnicity, genealogy, and skin color. Throughout this book I use "black Creole" and "American black" to mark the distinctions between the two groups of New Orleanians. These terms are imperfect and represent the limitations of language when describing complex constructions of race and ethnicity in New Orleans.[42]

As John Blassingame has explained it, "The association of color with a certain social class was due primarily to historical accident and was not immutable."[43] Class and color have never fit neatly in New Orleans; and color itself is not what divided social and economic classes, or black Creoles from American blacks in the city. Nonetheless, black Creoles had greater access to skilled trades, wealth, and education. (And although this was still true by the 1930s, it was less so than in the 1860s.) These complex negotiations of class and color were both Caribbean and southern in character.[44] Because of this, New Orleans has long been noted as an exceptional city. Yet in some ways crucial to this project, New Orleans was also typical of other southern cities. Although New Orleans' history of *gens de couleur libres* is specific to Louisiana, the history of black Creoles in New Orleans speaks to conflicts of class and color in black communities throughout the South, particularly in Washington, D.C., and Charleston, South Carolina. Therefore, larger lessons about how segregation worked in a variety of segregated cities may be drawn from this study.

Sexuality

Sexuality, this book's second theme, helps me uncover wider networks of power that shaped black girls' everyday lives and subjectivities and provides the framework for understanding the double bind in New Orleans. Investigating sexuality allows for space to talk about the ways in which young black women experienced violence in their lives but also highlights the cultural constraints of respectability.

I work with a broad definition of sexuality, one that encompasses more than simply "sex." I understand sexuality to be the various social and cultural restrictions related to sex that constrain people's behavior by literally disciplining their bodies but that also allow for places of intimacy and pleasure. My attention to sexuality is also closely related to my interest in racial subjectivities because the development and maintenance of racial categories have been historically tied to the regulation of sexuality. This nexus can be articulated as "racialized sexuality"—that place where "the deployment of sexuality intersects with the deployment of race."[45] Throughout this book, I understand sexuality in this way, as always already connected to the politics of race.

Because black women and girls have often avoided overt discussions of sex, sexuality, and bodies in public space, sources relating to their histories of sexuality are sometimes difficult to find. As a methodological strategy, I read all sources carefully for moments of silence. An oral history interviewee, for example, who asked the interviewer to cease recording for a moment just as she began to speak about sexual harassment may have been asking for the privacy to relate her own painful experience. Meanwhile, a black girl interviewed by a sociologist might have been attempting to discuss rape and race but only when safely couched within another story—a story about how white men refuse to remain in their proper "place." My method of reading silence requires analysis of when, where, and how these silences occur. At times they exist in vocal intonation, in deliberate gaps in narration, or within stories that focus on secrets. Attention to these types of silences provides a technique to interrogate and challenge the culture of dissemblance, revealing exactly where and how sexuality was central to young black women's coming-of-age.

Even though the culture of dissemblance hid much about the sexual lives of black girls and young women, there were also public discussions of black female sexuality in 1930s–1950s New Orleans. These public discourses of sexuality were most often related to the policing of black bodies by whites or by middle-class African Americans. From the turn of the century to the 1950s, questions of delinquency among youth—both black and white—dominated sociological and popular discourse.[46] So-called wayward girls were often marked as delinquent through their sexuality and bodies. Therefore, the conversations about race and female delinquency provide one avenue for exploring the importance of sexuality in black youths' lives. Discussions of black delinquents in New Orleans among the local law enforcement and charity systems demonstrate how black girls' bodies were disciplined at both the state and religious level. At the same time, discourses of respectability were also public, leaving traces in the archive. Respectability was a central topic of discussion in black newspapers as well as among black intellectuals and activists at the time, who left behind writings and archives.

Although all girls—black and white—faced expectations about the "proper" way to behave and act, the politics of respectability were entangled with a specific racial politics. As Evelyn Brooks Higginbotham explains, "Respectability demanded that every individual in the black community assume responsibility for behavioral self-regulation and self-improvement along moral, educational, and economic lines; the goal was to distance oneself as far as possible from images perpetuated by racist stereotypes."[47] At every moment, the culture of respectability was intertwined with what it meant to be a black American in the early twentieth century and with expectations for personal and group advancement in a world that looked on blackness with scorn.[48] Therefore, for young black women in particular, lessons in respectability were undergirded by hopes for political and social equality. African American gender historians have discussed discourses of respectability by analyzing textual sources such as clubwomen's and churchwomen's writings, urban reform, etiquette manuals, and literature.[49] This book, however, focuses on how these discourses constrained young women and girls' daily lives, how girls and young women interpreted them, and how the discourses of respectability provided, at times, avenues of positive self-identification.

Methods from the study of sexuality allow me to do more than outline the ways in which black girls' bodies were disciplined by Jim Crow society and by the politics of respectability. By making use of methods from the study of sexuality that focus on intimacy, pleasure, and love, I am able to explore how black youth in New Orleans created small moments of pleasure and play in their lives. Pleasurable sexuality also existed within the double bind. To uncover moments of pleasure, I turn to sources authored by black girls in small spaces of freedom. Photographs that detail dances, romantic writings, and adolescents' reading materials all help me begin to open up a space to talk about sexuality and pleasure. Exploring pleasure and subjectivity in this way, I am able to rethink "racialized sexuality" to include a politics of pleasure. Such a focus has been lacking in most studies of racialized sexuality during Jim Crow. For example, Danielle McGuire's work on civil rights activism, *At the Dark End of the Street: Black Women, Rape, and Resistance*, does not have a framework that allows for the existence of sexual pleasure in black women's lives. Her focus on violence and activist responses necessarily highlights trauma, particularly at the community level.

Many historians have noted that "sexuality has increasingly become a core element of modern social identity, constitutive of being, consciousness and action."[50] For young black women in New Orleans, sexuality dominated their subjectivities. Whether they were defined as respectable or as delinquent girls, this book shows how they came to understand themselves in relationship to sexualized categories.

Affect

Nina Simone, who grew up in Jim Crow North Carolina during the 1930s and 1940s, was asked as an adult if she "felt" injustice as a child. Simone responded emotionally, "All my life. Ever since I can remember. Even when I first started to take piano lessons, I felt it then. I knew what I was thought of. And I had to go across the tracks to the white side of town to even take my music lessons. And every Saturday that I did it, I felt it. I felt it all my life."[51] This book's third theme, affect, explores black girls' subjectivity by focusing on their emotional lives. What did it feel like to be a black girl living under Jim Crow? What does it feel like to be black when blackness connotes second-class citizenship? W. E. B. Du Bois asks the question in this way: "What does it feel like to be a problem?" His answer to this question, double consciousness, remains a central framework for understanding black identity:

> The Negro is a sort of seventh son, born with a veil, and gifted with
> second-sight in this American world,—a world which yields him
> no true self-consciousness, but only lets him see himself through
> the revelation of the other world. It is a peculiar sensation, this
> double-consciousness, this sense of always looking at one's self
> through the eyes of others, of measuring one's soul by the tape of
> a world that looks on in amused contempt and pity. One ever feels
> his two-ness,—an American, a Negro; two souls, two thoughts, two
> unreconciled strivings; two warring ideals in one dark body, whose
> dogged strength alone keeps it from being torn asunder.[52]

This feeling of blackness, in Du Bois's theoretical framework, is highly gendered. For him, the white world's vision of the black self stifled the natural physical and intellectual powers of black men, causing them to appear and feel weakened and unmanly: "The black man's turning hither and thither in hesitant and doubtful striving has often made his very strength to lose effectiveness, to seem like absence of power, like weakness. And yet it is not weakness,—it is the contradiction of double aims." Du Bois places the problem of double consciousness into the problem of masculine coming-of-age, of gaining social power; he argues that the "longing to attain self-conscious manhood" is the history of the American Negro.[53]

Crescent City Girls builds from Du Bois's question—how does it feel to be a problem?—but reframes the question from the standpoint of a young black woman. This attention to gender changes our very notion of double consciousness. Black girls, too, are looking at themselves through the eyes of others. In New Orleans, they saw themselves through the eyes of whites but also through the eyes of middle-class blacks who attempted to regulate their behavior, bodies, and sexuality. This feeling—of being stuck within the double bind—helps us understand the structure of black girls' emotional lives. By examining a wide range of sources through the lens of cultural studies, including interviews with children, children's fictional writing, oral histories, delinquency records, newspapers, and social workers' reports, *Crescent City Girls* pushes past the culture of dissemblance that shielded black female inner worlds to discuss both trauma and pleasure in young black women's emotional lives.

Such a project is crucial not only for uncovering the trauma of racial violence—and thus the segregated South's true character—but also for understanding the legacy of that violence today. Furthermore, by investigating emotions, *Crescent City Girls* takes seriously black girls' full personhood. As Nell Painter underscores in her essay "Soul Murder and Slavery," "the first step is to think about slaves as people with all the psychological characteristics of human beings, with childhoods and adult identities formed during youthful interaction with others."[54] My first step, then, has been to always treat black girls as full human beings with a wide variety of emotions, including both fear and pleasure. My attempt to look at emotional worlds has been aided by the recent turn to "affect studies" in cultural studies, histories of emotion by early modern scholars, as well as by scholars of African American life who have interrogated the links between trauma and memory, particularly in the history of American slavery.[55]

New Orleans in Black and White

Youth growing up in urban New Orleans encountered a racial geography marked by various neighborhoods and spaces—whites dominated some spaces, blacks others, but many spaces were interracial. As one memoirist has written, "It's not easy to pin down the essence of New Orleans, because in many ways it is a city of contrasts and contradictions."[56] The racial ideology of the Jim Crow city was full of "contrasts and contradictions." New Orleans was at once racially diverse, with a population more dynamic than simply "colored" and "white," while simultaneously strictly segregated along those two axes. Officially, black New Orleanians made up 27.2 percent of the population in 1930, while whites accounted for 69.4 percent.[57] This racial breakdown remained relatively steady throughout the 1930s and 1940s, even with the outmigration of black southerners to northern and western cities during and after World War II. However, a simple breakdown of "colored" and "white" cannot capture the deep complexity and diversity of the city's racial geography and history.

The black population of New Orleans was multiethnic and varied, resulting in muddy, if not fluid, racial categories. As a teenager, Eileen Julien left segregated New Orleans to attend college in New England, but her girlhood in New Orleans influenced her racial subjectivity. In college she became politically active, but, as she explained, her sense of blackness was "different from other black students. . . . For them, black and white were hard and fast opposites; for me—even as I knew the scourge of racism—they were tendencies on a continuum. There were too many blurred categories back home, too many shades in my own family and an acceptance of those shades as entirely normal, something that would begin to make better sense [much later], when I picked up Gwendolyn Midlo Hall's *Africans in Colonial Louisiana*."[58] Hall's pathbreaking work explains the historical foundation for black cultural diversity in New Orleans by detailing the ethnic diversity of Louisiana's enslaved population, the influence of the French and Spanish, and the creolized culture that developed; importantly, the book marked Louisiana as the most "African" colony.[59] Arnold Hirsch has since extended the analysis of black cultural and ethnic diversity between "Franco-Africans" and "African Americans" into the twentieth century. The harsh realities of Jim Crow, he argues, sought to "submerge what remained of a stubbornly persistent sense of ethnic difference in the black community" between black Creoles and American blacks.[60] Thus, segregation in New Orleans officially divided the city simply between white and "colored," while black cultural life simultaneously marked black neighborhoods, institutions, and even some schools as American black or black Creole.

Whiteness in New Orleans was also diverse: there remained a small but culturally significant Jewish population in the city as well as a sizable immigrant population. Jewish settlers had come to colonial New Orleans as early as the eighteenth century; in the 1930s, the Jewish population was about 1.5 percent of the total.[61] During segregation, whites-only clubs and social organizations refused Jewish New Orleanians.[62] The city also had diverse immigrant communities; according to the census, the "foreign born" population was at 9 percent in 1900, 8 percent in 1910, 5.3 percent in 1920, and 3.1 percent by 1930, remaining steadily there through the early 1950s. Because of this, New Orleans was home to many first- and second-generation children who made up diverse white ethnic (Italian, Irish, German, white Haitian) and minority (black Haitian, Mexican, Chinese) populations.[63] Therefore, understanding the city as white and "colored" is only a starting point. White segregationists fiercely inscribed this binary onto the city, but within the strict separation there existed a history and culture much more complex.

Indeed, the city was one of "contrasts and contradictions" because this racial, ethnic, and cultural diversity existed alongside Jim Crow's white/"colored" racial binary. Segregation was an unrelenting project, endlessly inscribing and reinscribing boundaries and barriers. A memoir written by two white New Orleanians demonstrates the danger of romanticizing the racial fluidity of New Orleans in the 1930s and 1940s. Their work erases black lives and describes the strict bifurcation of race in the city despite its diversity. "Racially, New Orleans was then a predominantly white community," they recall. "Almost seventy percent of its citizens were white and thirty percent were black. Demographically, it was the most integrated city in the United States with blacks and whites living in close proximity in almost every residential area of the city. That was as far as integration went, however."[64] That the authors can at once declare New Orleans a "white community" in one sentence and then speak of the "integrated" nature of the demographics in the next suggests that they understood very little about black New Orleans. Nor did they see black New Orleanians as a constitutive or vital part of the larger New Orleans community. In their childhood, black and white were strictly separated socially; they have few memories of blacks or black culture outside their interactions with their maids or nannies.

Some memoirists or oral history interviewees remember more than just integrated neighborhoods; some also recall integrated play as young children. This play, however, had its limits. In an oral history interview, Joycelyn

Hyman and Ann Stuart recalled playing with white children in elementary school. Stuart remembered that in her neighborhood this integrated play ended around junior high school. It was then that the white kids "pulled away," becoming distant or unfriendly.[65] Hyman also interacted with white children in her mostly white neighborhood. They would play marbles and baseball, and the white kids would even come over to her house to watch a small black and white television. In the 1940s, few families, white or black, owned television sets in her neighborhood. But by the time she entered the seventh grade, all of her white friends had stopped speaking to her. Hyman recalled, "All of a sudden you could hear the word 'nigger' in my community." At that moment, for Hyman, "everything changed; it was very different. I mean, very, very different."[66] In remembering the moment when the white children stopped speaking to her, Hyman slowly chose her words, her voice grew serious, and her eyes watered. She attempted to communicate the emotional weight of the isolation she felt at the time, knowing it was because she was "colored." The years of junior high school were extremely difficult for her; this was an emotional lesson to be learned, a lesson highlighting the difference between black and white in the city. For Hyman and other black girls, "integrated" neighborhoods of New Orleans also carried lessons of social segregation. As this complex racial, ethnic, and geographic history shows, the city's black and white populations overlapped even when they did not interact. Black girls navigated these "contrasts and contradictions" in a demographically diverse city.

THE ECONOMIC AND POLITICAL backdrop to this story of black girlhood in New Orleans is the Great Depression of the 1930s, the social transformations of World War II and the postwar era, and the Great Migration of black southerners northward and westward. These changes affected all New Orleanians, but for many black women and men, change was uneven and racial violence and economic injustice remained constant themes. Of the Great Depression, one Works Progress Administration informant in New Orleans mused, "I got through the Depression all right. It doesn't do to complain about things—anybody'd better just keep goin' and make the best of it. As far as the Depression is concerned, the colored man has always had a hard time. If a man has a large salary and it's cut off, it makes a big difference. But the colored man hasn't. So he gets along about the same as usual."[67] The Jim Crow realities of the Great Depression and that of the postwar period took a slightly different shape for black children. By the late 1940s, facing lawsuits from the NAACP, the city invested more money in segregated facilities for black citizens. City officials opened a new public (industrial) high school for blacks, created some playgrounds, and improved Lincoln Beach for black bathers.[68] But still, much of this "improvement" was reactionary rather than visionary: the city sought to defend the segregated racial order. Adam Fairclough has investigated the entrenchment of segregation during these years in New Orleans, even in the face of black radicalism. "As the expanding industrial economy absorbed the white unemployed," he explains, "blacks found themselves squeezed between job discrimination on the one hand and the termination of New Deal relief programs on the other."[69] Black New Orleanians were "thrown off relief rolls" without secure job prospects.

Crescent City Girls thinks through these changes in the cityscape during the 1930s, 1940s, and early 1950s. At the same time, the book is a synchronic history, deeply interested in the moments of black girls' daily lives that characterized racial segregation throughout the period. The chapters do not proceed chronologically; rather, each chapter works to exhibit a different aspect of the double bind, providing a dense network of power relations along the lines of gender, race, and sexuality in Jim Crow New Orleans. The analytical strands of geography, sexuality, and affect are woven through every chapter, although each chapter has a particular focus.

The first two chapters of the book begin with the theme of space as a way to introduce New Orleans. Chapter 1 maps the geography of Jim Crow New Orleans, where black children learned the difference between "white" and "colored." To understand the politics of segregation, black children mapped the world around them. These maps helped them learn how color and power related to their lives and assisted them in developing their sense of self in relationship to their place in the city. Chapter 2 analyzes young black women's experiences on two specific streets in New Orleans: Canal Street and Rampart Street. These two streets demonstrate how black girls learned lessons of racial difference that were constructed through street harassment and insult. The streets demonstrate the spatial relations of sexuality. Black girls knew, for example, the spaces that carried the threat of insult, sexual violence, and sexual harassment; the spaces where young women were defined as "respectable" or "bad"; the spaces where black girls were defined as outsiders; and the spaces that provided some measure of safety. Together, chapters 1 and 2 lay out the geography of the double bind. On the one hand, the chapters show aspects of the gendered violence of segregation: street and sexual harassment. On the other hand, the chapters delineate the physical space of middle-class respectability in the city.

Chapter 3 explores incidents of interracial sexual violence as well as the contradictions young black women faced as they attempted to act respectably in the face of sexual violence. At the center of the chapter is the story of the attempted rape of fourteen-year-old waitress Hattie McCray by a white police officer, Charles Guerand. Hattie McCray's and Charles Guerand's histories reveal the inner workings of gendered Jim Crow violence, particularly the ways in which black girls' bodies were subject to assault by white men.

Chapter 4 analyzes the emotional toll of the double bind in the lives of two black girls living in downtown New Orleans—Jeanne Manuel and Ellen Hill—who were interviewed by social scientists while they were teenagers in 1938. By investigating their life narratives, we learn that sexuality, and more specifically chastity, were at the core of the girls' subjectivities. Both were concerned with maintaining the designation of a "nice girl" living in a nice space and constantly feared that they might lose their respectability. Chapter 5 turns its attention to delinquent girls at the House of the Good Shepherd, a Catholic delinquency home for black and white girls. The Sisters of the Good Shepherd, who ran the home, along with the Jim Crow municipal authority, stigmatized black girls' bodies by marking the youth in their care as "sexually delinquent." The chapter provides a glimpse into the world of young women who did not live up to middle-class standards of "niceness" and explores the various forces shaping their choices, transgressions, and vulnerability to abuse and mistreatment. In this way, the chapter examines those girls who, although they trespassed the boundaries of respectability, negotiated the double bind all the same.

Chapter 6 explores pleasure in black girls' lives. Because of the culture of dissemblance and silence that continues to construct black women's sexuality, finding sexual enjoyment and satisfaction in black women's lives is crucial in reconstructing their inner worlds. As chapters 1 and 2 demonstrate, during segregation black girls had to carefully figure out places in the city where they were allowed and welcome. But if space was an important regulatory feature of Jim Crow New Orleans, then finding spaces of freedom and pleasure was equally important for young black women. Chapter 6 focuses on three pleasure cultures in black girls' lives: the reading and writing culture of romance stories, the dance culture as evidenced at the local "colored" YWCA, and the pleasure cultures of Mardi Gras. I argue that these pleasure cultures show "make-believe worlds" that black youth created to forge moments of intimacy away from the violence of Jim Crow.

In the end, *Crescent City Girls* opens up a way to understand black girls' coming-of-age in the Jim Crow South. In so doing, I hope to complicate understandings of life in segregated America. Recent discussions in American politics that focus on "reverse racism" often elide and ignore real histories of trauma related to racial discrimination, segregation, and violence. In public discourse, the history of Jim Crow has been erased despite the fact that people live every day with the memories and scars of growing up during the Jim Crow era. With *Crescent City Girls*, I hope to bring to light one piece of the history of American segregation.

CHAPTER ONE

Suppose They Don't Want Us Here?
Mental Mapping of Jim Crow New Orleans

*And as I would be going to Dryades Street with my father . . . I would spell
out words. And one word that I kept seeing was spelled c-o-l-o-r-e-d. And I was
trying to sound out the word and I was saying col-o-red. What is col-o-red?
And he told me, "That's colored, and it means you." And I was looking at the
signs that were marked for my use that looked different from things that had
"w-h-i-t-e." And I always wanted to know why these things didn't look as
nice . . . so my father was trying to help me understand the kind of society
in which I had to live. And he just told me that no matter what other
labels placed on me, I determined what I was.*
—FLORENCE BORDERS INTERVIEW, BEHIND THE VEIL
ORAL HISTORY PROJECT (1994)

Growing up during segregation, Florence Borders discovered that she was
"colored" in the space of urban New Orleans.[1] As she traveled across the city
and practiced her reading skills, she came to understand the meaning of
race. The letters in the word "colored," the sounds they made when strung
together, and the quality of the things those letters marked taught her complex lessons about her place in Jim Crow society.[2] Borders's father simultaneously helped give meaning to the word "colored" as he attempted to teach his
daughter to see herself as more than the narrow definition that hung from
the signs she sounded out.

Geography and corresponding spatial relationships introduced Borders to the terms "colored" and "white." She encountered the signs
away from her home and neighborhood. As her recollection illustrates,
girls learned what it meant to be "colored" in New Orleans and in the
American South in both private and public spatial encounters. Everywhere they turned, they saw signs that marked them as outsiders, public
benches they could not sit on, and dressing rooms where they could not

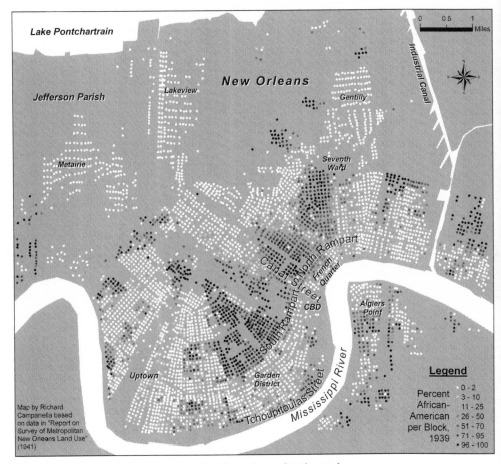

FIGURE 1.1. New Orleans' population distribution by race, 1939
(map by Richard Campanella)

try on clothes. This was the reality of racial segregation and part of the violence of the double bind.

Mental Maps and the Politics of Place

"I am struck by the centrality of space—the rhetoric of spatiality—to the locations of identity within the mappings and remappings of ever changing cultural formations," observes feminist scholar Susan Friedman.[3] This "rhetoric of spatiality" was especially intense in segregated southern cities. The Jim Crow state effectively controlled space and employed spatial language—boundaries, borders, insides, and outsides—to create a biracial order. The biracial order flattened New Orleans' racial and ethnic diversity by dividing the city into only "white" and "colored."

The ideology that whites and blacks must always be completely separated emerged during the waning days of Reconstruction.[4] For white supremacists in the city, spatial separation ensured racial dominance while spatial proximity became a metaphor for racial equality. In 1892 a white New Orleanian declared, "We of the South who know the fallacy and danger of race equality, who are opposed to placing the negro on any terms of equality, who have insisted on a separation of the races in church, hotel, car, saloon, and theater . . . are heartily opposed to any arrangement encouraging this equality, which gives negroes false ideas and dangerous beliefs."[5] Even figuratively, race relations between blacks and whites came to be understood spatially, as W. E. B. Du Bois elegantly framed it in 1903: "The problem of the twentieth century is the problem of the color line."[6] But children in New Orleans did not experience the segregated space around them in two dimensions. They did not encounter simple, flat lines; instead, the world around them was alive with the three-dimensionality of space, influenced by social encounters, emotions associated with places, and the physicality of bodies—big bodies, barely visible bodies, bodies marked by their color.

Black girls in New Orleans developed mental maps that helped them understand themselves and their racialized city. As architectural historian Rebecca Ginsburg describes, mental maps are "multi-layered" and "fragmented." They are multiple, conceptual scales of the city and its buildings, streets, ecology, play areas, and people imperfectly meshed together.[7] Children's mental maps are not to scale, nor do they correspond neatly with cartographers' mappings of the city. Instead, they reflect children's own experiences, their cognitive development, and their growing sense of the world around them. During Jim Crow, mental maps provided "imaginative order" to black girls' worlds and helped them form a growing "awareness of racialized space."[8] This awareness of race, geography, and place is clear in playwright and activist Endesha Holland's remembrance of Jim Crow Mississippi: "Although I didn't know it then," she recalled, "the houses in Greenwood gave me my first lesson in race. I learned that color and money went together. I learned that houses had skins, just like people, and just like people they were segregated by color and money."[9]

Just as Endesha Holland did in Greenwood, Mississippi, children in New Orleans placed themselves, their homes, and their bodies on mental maps, thus defining themselves and their place in the city. Herbert and Ruth Cappie, both teenagers in New Orleans during the 1930s and early 1940s, articulated the complex and ever-shifting notion of "place" they dealt with as they came of age during Jim Crow. Herbert Cappie noted, "The most difficult thing about segregation was in knowing one's place. In New Orleans, my place may have been over here, and in Alabama it was in another place over there. You had to know how to deport yourself in different places." Ruth Cappie added, for emphasis, "That's like in foreign countries."[10] Segregation and race-making in one Jim Crow city was not exactly the same in the next. Further, different spaces within a single Jim Crow city might have vastly different rules for the proper "place" for black citizens. This made mental maps all the more important for black children. Indeed, white children did not have to conceptualize urban space in this way. For instance, white memoirists often remember exploring New Orleans' streets with freedom and abandon and without fear.[11] But, as the Cappies' interview demonstrates, place in legally segregated cities was extremely complex for black children; one had to constantly learn and relearn the proper space for and deportment of "colored" citizens, or they might be arrested or harassed by city workers, officers, sheriffs, or white citizens more informally policing the streets. Figuring out one's place was made more difficult by the fact that spaces and the meanings associated with them, though seemingly self-evident and stable, were never fixed.[12]

In New Orleans, black children moved about in a topography marked by color and thus had to figure out their "place" in every space they entered.[13] Rather than simply noting the city's population distribution, Figure 1.1 visually demonstrates the complexity of moving around a segregated city, of moving from black space to white space, to gray space and back again. As black children moved through segregated spaces—through white neighborhoods, black neighborhoods, and interracial neighborhoods—they learned about the relationship between color, gender, and power. As black bodies were in motion, so too were their senses of self.

Black children in New Orleans developed mental maps of the city reflecting the racial-sexual domination of space. For black girls, this influenced things as mundane and yet as significant as their movement through the city and their bodily comportment. In the autobiographical essay "Growing Out of Shadow," Margaret Walker remembers coming to a realization of "what it means to be Black in America." For her, shadows represented the space of Jim Crow—restricting childhood movement and growth. Walker's essay begins by reflecting on childhood encounters, moments of learning about proper place. Walker, who lived in New Orleans as a girl, writes, "Before I was ten I knew what it was to stay off the sidewalk to let a white man pass;

otherwise he might knock me off. I had had a sound thrashing by white boys while Negro men looked on helplessly."[14] Walker learned early how to walk the city streets deferentially. She learned where her body belonged in relationship to whites, whether they were men or boys. Walker's encounter with white boys on segregated streets demonstrates the ways in which black girls' mental maps had to represent racialized and gendered power in the city. Geography influenced black girls' subjectivities, bodily comportment, and sense of place in New Orleans. Black girls sometimes walked the city streets carefully, figuring out where they belonged.

Mapping Black Girls' Neighborhoods:
Uptown and Downtown Children

In the pages of the nineteenth-century *African Methodist Episcopal Church Review*, tourist Willietta Johnson described a charming, scenic New Orleans. She explained that the city was "cut by Canal Street into two phases of life, two epochs of history, and two methods of thought." French and Spanish culture survived in the slice of the city below Canal Street, which was full of Old World splendor, foreign chatter, and "beautiful women, convents, chapels, cemeteries and seminaries, all of which are tinged with an oriental charm." "The upper portion of the city," she wrote, housed the garden district and "the beautiful as well as the characteristic southern home, planted in lovely lawns."[15]

Willietta Johnson visited New Orleans in 1893. *Plessy v. Ferguson*, the case that eventually enshrined "separate but equal," was already winding its way through the court system. New Orleans railways had separate cars for different races, and the city was well on its way to Anglo-Americanization and eventually to solidifying legalized segregation. The ugly underbelly of the city was invisible to Willietta Johnson or, more likely, was not a part of the enthralling, exotic portrait she wished to create for her readers. Although her account was more flawlessly poetic than reality, one thing Johnson took note of was true—Canal Street demarcated the middle of the city, separating two ways of life.

New Orleanians reveal a particular geographical knowledge of the metropolis; their memories provide insight into the symbolic importance of the city's streets. Oral history interviewees constantly referenced Canal Street and, like Johnson, represented it as a cultural crossroad. Interviewees described who they were and where they came from by beginning with "uptown" and "downtown." One oral history interviewee, for example, responded to the question, "Where did you grow up?" with, "In the uptown section. As a matter of fact, I was born within about fifteen, twenty blocks from here, in the uptown section of New Orleans."[16] Canal Street was the functional dividing line between the uptown and downtown sections of the city and between two socially distinct black communities.[17] Even white New Orleanians felt this way. In the joint memoir *Uptown/Downtown*, two women who grew up in the city noticed that "in comparing notes about our growing up years we discovered that while we shared the same unique culture and customs of New Orleans, we often experienced them differently. One of us had an 'uptown' experience and the other had a 'downtown' experience."[18]

This sense of place, of marking oneself as uptown or downtown, gave New Orleanians a way to describe who they were and deeply informed their subjectivity. But, according to civil rights activist Charlayne Hunter-Gault, the impulse to "place" oneself geographically is a feature of southern subjectivity more broadly. In her memoir *In My Place*, in which she recalls her coming-of-age as a black girl in the Jim Crow South, Hunter-Gault continually plays with the idea of "place" and its many meanings. Of placing oneself in one's community and personal history, she says, "Ask any Southerner where he is from and he will tell you every place he has ever been from. I am no exception. I always say, 'Well I grew up in Georgia, but I'm from South Carolina.'" Hunter-Gault argues that the multiple places and geographies she associated with gave her a "strong sense of place."[19] Similarly, in *From the Mississippi Delta*, Endesha Holland begins her life story with the specificity of place—she first describes Gee Pee, "the roachy heaben o' de Delta," a respectable black neighborhood in Greenwood, Mississippi.[20]

Because of the bifurcation of uptown and downtown in New Orleans, black youths' mental maps began with their neighborhoods. But these maps began to expand once they ventured into new sections of the city or met youth from other parts of town. Children and adolescents often met at Catholic schools: some would travel uptown to go to Xavier Prep; others would travel downtown to go to St. Mary's. Likewise, many teenagers came together because throughout the 1930s, the city had only one "colored" public high school, McDonogh #35 (an industrial high school, Booker T. Washington, opened in the early 1940s). Florence Borders, who graduated from McDonogh #35, explained the cultural divisions within black society: "Generally you were an uptowner or a downtowner, all across the board. And when we got to 35, we met people for the first time who were in our age group, and in our class, and from another section of the city. But there was always a consciousness of being an uptowner or a downtowner. . . . One of the girls who was in my class married a '*downtown boy*.'"[21] Borders laughed and used vocal intonation to imply that a "downtown" boy was scary, different, and possibly even dangerous. She did so lightheartedly, but her narrative pointed to the fact that perceptions of the difference between the two sides of the city were extreme enough to remark on inter-neighborhood dating. Uptowner Millie McClellan Charles also spoke of McDonogh #35 as a cultural meeting ground between two separate communities. "I had never known the other high school kids that were below Canal Street until that happened, because I never traveled below Canal Street, except for with my grandmother who went to the French market every Saturday," said Charles. When she arrived at the school, she "marveled at the fact that they had lifestyles that were different. They were predominantly Catholic. The Creole mentality was very strong there."[22] Charles's reference to "lifestyles" and "mentalities" highlighted the distinct notion of a bifurcated New Orleans: from Charles's view, the kids from downtown thought about and saw the world differently.

A complex mixture of class, color, ethnicity, and histories of migration patterns divided black uptown children from black downtown children. Many of the black downtown families had lived in New Orleans for generations, their ancestors a blend of African, French, Spanish, and Caribbean migrants. As such, a majority of the downtowners identified as Creole. Black youth placed ethnic and cultural difference, then, on their mental maps of the city. Louise Bouise, who grew up in the downtown Treme neighborhood, described the difference between downtowners and uptowners as primarily an ethnic difference: "[Canal Street] was the sort of dividing line between the American blacks, as some people refer to them, and the Creole blacks. And more or less, the Creoles lived on this side of Canal Street, which we call the downtown side; the American blacks lived on the uptown side, or the other side of Canal Street."[23] Bouise contrasted the term "Creole blacks" with the phrase "American blacks," noting the difference between those she identified as Creole and those who were not. "American" in her usage stood in for an anglicized, Protestant, and Other. American blacks were not like the people she grew up around; instead, they lived on the "other" side of Canal Street. She mapped the difference between these two groups of New Orleanians onto the streets, explaining the categories geographically by placing "American blacks" in uptown New Orleans.[24]

In fact, black Creoles and American blacks lived on both sides of Canal Street. But most blacks (and whites) who lived in uptown neighborhoods were (relatively) recent migrants to the city. Their families often came from small towns throughout Louisiana and Mississippi looking for better education, work, a little more opportunity, and a lot more excitement.[25]

Black New Orleanians often associated the Treme and the Seventh Ward, two downtown neighborhoods, with black Creole culture. The Treme was located just "downtown" of Canal Street, bounded between North Rampart and North Broad Streets. Marie Boyer Brown grew up on St. Phillip Street "in the heart of the Treme." Brown identified herself and her family as Creole. Notably, she described her mother as both "brown-skinned" and Creole.[26] Marie Boyer Brown made explicit the distinction between skin color and ethnicity in her interview. By noting that her mother was darker in color, she wanted to explain that Creole, in New Orleans, did not designate skin color alone, despite local and national myths that either claimed black Creoles as nearly all white-looking or defined "Creole" as a racial type. Instead, Brown characterized Creole as a culture (which included a shared set of values, language, and religion) and as an ethnicity. As a girl, Marie Boyer Brown's elderly relatives and friends, for example, spoke "Creole" and went to a Catholic church. The family's genealogy, according to Brown, traced back to France, Africa, and Haiti. Marjorie Pajeaud also grew up in the Treme and defined Creole outside of mere skin color by explaining, "Creole is a form of life, a form of culture."[27]

Lilli "Tiny" Braud grew up in uptown New Orleans, and her family also identified as Creole. Braud's own mental map began in uptown New Orleans, and she identified herself as an uptowner. Her interview illustrates local black geographical knowledge of New Orleans' neighborhoods and the way color and ethnicity combined to define a sense of place within black New Orleans. Braud was raised in a comfortable Creole family and was able to attend Xavier University Preparatory School, the black Catholic high school. Yet as a teenager she went to all of the American black clubs and restaurants located in uptown New Orleans. Still, people continually classified her in terms of neighborhood and skin color. "When I tried to go into some of the black places," she explained, "they didn't want me. Because they said they couldn't come into ours. . . . But see, everybody, if you were light, they just assumed you were from the Seventh Ward." When she met resistance at the bars, Braud would announce: "I don't live in the Seventh Ward! I live in the Thirteenth Ward! And I'm going to go to this place."[28]

By stating that she was not from the Seventh Ward (downtown), Lilli Braud identified herself as a certain type of black New Orleanian. Despite her light skin, she wanted to identify with the black community uptown—the community she grew up in. By insisting that she was not from the Seventh

Ward, she also rejected the exclusiveness of the downtown Creole community and culture. Braud's identity was certainly fluid; she went to a private Catholic school and made friends with many of the downtown black Creole girls but continued to associate with black uptowners and people from all backgrounds. Braud always thought of herself in the broadest of terms, evidenced by her bridging of uptown/downtown cultures. At the same time, Braud's experience also reveals how the physical body is mapped to spaces within the city. Her encounters at black clubs illustrate the ways in which the lived body interacts with space. "The lived body," explains feminist theorist Iris Marion Young, "is a unified idea of a physical body acting and experiencing in a specific sociocultural context; it is a body-in-situation."[29] The lived body is a body in space. Braud's pale skin, light brown hair, and hazel eyes signified a certain relationship to the city. Her physical body gave her access to Creole spaces and even to white-only spaces. And American black New Orleanians looking at her assumed that her body belonged in the space of downtown New Orleans.

Canal Street, then, separated two black communities with distinct identities; which side of the street one was from became shorthand for the community with which one identified. The institutions associated with each community helped define social life and girls' experiences with the city. Downtowners had Catholic churches, parochial schools, and social clubs such as the Autocrat Club, known for its exclusivity. Uptowners congregated at Baptist and Methodist churches and clubs such as the Dew Drop Inn. Of course, as Lilli Braud's interview makes clear, the distinctions between uptown and downtown were never totally clean and clear; there was always overlapping and interweaving. But the divisions were stark enough to discourage inter-neighborhood dating and to sustain the stereotype that all (or most) black Creoles lived downtown. As a consequence of these distinctions, Canal Street became an important geographical marker in black girls' lives, defining whether they were an uptowner or a downtowner. Yet no matter how distinct the black communities were from one another, white New Orleanians defined both uptown and downtown black girls as "colored." If girls went to public schools, the Jim Crow laws forced them to go to colored public schools. When brown-skinned girls walked the streets, whites identified them as colored girls. In this, it did not matter which neighborhood a black girl came from.

To better explain the process of mental mapping for black girls, I would like to turn to raced understandings of place in two particular New Orleans neighborhoods: the French Quarter in downtown New Orleans and the riverfront neighborhood along the Mississippi River in uptown New Orleans.

Black Girls Mapping the French Quarter

Dolores Aaron spent her teenage years living in downtown New Orleans in the French Quarter with her mother and sister. This was rare. Very few black families lived in the French Quarter. Indeed, the French Quarter, or Vieux Carré, was less than 5 percent black.[30] Aaron identified the area as "an entirely white neighborhood." And although she spent her teenage years in the French Quarter, she also strongly identified with the Treme—the neighborhood where she spent her childhood years. The Treme provided her with her closest friends and her leisure activities. She did not have friends from the French Quarter, and her family "did not visit anyone because people didn't visit." Aaron explained, "People were right next to you [and would have] polite, short conversations. Most of the residents there were white, and they weren't mingling with black people anyway."[31] As a child, Aaron's mental map of Jim Crow New Orleans noted the whiteness and aloofness of the French Quarter, especially in comparison with the Treme.

Despite the whiteness of the French Quarter, black girls moved through the neighborhood. A few, like Aaron, lived in it or nearby. Some who were able to pass for white went to shops, stores, or museums in the French Quarter. Many others were familiar with the area because they attended the black Catholic girls' school located in the heart of the neighborhood: St. Mary's Academy. The Sisters of the Holy Family, a black order of nuns established in 1842 by a free woman of color, operated St. Mary's Academy. The Sisters had bought the building in the French Quarter in 1881. Along with St. Mary's Academy, the Sisters also ran an orphanage in the building.[32] One magazine claimed that when the convent moved to the French Quarter, the motherhouse became "the first and only Negro-owned property in the Jim Crow–ridden French Quarter."[33]

St. Mary's students' mental mapping of the French Quarter included the complex history of race in New Orleans, mingling space and time. The building that housed the Sisters of the Holy Family and their students was famous for once having been the Orleans Ballroom. Accordingly, the convent's "cypress floor, three feet thick, [was] said to be the finest dancing floor in the world."[34] By the time black girls in the 1930s and 1940s walked into their classrooms, the site was infamous for once having housed quadroon balls—dances where wealthy white Frenchmen met their mixed-raced concubines.

This system of concubinage was known in New Orleans as *plaçage*. (Even the founder of the Sisters of the Holy Family, Henriette DeLille, had found herself in that situation. She was one of the free young women of color in a relationship with a white man until she unbelievably found a way to make her own path, establish a radical religious order, and dedicate her life to helping educate and protect the enslaved and free black population.) The convent's building, the former Orleans Ballroom, was steeped in myth and nostalgia. As Monique Guillory suggests, "The 'history' of the building—what actually happened or did not happen there during the nineteenth century—is secondary to the myth of the balls that has firmly taken root." Today the building is a hotel that recounts the history of the quadroon balls and of the Sisters of the Holy Family. Guillory argues that the building is one of those spaces that Michel de Certeau defines as "a crack in the system that saturates a place with signification and indeed so reduces them to this signification that it is impossible to breathe in them."[35] But during Jim Crow New Orleans, black girls learned and played inside the building, just as black nuns lived and worked there.

Even during the Jim Crow era, the nuns working in the building and the girls going to school there were aware of the "historic" indecency of the site. A 1904 article, for example, in *National Magazine* recalled the mythical history of dancing quadroons and *plaçage*. The article noted an engraving on the building's walls, a perpetual reminder of the past: "Always in sight, as a constant reminder that the whiteness of their lives must wipe out the stain left by the beauties gone before, is the inscription: 'I have chosen rather to be an object in the house of the Lord than to dwell in the temple with sinners.'"[36] In 1947, white travel writer Eleanor Early also perpetuated the myth of the Orleans Ballroom and the quadroons—"women so beautiful, so notorious and so terribly hated" by white women—who danced there.[37] On her trip to New Orleans, Early visited the Sisters of the Holy Family to learn more about the history of *plaçage* and to see the ballroom for herself. "The sweet-natured nuns graciously showed me through their convent, and I expect they would show you, too," wrote Early. Still, Early understood that her presence and the quadroon balls of the past were intruding on the Sisters of the Holy Family's present. Early told her audience, "I hope you will not bother them when they are busy with their classes. If you do, you should leave an offering for their orphans. The nuns are naturally a bit self-conscious when visitors want to talk about the Quadroons. But I asked questions like an Inquiring Reporter, and they were very courteous." Taking advantage of the Sisters' hospitality and her own whiteness, Early continued asking questions about the racial past and its hauntings of the building's geography.

Throughout her story of the Orleans Ballroom, Eleanor Early referenced the Sisters' reticence. The Sisters had good reason to be "self-conscious" of a racial history that emphasized sex between white men and unmarried free women of color. In an oral history interview, two St. Mary's graduates, Joycelyn Hyman and Ann Stuart, remembered that the nuns "kind of kept that [history] under wrap." Stuart believed that they were "kind of embarrassed" by the history of the quadroon balls. Hyman recalled that the nuns "didn't talk about such things. As a matter of fact, they would sometimes shush us. If they would overhear a conversation they would say, 'Shhh you can't talk about that.'"[38] The black nuns wanted to teach their students how to be proud, decent, and respectable. The geography of the ballroom may have made their convent famous, but it distracted from the Sisters of the Holy Family's mission.

But even though she knew that the Sisters were uncomfortable with the history of the ballroom, Eleanor Early continued her questions during her tour of the convent and school. Early wrote, "When we were in the courtyard I had wanted to talk about the Quadroons. Sister Gilbert, stooping to touch a pansy face, wrote with her finger among the walking iris, I had thought she did not hear me."[39] Early told her readers a story of a duel fought by two white men over a quadroon woman at the ball. On her visit to the convent, she asked to see the bloodstain, a reminder of the duel and the racial history of the building. According to Early, "One of the nuns showed me the stain, but she did not want to talk about it. When the Holy Family took over the Salle d'Orléans, the ballroom was purified and the garden blessed. And every morning and every night, at Holy Mass and benediction, the sisters pray for the souls of the Quadroons and for the remission of their sins."[40] If the Sisters did show Early the bloodstained ballroom floor, then she was taken into the Sisters' living quarters. The old Orleans Ballroom was where the Sisters slept, in dormitory style.[41] For Early, the geography of the convent spoke specifically to the racial past. In this way, antebellum geographies haunted Jim Crow geographies.

The geographies of racial inequality and of sexual exploitation permeated the space of the convent and school through ballroom floors, bloodstains real or imagined, and white visitors intent on resurrecting a "romantic and appalling" history.[42] Eleanor Early told her readers of the single-mindedness of the Sisters, claiming that "for more than fifty years, ever since they bought the place, the nuns have scrubbed and scrubbed, saying prayers upon their knees for the wild young men who danced and loved and fought, and for

FIGURE 1.2. Sisters of the Holy Family, ca. 1899
(courtesy of the Library of Congress)

the beautiful girls they fought over."[43] Early's representation of the Sisters'
relationship with the quadroon balls emphasized a history of romance and
madness; for Early, the Sisters themselves existed in this present-past.

But the relationship between the convent, St. Mary's Academy, and the
Orleans Ballroom is more complex than Eleanor Early could understand.
The Orleans Ballroom represented black dispossession, where women of
color with few choices for advancement were forced to look to white men for
love and protection. But the process by which black women in New Orleans
were segregated, alienated from the landscape, and dispossessed (represented by the ballroom and Jim Crow just outside its doorways) coexisted
with a history of black survival, pride, and religious fervor (represented by
the history of the black Sisters of the Holy Family; their founder, Henriette
DeLille; and the girls inside St. Mary's Academy). The past haunted the present but also made way for a new black geography within the convent. As
Katherine McKittrick explains, "The various kinds of madness, the pathological geographies, the dismembered and displaced bodies, the impossible
black places, the present-past time-space of cartographers, the topographies
of 'something lost, or barely visible, or seeing not there'—these material and

metaphoric places begin to take us" inside of black geographies and black subjectivities.[44] A 1961 article in *Ebony* magazine about St. Mary's Academy emphasized this "impossibility of black places" and their ability to encompass the present-past. "Once known as 'the bawdiest house in the nation's bawdiest town,'" the author explained, "it now is as famous for its virtues as it is infamous for its lurid past."[45] The memories of the Orleans Ballroom permeated the space of the French Quarter and the school's building, but *Ebony* was quick to point out the Sisters of the Holy Family's resistance to traditional geographies that sexualized black female bodies.

So, unlike the women who allegedly danced in the halls in the nineteenth century, the girls of St. Mary's Academy were not in the building to highlight their beauty or sexuality. Instead, they were there to learn how to be proper girls—educated in academics, right conduct, and modesty. The Sisters paid special attention to the geography of the body, teaching the girls to conform to rules of respectability. Joycelyn Hyman believed that by emphasizing the geography of the body, the Sisters taught students pride. The Sisters believed "in being honest, in standing tall, in holding your head up."[46] Sister Claire, a former student who later became a Holy Family nun, also remembered the lessons she learned as a student: "The nuns taught us what it means to be a woman. And they didn't give us a long lecture. When a woman came out of her house, she's always to look good and always [have] a certain decorum."[47] The Sisters enforced strict rules about the uniforms and the behavior of the students. For example, the students wore long sleeves and skirts in every circumstance—including in the heat, when participating in athletics, or in sickness—and girls had to wear thick tights underneath their skirts after the age of twelve.[48] According to students who went to St. Mary's, the nuns were "strict disciplinarians" but also taught by example. Students learned by observation how they were supposed to act, walk, and move their body in space. As Ann Stuart explained, the students also knew what they were *not* supposed to do: "Walk a certain way and carry yourself a certain way and be aggressive a certain way. Oh! We knew better than that. And you learn by deductive aspects, you know; you copy others and you copy the nuns. And they all wanted us to be nuns." The space of the school, for the girls inside, was a space saturated with notions of religiosity and righteousness. The building's past history of "bawdiness" was starkly juxtaposed with the decorum of the school and the girls inside.

The *Ebony* piece on St. Mary's Academy and the Sisters of the Holy Family not only highlighted the historic indecency of the Orleans Ballroom but also noted the contemporary "vice" of Bourbon Street—only a few streets

OLD TRADITION AND CULTURE

prayers yielded the payments that fell due on their newly purchased home. But their determination to hold on to their possession equalled their predicament. After obtaining special permission from Archbishop Francis X. Leray, they went North and East to beg for alms until on Oct. 4, 1889, the last note was paid.

Almost simultaneously with the liquidation of their debt, another burden was lifted—a burden the Sisters had carried in frustrated silence for the past eight years. The relief came in the form of a fire that destroyed the Faranta Circus on the adjoining lot, which until 1859 had been occupied by the Orleans Theater. Until the day of the blaze, the circus had been of particular nuisance value to the quiet existence of the nuns and pupils at the academy, and the cause of many a prayer for divine intervention and removal of the obstacle. Wrote a nun in describing the sad state of affairs that prevailed at St. Mary's in its infant days: "At nights, the lights from the hippodrome casting their glow over the statue above the altar together with the screams of the spectators often interrupted the devotion of the Sisters and seemed to represent a constant war between the powers of Light and Darkness. But the circus was doomed. It went down in God's good time." The Sisters' subsequent acquisition of the lot and the construction of a new wing appeared ample compensation to them for the years of agony they had endured because of their former noisy neighbor.

Since then, St. Mary's Academy and the religious community have grown steadily. The latter now operates a vast number of schools, orphanages and homes for the aged. Twenty of these are in New Orleans. Others are in various parts of Louisiana, Texas, Alabama, Oklahoma and as far away as British Honduras.

In 1955, the Sisters vacated St. Mary's to move into their donation-financed, $1 million Mother House at the outskirts of the city, a move that provided room for 100 additional pupils at the school.

Despite the popularity of the academy, keeping it out of the red has presented a perennial struggle to the Sisters. As a result, they recently considered a $315,000 offer from local white businessmen to sell their property, though its commercial value has been estimated in the area of $1 million. Pupils, graduates and friends of the academy throughout Dixie and beyond worried—then sighed with relief when they heard that the nuns had turned the offer down. Despite their bitter financial struggle, the Sisters resolved to carry on with the hard task they had begun 80 years ago, namely "to pay the utmost attention to the religious, moral and literary improvement of children entrusted to their care."

Balconied facade of former Orleans Ballroom (r.) on Orleans Street has remained unchanged since building was erected in 1817. Adjacent brick structure, extending to Bourbon Street, was added to academy after zealous Sisters acquired lot in 1889.

Bourbon Street strip joints within shoe's throw of St. Mary's form sharp contrast to austere religious life at school. Among major tourist attractions in city's French Quarter, street has been put off limits to all Maryites by academy rule.

During fire drill (L.), academy's ban on Bourbon Street is temporarily lifted to facilitate speedy evacuation of girls from school building.

Fancy iron work on balcony at intersection of St. Peter and Royal Streets is vivid reminder of city's Creole past. Night spots in Quarter bar Negro patrons but employ Negro waiters and musicians.

Continued on Next Page   59

FIGURE 1.3. Page from *Ebony Magazine* showing St. Mary's students, December 1961 (courtesy of Johnson Publishing Company, LLC)

away from St. Mary's. A series of photographs showed the geography of sin within the French Quarter and the girls' placement in it (see Figure 1.3). The photographs in the article depicted "strip joints within a stone's throw" on Bourbon Street and show the St. Mary's girls walking along the street for a fire drill, despite the "academy's ban on Bourbon Street."[49] Black girls who walked through the French Quarter, then, mapped not only whiteness but also vice. Black schoolgirls were expected to walk in a way that demonstrated their respectability and decorum, steering clear of seedy corridors.[50] Sister Claire remembered that the Sisters told the students, "'When you come out of school, walk with your head down. Do not look right or left.' And it was modesty; . . . they didn't want us to see anything that was happening on that street next to us. . . . It had to do with . . . keeping yourself . . . safe from outside negative influences."[51] Dolores Aaron also emphasized the immorality of her neighborhood in her oral history. "The ladies were out there hustling and calling men into the doors and that kind of thing," she recalled. "But there were no black people doing that at the time [in the French Quarter]."[52] Just like the girls at St. Mary's, Aaron could not walk down certain streets in the French Quarter, streets that her mother considered too sinful.[53]

But even as the French Quarter represented sin, it also represented a certain safety. Aaron remembered the neighborhood as a safe place to be "because they took care of the white folk; we just happened to be black folk." She took a certain pride in growing up in an area that contained few black New Orleanians; she also took pride in living in such a historic neighborhood.[54] Students at St. Mary's were also proud of their location in the French Quarter, in their building, and in the Sisters of the Holy Family. Joycelyn Hyman suggested that as young women they liked going to school and "just being in the French Quarter; and, of course, we were right down the street from [St. Louis] Cathedral. We were right at the back entrance of the cathedral. It meant a lot, being in the French Quarter; I think we thought we were special."[55] Of course students from St. Mary's never went inside the cathedral, built in 1727, because of segregation.

Much of the pride that students felt about going to school in the middle of the French Quarter also had to do with the Sisters of the Holy Family, who made the students feel special. The Sisters encouraged the students to develop a subjectivity based on their respectability and exceptionality. Sister Claire remembered that although the Sisters never talked about race explicitly, "everything they did said, 'You are as good as anyone else. You are as smart as anyone else; you're as competent and as talented as anyone else.' And they prepared you to be that, because they themselves grew up [black] in the [segregated] society. . . . They know where to go, where not to go; they know what to say, what not to say; when and how to achieve their purpose. And they did it very well."[56] This lesson, as Sister Claire explains it, was spatial. The Sisters taught the students that they were "smart" and "good," and the Sisters knew "where to go" and "where not to go" based on the rules of segregation. The Sisters knew how to follow the racial rules and how to bend the rules. To do this, one had to understand personal geographies of the body (bodily comportment) and geographies of segregation (the city and streets). Indeed, the Sisters obeyed the bodily rules of segregation by knowing where not to go just as they disobeyed them by walking confidently and claiming a sexual modesty for black girls and women. In this way, the Sisters taught the students to find a comfort within themselves, in the space of the French Quarter, and in the larger city. Ann Stuart remembered, "When we left St. Mary's and I went to Xavier [for college], I was very secure. I felt I was ready. I was pretty ready."[57]

The history of St. Mary's Academy and Dolores Aaron's interview demonstrate the complex nature of mental mapping for black girls in Jim Crow New Orleans. Their maps not only contained geographic markers, streets, and buildings but also consisted of the racial makeup of the areas in town and the present-past. They knew, as they walked through the French Quarter, that it was a place for "white folk." As they walked through the French Quarter, they also mapped virtue and vice. This vice had a history, related to race and white supremacy represented through the history of quadroon balls. But the vice also had a very real present, represented through a white-owned "red-light district" just down the street from the black motherhouse.

Black Girls Mapping the Riverfront

The uptown riverfront neighborhood ran along Tchoupitoulas (pronounced Chop-ə-too-ləs) Street, and Tchoupitoulas ran along the Mississippi River; so the story of Tchoupitoulas is, in part, the story of the river.[58] Textile factories, cotton mills, cigar factories, ice companies, lumberyards, and asbestos and chemical storage facilities were located along the river side of the street.[59] These industries were part of the activity of river commerce. Opposite this industrial corridor lived both white and black families with Anglo surnames; as one geographer has noted, the "noisy, smelly, objectionable riverside port facilities . . . attracted inexpensive housing and, ergo, an economically poorer class of people."[60] The white fathers tended to work at the factories, for the oil companies, or, less frequently, for the city. The black fathers of the neighborhood worked as manual laborers at the factories or labored on the docks, on the wharfs, or for commercial ships while their wives, mothers, and sisters worked as domestics for white families or cleaned and cooked for local companies. Although the area was "interracial" in some sense, the uptown riverfront neighborhood along Tchoupitoulas was nevertheless divided by race (see Figure 1.4).[61] The map of the riverfront extension project demonstrates the ways in which some "integrated" neighborhoods nonetheless followed rules of segregation. The numbers inside of the blocks represent the percentage of African Americans living on the block. What is striking about this pattern of racial segregation is that black families lived in clusters surrounded by white families: one block, for example, contained 92 percent black families, while the surrounding blocks contained zero black families.

American black girls who lived in the uptown riverfront area learned to map the city and its spatial power through their play and movement inside of their neighborhood. Black girls living along Tchoupitoulas navigated the streets, discovering where they were and were not wanted. An after-school program, the Kingsley House Extension Project, provides a window into black girls' constant conflict with neighborhood white children. Disputes and conciliation contributed to black girls' mental map of the city, their lived body experience, and their sense of self as they constantly assessed the level of exclusion and safety in the places they occupied. In this way, black girls learned to impose meanings on the geography of New Orleans based on race, power, and privilege.

Founded in 1896, the original Kingsley House was a settlement home located in uptown New Orleans near the central business district. The settlement home worked with white working-class children and women, particularly Irish and German immigrants and migrants to the city.[62] Kingsley House created safe play spaces in order to socialize children because social workers believed proper play spaces were good for children's development.[63] They sponsored dances and play activities and established playgrounds for the white children of the neighborhood. In 1945 the directors of Kingsley House decided to open an "uptown riverfront extension project" for the children of textile workers at Lane Cotton Mill farther uptown on Tchoupitoulas Street. Because there were so many children in the area with nowhere to play, they decided to make this a "biracial" project: primarily white children would be served, but black children would be allowed to play on special, separate days.[64]

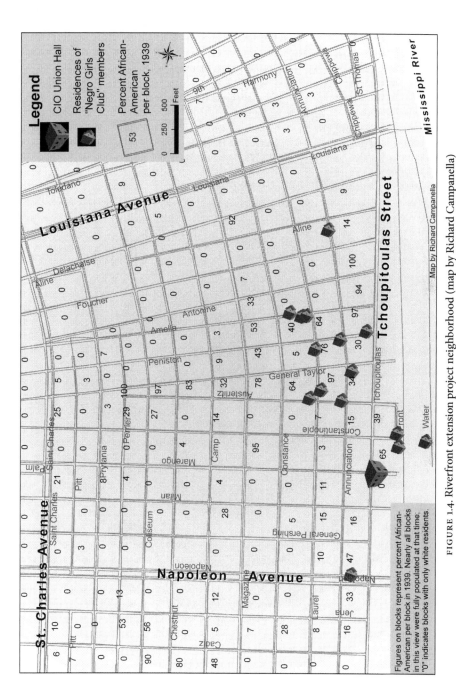

FIGURE 1.4. Riverfront extension project neighborhood (map by Richard Campanella)

To staff the extension project, the Kingsley House directors decided to hire a female social worker from outside of the New Orleans area because it would have been difficult to find a white local worker who was both qualified and willing to work with both groups of children. Constance Grigsby, originally from Des Moines, Iowa, was the first leader of the riverfront Kingsley House Extension Project.[65] The white social workers employed by the Kingsley House provide insight into the segregated space of uptown New Orleans. From their point of view, we can see the conflict between black and white children over the ownership of local streets. This perspective is often missing from oral histories and autobiographies. Adults thinking back on segregated New Orleans tend to emphasize moments when white and black children played together peacefully and coexisted on city streets. These memories usually come from early childhood, before children started at segregated schools.[66]

White writer and journalist Eva Augustin Rumpf, too, remembers an interracial neighborhood with an air of racial accord. Rumpf grew up in the uptown riverfront neighborhood in the 1940s—the exact time and place of the Kingsley House Extension Project. She lived only a few doors down from some of the black girls who played at the CIO building. Her memories highlight not exactly racial harmony but more a kind of peaceful coexistence between black and white neighbors. In her autobiography, *Reclamation: Memories from a New Orleans Girlhood*, Rumpf writes:

> In my Uptown neighborhood on Laurel Street, one could pass
> through several blocks of white families, then suddenly come upon
> blocks of black families, then white ones again, and so on. Our house
> at 3950 Laurel was in the last block before the next group of Negro
> residences, so we were accustomed to interactions as accepting and
> respectful neighbors. When colored folks walked past our front gate
> as we sat on the porch, my parents always greeted them with a cordial
> "good evenin.'" The eight blocks that I walked to Howard School took
> me through a Negro neighborhood, which I traversed alone as a
> youngster without feeling any fear. My mother saved our well-used
> but out-grown clothing for a colored woman with several children
> who lived in the next block, and I would be sent to deliver the bundle,
> which the woman politely accepted. If she felt any insult at being
> given the dubious gift, she succeeded in graciously masking it.[67]

This memory of the riverfront neighborhood is telling. Even as Rumpf describes an interracial geography, she also clearly delineates the ways in which the neighborhood was segregated between "white" and "Negro" sections, just as the map in Figure 1.4 clearly shows. Indeed, these white and black blocks become "neighborhoods" within neighborhoods in Rumpf's retelling, starkly dividing the groups of white and black houses. Her story also highlights white girlhood and subjectivity. She remembers feeling safe and comfortable in her neighborhood; security is central in her recollection. However, Rumpf was not allowed to walk on Tchoupitoulas because that was where, as her mother told her, the immodest Irish lived.[68] Even though she remembers ethnic and racial discord at moments of her telling, Rumpf's memories emphasize a type of unity between whites and blacks within her neighborhood.

In contrast, the social workers' viewpoints allow us to observe the violence that took place on the streets between black and white children. Because the social workers were not from New Orleans, they tended to report conflicts that were normal for the children of the neighborhood but appeared extreme and tense to the social workers. Their daily reports focused on both the mundane and the extraordinary. Furthermore, as social workers, they were trained to see and address the problems children faced.

The Lane Cotton Mill CIO Union Hall housed the Kingsley House Extension Project, which began by working exclusively with the white children of the neighborhood. In 1946, social worker Constance Grigsby and local black leaders discussed the possibility of including the riverfront black children in the after-school program. The local men emphasized the need, explaining that the black children had few places to play. But they worried about adding a black play day at the CIO hall because it would create "too much friction with the white folks and might lead to trouble." For these local black leaders, it was important that they not antagonize an already hostile white community. The fathers who attended the meeting described how their children walked to school, traveling on specific streets so they would not be beaten up by white children policing the neighborhood.[69] These fathers already understood the geography of the neighborhood as divided by race, even though black and white families lived on the same block.

Meanwhile, local white residents strongly discouraged the project from the start. Grigsby asked the neighbors if allowing black children to share the union hall—yet use it on separate days, "of course"—would be acceptable. She reported a local neighbor's response:

He did not come out and say that he thought it was impossible, but said that it would have been easier if we had started the two at the same time. At this point it would be taking away a day from the white children and might cause a good deal of friction. [He] emphasized the need to educate parents and children of the neighborhood to the idea of having such a program before starting it. [He] said he could see where the thing might hold all to dynamite if not very careful.[70]

The very threat of "dynamite" was a spatial threat. The white neighbor's use of the word suggested that if black children played in the union hall, there would be disorder and violence on the streets.

Kingsley House never secured a separate play area for the black children, so the social workers decided that the white and black children would have to share the same union hall on Tchoupitoulas despite the white residents' opposition. Black girls aged eight to fourteen would play on Wednesdays after school, black boys on Saturday mornings, and white children at all other times. The program was "progressive" because not only did the white and black children use the same building, they also used the same toys and the same restrooms.[71] This made the union hall a shared space. Yet the notion of having playtime scheduled based on race exposed the curious logic of Jim Crow. Once the new "biracial" program was officially announced to the white community, some children said they would not be able to play in the union hall after the black kids had played inside.[72]

From the biracial program's inception, controversy centered on which group of children, white or black, owned the play space. On the first Wednesday (black girls' day), the white children stood by, closely watching the eight black girls who showed up to play with the toys. Constance Grigsby reported, "There were quite a few white children hanging around and watching [the black girls] at their play which seemed to make the girls quite self conscious during most of their play. Some of the younger boys who were hanging around began making very cutting remarks like, 'Don't you break that you nigger,' and 'Dirty old things,' and I had to send them away quite briskly."[73] As the black girls tried to play, the white children possessed the space and attempted to physically intimidate them. The white children felt comfortable standing in the entrance of the union hall and occupying the street outside and the building. Thus they also occupied the union hall visually, a constant reminder of who had power. Even some of the white parents came by, just to look in on the black girls and assess the situation.[74] The white boys' visual possession of the space made the girls noticeably distressed. Having whites visually occupy the space reminded the black girls who belonged and marked the girls as visitors and interlopers. Black girls' mental maps of their neighborhoods would have noted this: in this particular space they were merely visitors.

As the program continued, more black children began showing up on their assigned days. On the third Wednesday of the new program, thirty black girls showed up for the Negro Girls' Club. The girls arrived before Grigsby, and while they played, a handful of white neighborhood children showed up, determined to disturb them. When Grigsby finally arrived, she found the white and black children ready to exchange blows.[75] The fight consisted of "nasty talk" on both sides. Grigsby called the altercation the "most tense" moment since the project's beginning.[76] That the black girls felt bold enough to fight illuminates either the intensity of the white children's words and actions or, just as likely, that the black girls routinely did not back down from the white children. The children knew one another. These were all local neighborhood children who lived around Tchoupitoulas Street. The resolution of the conflict was only temporary—the white social worker showed up and told the white children to leave. However, to control the situation, she told the black girls not to show up early, reinforcing the idea that the play space belonged to white children by default.

Soon, the conflict over the union hall spilled into the surrounding streets. A few months later, a group of white boys taunted the girls with "aggravating remarks" during a Negro Girls' Club meeting. The girls responded to these remarks by "talk[ing] back" to the boys. The social workers attempted to redirect the black girls but could not defuse the argument. Meanwhile, a white girl, May Rose, threw a rock over the fence toward the black girls. In response, the girls ran after her, calling her a "son of a bitch." An instructor reported: "They stopped at the corner. . . . Those who had run outside came into the hall again. They were irritated but not apparently really disturbed. With a fair amount of encouragement . . . they got settled in chairs for the meeting."[77] Just as the girls readied themselves for their club meeting, May Rose and two white boys came back, calling names through the doors of the union hall. Throughout the conflict, Grigsby noted that the black girls remained "calm" but "annoyed."[78]

The social worker's designation of the black girls' emotional state as "calm" exhibits how girls learned to deal with racial conflict during segregation. Most likely, the girls were used to the way the white neighborhood children treated them. Fending off insults from girls like May Rose was common. Even though the girls remained somewhat calm (they did, after all, chase May Rose down the street and call her names), they had to listen to the offensive words coming from their white peers. A student intern reported on the insults by white children and the varied reactions from the black children: "The colored children cannot express their hostility but must take the insults of the white children to keep what little they have."[79] Black girls' responses had to be measured because their use of the play space was always in question. The verbal fight reveals a physical aspect of black geographies of segregation. The black girls' bodies inhabited the play space in specific ways: they could not be overly aggressive. Rarely in the archive are bodily movements in space made clear. Yet in brief moments like this fight, black girls' "modalities" of "body comportment, manner of moving, and relation in space" are unveiled.[80] The "calm" yet "annoyed" description of the girls' emotional state speaks to the ways in which they might have fought back physically, but ultimately they had to return to bodily control. Clearly, the girls had learned to alternatively fend off and then ignore verbal insults from whites.

The week following the hectic street chase, the Negro Girls' Club hosted a Halloween party for their friends. A Kingsley House instructor "police[d] the streets" to keep the white boys and aggressive children away. Nevertheless, the white boys threw firecrackers into the union hall and shouted, "The Nigs ought not to be allowed to come [here]."[81] The insults coming from the white children were no longer simply verbal; they had turned physically violent. Despite the instructors' warnings, the white children wanted to mark the union hall as white-only territory. The erupting firecrackers delivered on one white father's earlier promise of "dynamite." The white boys' behavior taught the Negro Girls' Club members important lessons about racial-sexual domination on New Orleans streets: white boys and men were dangerous to their safety. The white boys' verbal threats and physical violence demonstrated the gendering of white spatial power in New Orleans—for the white boys, it was appropriate (or funny) to harass a group of black girls. They did not think of the black girls as children, like themselves, who might be hurt or injured. Interestingly, the conflicts over space were not nearly as intense on the black boys' play days. Sometimes the white and black boys even played football together.[82]

Social worker Constance Grigsby had a difficult time adapting to the racial dynamics of the uptown riverfront neighborhood. She found the black residents and their children respectful and "clean." At the same time, she worked every day with the white children. At the beginning of July 1946, Grigsby claimed that there was "little community antagonism" from whites but admitted that "occasionally when I am walking down the street a group of younger children who do not attend the program call 'nigger girl,' but this is the only indication I have had of such feeling (which of course does exist)."[83] The depth of local hostility remains unclear. However, that the name-calling came from children rather than adults is telling. The adults of the neighborhood, black and white, men and women, worked long hours. They had little time to themselves or to spend with their children, supervising their play.[84] If white adults felt hostile toward Grigsby, most simply kept their distance. Still, the archive suggests at least some tension between the white adults and the Kingsley House Extension Project: toward the end of July, the white chairman of the neighborhood advisory committee for the extension program quit in protest of the biracial program.[85] Meanwhile, Grigsby worked to keep one of the neighborhood's white mothers loyal to the program, explaining, "It is very important that she see it our way because she is very influential in this neighborhood."[86] Not long after Grigsby recorded the calls of "nigger girl" and her problems with the advisory committee, she quit.

By the beginning of 1947, Kingsley House hired new social workers Joy Coombs and a "Mrs. Kelley."[87] Coombs and Kelley were better prepared to deal with the white parents and spent much of their time negotiating the racial tensions in the neighborhood. Rather than ignoring or downplaying white racism in the neighborhood, they used the ideology of racial segregation and separateness to open up a space for the black children to play.

Kelley's work with the white girls made clear the complex negotiation over space and place in the riverfront neighborhood. One afternoon during the summer of 1947 (the second summer of the extension project), the white girls were "persistently" trying to come into the CIO union hall. The black girls had left the hall to go on a hike, and so the black boys were inside playing pool. Kelley recorded her conflict with the white girls:

> The girls (white) insisted that they had to come in and play jacks
> on the big table. . . . I repeated that they will not stand for any
> colored children coming in on the other days and that I could not in
> fairness let them in now. I also said that I knew their mothers were
> all critical of the program because it includes Negro children and
> that they would indeed be upset if they knew their daughters were
> actually playing in the same room with big Negro boys. The girls
> answered haughtily that their mothers "would never know a thing
> about it."[88]

In order to get control of the union hall from the white girls (who constantly showed up on the black girls' day), Kelley used racist language to convince them to stay away. Explicit in this language was a definition of black manhood as sexually dangerous ("big Negro boys") and, thus, an emphasis on the importance of protecting white daughters. In this way, the white girls learned from the social workers the power of racist language that worked to define black men and boys as inherently perilous. The white girls, though, were not afraid of the boys.

Kelley acted on her threat to tell the white girls' mothers that they had played near "big Negro boys." At first the white mothers were unfriendly; according to Kelley, they "were suspicious . . . only [one] asked me to come in. The others all held the door open just a crack. I said frankly that I knew I wasn't popular with the girls and that I knew they were calling me a 'nigger lover' but that I wanted to explain the real situation." Kelley proved to the white mothers that she was neither a "nigger lover" nor someone who supported an integrated play environment. She manipulated the discourse of racial segregation for her own "progressive" purposes in order to argue that the white children needed to give up the space of the CIO union hall for a couple of days a week. Kelley told the mothers she "was sure they would not want their daughters playing in such close quarters with the Negro boys. They were all horrified at the very idea and thanked me for coming to explain."[89] In her reports, Kelley, unlike Grigsby, made clear that the white mothers' rejection of interracial play and "closeness" between whites and blacks supported racist notions of blackness.[90] At the same time, Kelley's language reified sexualized assumptions about blackness and whiteness and superimposed that language onto children's bodies. The very threat of "such close quarters" implied a sexualized atmosphere within the union hall building. At the core of her argument lay the assumption that segregation was meant to separate black boys from white girls.

Because the social workers spent so much time negotiating with white children over control of the union hall, they were unable to forge an intimate relationship with the black girls. Unlike the black Catholic children who confessed to white priests and, depending on their school, might be taught by white nuns, black Protestant girls rarely had intimate relationships of any kind with whites in their neighborhood. Because public schools were segregated by race, black children going to public schools in New Orleans were taught by black teachers. The majority of black children living near Tchoupitoulas rarely, if ever, confided in white adults. Additionally, the conflicts with white children over space marred many of the black children's activities, causing awkwardness between the social workers and the black children. Joy Coombs believed that the black girls had "criticisms of the program that they don't want to express for fear of being thought unappreciative, partly because the leader meets with them only once a week, and then in a large group. . . . Most of the girls are reserved toward the leader and felt unsure of acceptance around the CIO hall and the white children."[91] Black girls' "reserve" again refers to bodily comportment in space. Coombs believed that the black girls' reserve was due, in part, because of the conflict over space. The black children had to navigate space in such a way that they were never quite sure if they belonged at the union hall. For black girls, figuring out their place was further complicated by the fact that the white children were always trying to remind them that they did not belong, even as the white social workers tried to make the black girls comfortable. This double message reveals the intricate ways in which black girls had to think about space: mental maps delineated spaces where they had to maintain emotional and bodily control versus spaces where they could feel comfortable and at ease.

Negotiations over space and place are evident in the black girls' trips outside of their riverfront neighborhood as well. The Negro Girls' Club took field trips around the city, illustrating how black children came to impose meanings on their environment relating to race, power, and privilege. One of the white social workers noted:

On the picnic and traveling to concerts [I am] often asked what places and equipment are okay for Negroes to use (the levee, swings in the park, residential sections). They need sound advice in this area. The older girls are quick to tell the younger ones if their behavior is not acceptable. Their admonition is in a moralistic generality; magic words "bad" and "nice" are their only explanation. The leader supposes that Negro children have to accept the behavior pattern expected of them younger than white children do and that standards of good public behavior are therefore a special need for them. The older ones probably have a particular interest in etiquette in general.[92]

The Kingsley field trips clearly demonstrate that although black children learned the rules of racial etiquette through interpersonal interactions with whites, they also learned the etiquette of space. Urban geography functioned as a teacher; it educated the younger children, telling them where they belonged and thus who they were. The built environment marked New Orleans' social priorities and power networks. Furthermore, the interactions between the older and younger girls demonstrates that age and cognitive development shaped black New Orleanians' encounters with and interpretations of space.[93]

The young girls were constantly figuring out their proper place and the attendant meanings of the spaces they inhabited. This had to be done carefully. Black children did not always have access to all the information they needed in order to know in which places they belonged. Part of developing childhood mental maps, then, meant figuring out "place" in a variety of unknown and possibly dangerous contexts. Importantly, white children did not have to do as much work to understand the meaning of space. Tiptoeing and careful movement through unknown spaces was part of black subjectivity. Moreover, the black girls' self-expression was limited at times; often, they had to act with controlled restraint in public spaces instead of with abandon or visible pleasure.

As they traversed the city streets outside of the Tchoupitoulas neighborhood, the younger girls took in information about new areas, expanding their mental maps. Children are not born with the ability to create complex maps of their environment; rather, they learn about the spaces around them as they grow, mature, and explore.[94] Moving around a city, children learn what is remote and what is near and then associate those distances with meanings. Black children in New Orleans might have learned early on in life that a white school was located near them—maybe just a few streets away or in easy walking distance—whereas the "colored" school that they would eventually attend was much farther away.[95]

Each new trip around the city helped younger girls involved with the Kingsley House Extension Project compose a mental map of the geography of New Orleans based upon race. The girls asked openly what their proper place was at the city parks and levees. The smaller girls looked to older girls for reassurance and guidance because it was never quite clear to them where they could safely travel. On one trip to the levee, the black girls sat on a log in the shade with the social workers. A younger girl asked if "colored people" were allowed in the space. The social worker reassured her: yes, colored people were allowed. Another girl chimed in, "Suppose they don't want us here?"[96] The girls' questions illuminate both the process of learning place in greater New Orleans and the restrictions they faced in the Tchoupitoulas riverfront neighborhood. For them, there was a difference between being "allowed" and being "wanted," a distinction they knew all too well from their play in the union hall. This distinction, then, affected bodily comportment and movement through segregated space. As they determined where they could and could not go and if they could swing on the swings or not, they tiptoed timidly and hesitantly. Black girls were accustomed to conflicts over space at the riverfront, in ways different, perhaps, from those of children who grew up in downtown New Orleans neighborhoods.

The Kingsley Riverfront Extension Project closed its doors in 1949, only two years after it began. Community antagonisms and vocal protests from whites in other parts of New Orleans killed the project. Social workers who observed the children, along with student volunteers from the local white women's college, Newcomb College, believed they had failed to create a safe play space for black children. Kelley deplored the situation, arguing that it was impossible to educate "children to more accepting attitudes in a neighborhood where prejudice is so rampant." Kelley further explained:

> Apparently trying to run a bi-racial program in accordance with what the community will accept is only erecting even more barriers between the white and colored groups. The distinction between "colored day" and "white day" . . . "my leader" and "your leader" . . . seems to be aggravating the rivalry between the two, instead of encouraging sharing of facilities and fair play. The colored children are becoming obviously more fearless about expressing their aggressions . . . which may be to some extent a healthy release for them, but which seems only to incite the white children to greater rejection, which, in turn, does nothing to help the Negroes.[97]

A student from Newcomb College agreed that the program could not last; she believed that "as long as the feeling between the two racial groups is as strong as it is in this neighborhood, a bi-racial program is a forced program." She, too, argued that prejudices were being "increased" by the Kingsley House Extension Project rather than abated.[98] Thus, the white social workers and volunteers viewed the violence in the neighborhood as being stoked by the program, even though the black and white fathers made it clear when the program began that dramatic tension already existed between the children. The social workers who witnessed the conflicts between white and black children may have been looking in on the normal play between the children in the Tchoupitoulas neighborhood.

The conflict on Tchoupitoulas Street clearly demonstrates the feelings of insecurity, resentment, anxiety, and anger for the majority of working-class, American black girls living, growing up, and playing in the area. Black girls learned to map their world according to race as they assessed where they belonged, knowing that each neighborhood in New Orleans had its own identity and thus racially defined spaces. Tchoupitoulas Street's racial patterns revealed intense hostility in an area some might define as "integrated." Yet the Kingsley House Extension Project shows the ways in which negotiation of place along the lines of race was incorporated into children's daily lives.

THE INNER WORKINGS OF Jim Crow rested on the control of social space and black movement within space; of less concern was the actual separation of black and white bodies. Black girls faced the task of learning about space, mapping racial order, and keeping track of their proper place. Meanwhile, all of this affected how black girls moved their bodies. Katherine McKittrick explains, "If we imagine that traditional geographies are upheld by their three-dimensionality, as well as a corresponding language of insides and outsides, borders and belongings, inclusions and exclusions, we can expose domination as a visible, spatial project that organizes, names and sees social differences (such as black femininity) and determines where social order happens."[99]

The shape and look of segregation in New Orleans began to slowly change in the late 1940s and early 1950s, as did black children's mental maps. Protest from African Americans in the city forced conservative whites to rethink black children's and youths' place in the geography of New Orleans. In July 1948 the *Louisiana Weekly* complained bitterly that "New Orleans Negroes were once again brought face to face with the reality that a 'voteless people are a hopeless people!' Democracy, Southern Style, was just a twisted and warped ideological concept which meant in effect that only white people are supposed to enjoy the municipally operated recreational facilities." The article noted that on Fourth of July celebrations, black New Orleanians had to congregate on the neutral space (median) on Claiborne Avenue because there were no other places to celebrate. The article linked southern segregation, the protection of "democracy" abroad, and municipal inequalities at home.[100]

In response to the protests over the problem of recreational space for black New Orleanians, the city began to develop *segregated* spaces for black children and youth to play. The New Orleans Recreation Department (NORD) began in 1947 with the explicit purpose of replacing delinquency with healthy sport activity. Indeed, NORD's "Negro Division" changed the relationship between space, play, and exclusion in the city. In 1952 the city pointed out in its NORD program report that before NORD, there was absolutely nothing for black children, then boasted of its "earnest and fruitful endeavor since 1947 to bring adequate facilities to the Negro population."[101] In this way, New Orleans city officials believed that by creating more "equal" separate spaces, they could stave off integration of white-only spaces; they also envisioned New Orleans as a leader among southern cities for recreation for children.[102] Consequently, by the 1950s, black children gained the right to certain NORD activities, and a separate "colored" swimming and amusement area at Lake Pontchartrain (Lincoln Beach) opened in 1954 as well as a few new "colored" playgrounds. These new segregated play areas, however, did not change the importance of mental mapping for black children. Black girls continued to carefully navigate space, making sure they were both allowed and "wanted."

CHAPTER TWO

A Street Where Girls
Were Meddled

Insults and Street Harassment

CLARITA REED: It wasn't easy. You just got hardened to it. You
always expected an insult, regardless.

INTERVIEWER: Daily?

CLARITA REED: Of course. Of course. If anyone tells you differently,
they're lying, 'cause it was . . . but basically that's what growing up
in New Orleans was.

—*Clarita Reed interview, Behind the Veil oral history project (1994)*

Born in 1922, Clarita Reed grew up in segregated New Orleans. In a 1994 interview, she struggled to narrate her coming-of-age during Jim Crow. To describe the psychological trauma of segregation, Reed first turned to her brother's experience—a more familiar story. She explained, "The black male wasn't safe." Reed lived in "mortal fear" that one day whites might accuse her brother of raping a white woman or that police officers might brutally beat him. In contrast to Reed's thick description of the dangers associated with boys' coming-of-age, Reed offered only a vague sketch of black girls' traumatic experiences with segregation. "The black woman could be insulted any time," she said. She mentioned the possibility of "insult" three times during her interview. These insults were gendered—something that black women and girls contended with. Yet Reed never gave an example of an insult she received or clarified what types of insults were hurled at black girls.[1] The precise nature of these daily insults—whether they were racial slurs or sexual harassment—remained unspeakable, lost to history. Instead of specificity, the ubiquity of insults comes across in Reed's interview; insults provided the background noise to black girls' daily Jim Crow life.

Other black women from Clarita Reed's generation who grew up in Jim Crow New Orleans remembered being insulted as well. These memories provided examples of the everyday trauma of Jim Crow life. Aline St. Julien explained in an oral history interview, "They treated you without dignity, you know? Your dignity was always hurt."[2] Olga Merrick remembered being called a "nigger" by a streetcar conductor and forced to give up her seat to a white woman at the age of twelve. She obeyed. "But I cried. Because my feelings were hurt. But there wasn't anything I could do," she recalled.[3] Dolores Aaron remembered whites calling her and her sister "monkeys." Her mother would turn the language of insult into "loving words" protecting the girls by responding in a sweet, singsong voice, "Yes, these *are* my little monkeys!"[4]

As Dolores Aaron's memory highlights, insults were not always sexualized. For black girls growing up in the Jim Crow era, the term "insults" carried with it multiple meanings. Sometimes the word "insult" functioned as a veiled reference to interracial sexual harassment. At other times "insult" referred to whites' purposeful attack on black women and girls' self-respect and pride (not allowing girls to try on clothing; requiring blacks to enter through the rear door; calling girls "monkeys," "dirty," "ugly," "nigger," and so on). Whereas sexual harassment functioned to call into question black women and girls' sexual respectability, insults to black women and girls' self-respect assaulted their gendered respectability, suggesting that black girls were not feminine. Therefore, sexual harassment and attacks on dignity were deeply intertwined. Audley (Queen Mother) Moore was born in New Iberia, Louisiana, in 1898 and spent time as a girl and young woman in New Orleans. In an oral interview in 1978, Queen Mother Moore discussed street harassment, verbal slurs, and sexual harassment. In her telling, the stories crisscrossed and intersected one another. Within the span of a few minutes, Moore remembered a white police officer who "asked" her sister for a date and a white male passenger on a train who called Moore a "nigger." After recalling her experience on the train, Moore stopped to explain the concept of insults to the interviewer: "There was struggles all the time, white men trying to molest us all the time; you had no peace from white men. I remember my brother . . . he went and got with the boss's son at the big sawmill, who had insulted me. That was an insult for a white man to say he wanted you; that was an insult. You see? And I remember he went and got him by the collar . . ."[5] Queen Mother Moore's insistence that "you had no peace" also appears in Clarita Reed's interview: "You got hardened to it," because black girls could be insulted "at any time," she explained.

Most of these insults took place outside of girls' homes—on the city streets of New Orleans. As black girls navigated the Jim Crow streets, they encountered physical and verbal insults. The auditory and tactile nature of space, then, also contributed to black girls' mental maps. On some city streets black girls might routinely walk by a cacophony of catcalls; on other streets they might have to withstand touching from whites or other physical assaults; and, as I explored in the previous chapter, on some streets black girls faced insults from white children. The insults taught black girls lessons in race, sexuality, and gender; through street harassment, they learned what it meant to be a "colored" woman in Jim Crow society. According to anthropologist Micaela di Leonardo, street harassment is the moment when a man (or men) approach and accost a woman (or women) in public space. Street harassment begins with "looks, words, or gestures" whereby "the man asserts his right to intrude on the woman's attention, defining her as a sexual object and forcing her to interact with him."[6] For black girls growing up during Jim Crow, this particular type of insult was a moment of encounter when girls realized their sexual and physical vulnerability. Often called "meddling" by black female New Orleanians, street harassment had a powerful racial component. White men had the power to insult black women in social space. But white men were not the only ones who harassed black women and girls; black girls faced insults from white women as well. Insults, whether from white men or women, marked black women and girls as insufficiently or improperly feminine or overly promiscuous. Street harassment, of course, could also be intraracial. There were places in the city's geography where black men commonly harassed black girls.

Tracing fleeting moments of street harassment and insults can be difficult for historians. But street harassment provides a window into the racial-sexual domination of space. Girls' relationships to men, to their own bodies, and to their sexuality changed based on their location in the city. Some areas of New Orleans were dangerous; certain geographies marked black girls as sexually available to grown men. Other places might be safe only for some girls, marking them as part of the "respectable" middle class. As a result, black girls' sexual subjectivities shifted as they moved across the city. At one moment they might identify as a naive schoolgirl; at another they might realize that they did not have access to performances of modern femininity. The history of insults is a reminder that black female subjectivity and a black female "sense of place was inflected by unspeakable (unmapped) and speakable (mapped) displacements."[7] For girls growing up under Jim Crow, these displacements were based on "racial-sexual domination," "uneven geographies," and moral geographies with their intraracial class biases.[8] Insults are often unmappable because, as Clarita Reed's interview indicates, although they existed everywhere in the Jim Crow landscape, they were also transient. But despite their impermanence on the landscape, insults remained with black girls, embedded in their knowledge of space, in their mental maps, and later in their memories of the meanings of southern segregation, racism, and coming-of-age. Following insults, therefore, opens up a multilayered understanding of Jim Crow New Orleans and black girls' subjectivity. This chapter, by thinking through geographic rejection, street harassment, and meddling, explores the multiple ways "insult" functioned in Jim Crow New Orleans. As we see how insults were placed on black girls' mental maps, New Orleans' uneven geographies come into view, geographies influenced by race, gender, and class tensions.

Canal Street: Exclusion, Rejection, and Harassment on the Main Thoroughfare

Canal Street is one of the most recognizable streets in New Orleans. It not only divided uptown New Orleans from downtown New Orleans but also functioned as a more symbolic dividing line between blacks and whites. This dividing "line" was not a two-dimensional line but a race-making spatial zone in which differences between black and white were created through geographies of exclusion and harassment. On this street, black girls learned important racial lessons centered on the logistics of Jim Crow. Most of the stores on Canal Street allowed blacks to shop but not to try on clothes, shoes, or hats; there were not many places for black New Orleanians to relax or hang out. "At one time blacks were shunned off the main street, Canal Street," explained Beverly Caitone.[9] Although blacks were "shunned," Canal Street was still filled with excitement. As a girl, Eileen M. Julien would go shopping with her mother on the street back "when Canal Street was *the* place, in fact the *only* place to go: Krauss, Maison Blanche, Krieger's, Godchauz's, Gus Mayer's, D. H. Holmes, McCrory's, Woolworth's."[10]

In 1930 Canal Street received a makeover; city officials and businessmen poured $3.5 million into modernization.[11] After renovation, the city celebrated with a festival, which included the first "lighting" of the street's new electric streetlamps. The spectacle of lighting Canal Street began with none other than Thomas Edison flipping a switch to turn on the streetlights (from his home in Florida) while local bands played, powerful white citizens spoke, and "thousands" cheered.[12] An ad in the *Saturday Evening Post* highlighted the magnificent transformation of the shopping district and dubbed the street "the White Way of the South." "Canal Street, New Orleans, has long been known as the widest and one of the finest business streets in America," the ad claimed.[13] Even the *New York Times* reported on the new lights of the "white way."[14]

Night Brings Light, , , , ,
to Historic New Orleans

WIDER than famed Pennsylvania Avenue, Washington, or the Mall, London, Canal Street, New Orleans, has long been known as the widest and one of the finest business streets in America. The lighting of such a thoroughfare is no small engineering problem.

City officials and business men of New Orleans desired a lighting system as efficient and beautiful as that of any city. Furthermore, it was desirable to clean up the curb-lines—to carry the trolley span wires of the four-track street car system on the lighting supports.

Union Metal, internationally known as builders of the greatest White Ways, was selected to handle this problem.

The new lighting system, recently dedicated, has transformed Canal Street into a brilliant avenue of light. From the tops of Union Metal Heavy Duty Standards, hundreds of lamps throw a sheen of brightness over the street. Night brings, not darkness, but light.

By day, the standards, commemorating in design the history of the city under four flags, add dignity and beauty to the street.

The old historic spots of New Orleans remain unchanged but commerce and industry swing steadily forward. Business thrives. Streets have a clean, modern appearance.

Ask Union Metal to show you how your community can obtain the same benefits which New Orleans is now enjoying.

THE UNION METAL MANUFACTURING CO., General Offices and Factory: Canton, O.
Sales Offices: New York, Chicago, Philadelphia, Cleveland, Boston, Los Angeles, San Francisco, Seattle, Dallas, Atlanta

Distributors
Graybar Electric Company, Inc.

General Electric Supply Corp.

Offices in All Principal Cities

Union Metal Design No. 9801 with General Electric Novalux Units

Canal Street, New Orleans, the White Way of the South. Union Metal Standards, installed by the New Orleans Public Service Co., supply the illumination. The success of New Orleans' great beautification program was due largely to the leadership of Mayor T. Semmes Walmsley, Commissioners William T. Hall, John Klorer, Paul B. Habans, City Engineer Bryson Vallas and the Canal Street and Association of Commerce Beautification Committees.

UNION METAL
ORNAMENTAL LAMP STANDARDS
ALSO DISTRIBUTORS OF KING FERRONITE STANDARDS

FIGURE 2.1. "Night Brings Light" ad from the *Saturday Evening Post* (from H. George Friedman Jr. Collection, courtesy of Union Metal)

But, as historian Tera Hunter has explained, "modernization and Jim Crow grew to maturity together in the New South."[15] The modernization of Canal Street worked to exclude blacks from the geography, and the "White Way" became a figurative description of Canal Street: a grand street for whites only. Despite the money poured into the boulevard, there were no "colored" public restrooms. Olga Merrick remembered, "When you got ready to go to the bathroom you had to come home because there was no bathrooms down there."[16] Local businessmen purposely excluded black New Orleanians when they decided to build "public comfort stations" that would "service the white people of New Orleans."[17] The message to black New Orleanians from white store owners, city officials, and local businessmen was clear: do not make yourselves comfortable, you do not belong here.

Because of the hostility experienced on Canal Street, it is represented as a geography full of insults. Canal Street is often featured in oral histories that describe life during Jim Crow. The street was an iconic site (not unlike the French Quarter) and therefore held a certain currency for New Orleanians and outsiders alike. By choosing such a symbolic place for the setting of their narratives of rejection, oral history interviewees were able to articulate the significance of the experience of insults to interviewers who were not from the city. Canal Street helped interviewees demonstrate the differences between "inside" their neighborhoods and "outside" in the world, where they felt the most vulnerable to the effects of segregation and racism. In these interviews, narratives of rejection are a common theme, revealing moments of racial learning in the segregated South.[18] These are moments when the teller of the story had been metaphorically (and sometimes literally) kicked out and marked as Other through a very public process. For black girls and young women during segregation, these moments of rejection were social encounters, taking place on the street or in front of other people.

Aline St. Julien narrated such a story of rejection and insult in an oral history interview. In the 1940s, after having a baby and getting back into shape, St. Julien proudly went to the department store Maison Blanche on Canal Street. Maison Blanche had a commanding presence on the skyline; the building stood tall, announcing the majesty of the shopping experience. St. Julien traveled to the department store to buy a bathing suit that might show off her hard-earned figure. The store "politely" refused to let her try on the suit, given that it was against store policy to allow "colored people" to try on garments before they bought them. Confronted by St. Julien's vocal protests, the store clerk sent her to see the assistant manager. For

Aline St. Julien, this story about a bathing suit described her relationship to segregation and her complex relationship with the city she loved:

> That was the first time I cried like a baby. I cried. The first time
> segregation made me cry. All those years you grew up knowing you were
> segregated. . . . I knew everyday that I woke up in my life that I wasn't as
> good as the little white girl living at that time in our neighborhood. . . .
> When they wouldn't let me try on that bathing suit I cried. But I wasn't
> crying just for that bathing suit. I was crying for all those years that I had
> suffered. And it had come to a head. You know . . . that woman whose
> clothesline broke and she went inside and shot herself? It wasn't that
> clothesline; it was all the things that had mounted through the years.
> And that's what happened to me. It just came down on me . . . but that
> one time I broke. I never cried after that.[19]

This narrative of rejection suggests how emotions are crucial to reconstructing the history of segregation and black female subjectivity during Jim Crow. Using the metaphor of the woman who committed suicide, Aline St. Julien explained how the constant denial of her dignity and the daily insults slowly tore down her defenses, causing psychic injury. St. Julien attempted to describe the effects of everyday trauma by explaining that she was not crying over the bathing suit. Instead, the bathing suit added to the "small violences of the spirit" she encountered in her daily life.[20] This memory illustrates the trauma of growing up during Jim Crow.[21] Traumatic events are often understood as "outside the realm of the ordinary."[22] But the daily insults, like the store clerk's rejection of St. Julien's personhood, were routine, representing "insidious trauma"—a trauma of the everyday. Everyday trauma assaulted a person's integrity. Rejection from Canal Street and all those things that had mounted through the years did violence "to the soul and spirit."[23]

Like Aline St. Julien, Lilli Braud chose to enter a Canal Street department store and try on merchandise, although she too knew Jim Crow's rules. Braud's story exposes the complex negotiation of space by light-skinned blacks in New Orleans. Lilli Braud was from a black Creole family, and her light complexion allowed her to *passé blanc* (pass for white) when she so chose. Like other oral history interviewees, Lilli Braud used Canal Street as a larger metaphor for troubles with segregation. She laughingly told about her experience as a teenager:

> It wasn't until you started venturing outside or going downtown to
> Canal Street and you tried to put a hat on your head [that incidents

occurred]. I had a girlfriend . . . [who was] very dark-skinned . . . , and I went all over with her, because she was kinda brave, you know. She was one of those girls uptown. She'd protect you! . . . JoAnne and I were [shopping] and she went off somewhere else in this store, and I am trying on these hats and this lady is helping me. And all of a sudden I turn and I say [to JoAnne, who was returning], "How do you like this one?" [The clerk] turned, she looked at JoAnne, she looked at me. Now this had been going on for a good ten minutes, [but] all of a sudden she said, "Oh, I am sorry, you can't try on this hat." So then I put on every expensive hat they had on that table. I put this on my head; I threw it down. I guess [the clerk] said [to herself], "I'm gonna leave this crazy lady alone." I said, "Don't you tell me that I can't. I've been standing here for fifteen minutes."[24]

Because of Lilli Braud's skin tone, she could disobey the signs that attempted to regulate black New Orleanians. However, her insistence on hanging out with whomever she wished (including dark-skinned friends and brown-skinned family members) meant that she would not pass into the white world unnoticed. Her refusal to cede ground to the store clerk was very likely made easier by her position in New Orleans as a light-skinned, middle-class Creole girl.

Even though Lilli Braud seemed relatively unaffected by the rejection she received from the store clerk, her tone and performance of the experience during the oral history interview exposed the insidious trauma implicit in experiences of rejection. As Braud began her story, she was talking fast, laughing, and acting out the parts. At the end, however, her words slowed; she became pensive, her tone somber. The story, though funny, dramatic, and defiant, was also serious. She ended gravely: "And that's the rebel in me. I knew I would get in trouble. You just weren't supposed to talk to white people like that."[25] As soon as she finished high school, Lilli Braud decided to move to California because she believed she could not accept (or survive within) the constraints of New Orleans.

Aline St. Julien and Lilli Braud and her friend JoAnne showed up at Canal Street department stores knowing that they would not be allowed to try on bathing suits and hats. Their actions took a considerable amount of courage; they put themselves out in public to be exposed by white store clerks as unequal members of New Orleans society. By going to stores like Maison Blanche and insisting on trying things on, Aline St. Julien and Lilli Braud pushed back against the geographic dislocation, the dominant narrative that they did not belong in that particular space of the city; they made themselves visible to the store clerks who attempted to marginalize them.

Another oral history interviewee, Dolores Aaron, described her experiences with rejection and revealed the way segregation continues to have a hold on her, influencing her current behavior. Aaron explained why she refused to shop on Canal Street:

> I hated to go shopping. I hated to go shopping. I hated it. 'Cause you could look at something, you could like it, [but] you couldn't put it on. And they had places where you could go try on clothes, and the sign up there would say "for whites only." The signs told you [that you] could not try on a hat, and you could not try on any clothes. So I hated to go shopping, and that is why Mama did most of our sewing for us. [Going shopping was] the worst thing in the world. And guess what, until today, I shop at two stores now. . . . It's just a carryover that I have never gotten over. . . . I buy [from] two black stores, Treasure Chest and Elegance, in Los Angeles. . . . I shop twice a year, and my friend in Los Angeles sends me things and I either keep them or send them back. That is what that has done to me. It's just like if I couldn't buy it then, I don't want it.[26]

The everyday trauma of segregation is evident in Dolores Aaron's description of Jim Crow shopping. In her interview, Aaron repeated the word "hated" multiple times; she could not overemphasize how uncomfortable she felt shopping in New Orleans. The "for whites only" signs in Aaron's story represented the refutation of her personhood. Those signs attempted to tell her who she was by explicitly stating what she could not do; and Aaron's repetition of the word "sign" exposed her insistence that those signs were meant to negate her right to that particular space (the dressing room, for example), to the very articles of dress the store sold, and, by extension, to Canal Street geography itself. In the resolution of this narrative, however, Dolores Aaron emphasized that she would not even shop in those stores today. Her current (at the time of the interview) refusal became a viable political protest against the geographic dislocation of past segregation. At the same time, she presented her refusal to shop at those stores as part of the trauma of segregation. She said, "It's just a carryover that I have never gotten over," as if her inability to shop regularly was something that had not been cured yet. She had not fully healed from her experiences of insult.

Many stories of rejection centered on Maison Blanche, a major department store in New Orleans. The narratives highlight the gendered and

FIGURE 2.2. Maison Blanche (courtesy of H. George Friedman Jr. Collection)

sexualized spaces of Canal Street while underscoring the struggle that young black women and teenagers faced in self-presentation. The space of Canal Street denied these women the opportunity to pleasurably engage in consumption, which was the main spectacle of the street. In so doing, the businessmen, city planners, and white saleswomen controlled who deserved the satisfaction of shopping, an activity that defined one's class and gender.

The centrality of shopping as a Canal Street leisure activity is apparent in a 1940s photograph (see Figure 2.2). Standing elegantly in the middle of the street is a young black woman dressed up in sling-back white heels and a printed dress. Her slicked-back hair has stylish waves and rolls. It is clear that she put effort into the way she looked for her trip to Canal Street. Her beauty and poise is a potent reminder of the nature of bodily performance and promenading in shopping districts. Canal Street was a place to be seen. For young women and teenage girls, the street offered a stage to perform sophisticated femininity: they were clean, cultured, and chic. Although this young woman presents a picture of modern fashion, representations of segregation simultaneously haunt the photograph, just as they did Canal Street. The West Line streetcar, shown in the image, divided its passengers based on race, and if the young woman boarded it, she would have had to sit behind the "For Colored Patrons Only" sign. The large, imposing presence of Maison Blanche sits in the background. In the photograph, the building beckons the viewer, just as it seems to do for the woman in the foreground. Maison Blanche was a building that could not be ignored; it asked that people come in, shop, and recognize its significance. Its very presence taunted those who could not comfortably shop inside while it signified a privilege for those who could. Segregation and insults on Canal Street, then, helped to define promenading as an activity for white young women and teenagers. Black teenagers could not leisurely shop and walk Canal Street without encountering insults, rejection, and harassment.

But not everyone came to Canal Street to shop. Mary Johnson described in an oral history interview the effect of rejection and insults on black working-class teenagers who had to travel across the city street.[27] After graduating from eighth grade, Mary Johnson gave birth to her first child, a son, who brought with him the responsibilities of adulthood. Soon thereafter, Johnson began working as a domestic in white families' homes to support her child. Her stories are perhaps more emblematic of the many unrecorded voices of working teenagers who did not leave written records about their experiences with segregation.

Johnson emphasized that every day she went to work, she had to ride the streetcar all the way down "to the end of Canal Street":

> Well, when I did start working . . . I went to work from eight in the morning. I came home [at] about four in the evening. But when we came from work, a lot of time we didn't have anywhere to sit because the white people had taken up all the seats. . . . So we had to stand up and crowd behind where the colored people was. A lot of times [the whites] didn't want you to even stand over them. It was on the streetcar, the Canal Street car. We had to stand up. But the streetcar driver, he didn't say anything about it. But we had a kinda hard time. We didn't have a too hard time getting to work, but we had a hard time coming back.[28]

As Mary Johnson told her story, the anger in her voice was palpable. With pointed vocal intonation, she emphasized that the white riders did not want the black riders to stand over them. The listener or reader of this story can all too well imagine the crowded black riders standing in the back behind the "For Colored Patrons Only" screen that demarcated the front of the streetcar from the rear. The white riders made clear their dislike of the black riders, snubbing the black women by suggesting that black bodies not be too close and that black arms not hold on to bars above their pristine white heads.

Just as black girls were made uncomfortable riding the streetcar down Canal Street, they also had to watch themselves as they walked down the street. White boys were known to harass black girls as they traversed its geography. In 1939 the *Louisiana Weekly* reported in a headline "White Boys Hit Schoolgirl: Was on Her Way Home When Hit in the Face." The newspaper article that followed is a rare instance where street harassment shows up in the "official" archive; here, street harassment was made visible and recorded for all to see. The *Weekly* reported that neighborhood white boys harassed black girls attending the newly built Claiborne Branch of the YWCA located on Claiborne Avenue and Canal Street. The white boys on the street forced black girls entering the Colored YWCA to recognize their power and control over the space of the street. In their violence, they marked black girls as objects at their disposal, objects unworthy of protection. The newspaper pointed to the regularity of the attacks and argued that the assaults were motivated by resentment among white residents who did not want the YWCA located on Canal Street.[29]

The Claiborne Branch's location toward the lake side of Canal Street helps explain some of the hostility girls faced as they attempted to enter the building. The structure was formerly a black teachers' training school, Straight College.[30] Behind the YWCA but occupying the same property sat Albert Wicker Junior High School, a "colored" public junior high school. Although these two important black institutions were near Canal Street, whites populated the homes that bordered them. According to the 1930 and 1940 censuses, not even one black family lived in the thirty-two homes surrounding the property.[31] The whites that lived along the property of the YWCA were working-class and middle-class whites; they engaged in labor at local factories, worked in white-collar jobs as clerks, and were employed by the city as firemen, city officials, streetcar drivers, and typists—all jobs denied to black New Orleanians. There were even white police officers in the neighborhood: policeman Henry Norton's house was directly across the street from Wicker Junior High School on Cleveland Avenue.[32] But the presence of policemen did not provide safety for black girls walking along the street. Indeed, the New Orleans police were notorious for hurling "insulting epithets" at respectable black women and girls.[33] The whites living on Canal Street and Cleveland Avenue did not want buildings for African Americans in their vicinity. Neighborhood white boys and girls owned the streets surrounding the YWCA and Wicker Junior High School. The *Louisiana Weekly* article made clear the way in which local white residents carefully policed Canal Street surrounding the YWCA.

Canal Street insults marked black girls as "colored" in an unequal society. Here, the racial-sexual domination of space defined black girls as outside the "normal" definition of proper women: they could not perform a modern and acceptable femininity and sexuality, as white girls did. The insults of Canal Street reinforced white supremacy and continually reminded black girls of their second-class citizenship. It is not surprising, then, that Canal Street became an important site of youth activism during the civil rights movement. In 1961–62, when local chapters of the Congress of Racial Equality and the NAACP's Youth Council, a group too radical for the NAACP leadership, began boycotts and sit-ins, one of their first stops was Canal Street— the symbol of white exclusion and geographic dislocation.[34] Civil rights activist and NAACP Youth Council president Raphael Cassimere remembered segregated Canal Street as a place of exclusion: "You kind of knew as you grew up where you had to go. You had a mental map because if you were in the wrong place and you needed to use the restroom or needed a drink of water, you couldn't use it." As he grew older, Cassimere was one of many New Orleanians who forced Canal Street businesses to fully integrate. "Integrating Canal Street was a street-based endeavor," he recalled. "One thing that most people need to realize is that this was an effort made by a lot of people, young people, older people, blacks and whites, Jews and Gentiles, Catholics and Protestants. And while there was a lot of sacrifice involved, there was also this feeling that something positive was happening."[35]

Rampart Street: Meddling and Intraracial Street Harassment

Not only does investigating black girls' experience with insults highlight black female dislocations in Jim Crow geographies based on race, but it also makes clear "negotiations of community" and "contests for civic space" within and among the black community.[36] In New Orleans, these geographic negotiations took place in many spaces, but one of these, Rampart Street, highlights gendered negotiations around street harassment and class tension within the black community. Rampart, along with Dryades Street, helped close the gap created by Canal Street's white-only consumption—Rampart was the "prime black street" instead of the "White Way."[37] Rampart Street ran both downtown (North Rampart) and uptown (South Rampart) of Canal Street. North Rampart marked the boundary between the Treme and the French Quarter. Of South Rampart, the 1938 Federal Writers Project (FWP) of the Work Progress Administration (WPA) city guide for New Orleans boasted, "South Rampart Street is the Harlem of New Orleans."[38] Like Canal Street, Rampart

Street functioned as a definitional space; Rampart illuminated gendered and class distinctions among black New Orleanians. Some black girls walked along the street undisturbed, while others were harassed.

Robert McKinney, a black writer, journalist (for the *Louisiana Weekly*, the *Chicago Defender*, and the *Pittsburgh Courier*), and FWP folklorist, wrote about Rampart Street as a contributor to WPA projects in the 1930s and 1940s.[39] Three white writers—Lyle Saxon, Edward Dreyer, and Robert Tallant—oversaw and edited his work.[40] Many of these folklorists and amateur historians blended fact with fantasy. McKinney conducted numerous interviews with black New Orleanians; some of the material appeared unattributed in collections such as *Gumbo Ya-Ya*.[41] McKinney and the FWP writers' vision of the social and cultural geography of New Orleans emerges from the interviews. For these men, Rampart Street was the center of black New Orleans, a place of unbridled sexuality, promiscuous women, erotic music, and gambling men.[42]

In the FWP narratives, the women of Rampart Street represented an exotic world of black sexual excess. In many ways, the descriptions of Rampart Street women are insults themselves, revealing very little about the young women's lives, experiences, or subjectivities. Robert McKinney described a twenty-two-year-old cook whom he interviewed:

> Mary was doing some fancy walking up South Rampart Street . . . keeping time with the hubbub and beat of the noisy street. . . . She was a spectacle to see, wearing green house slippers, a tight short black dress that had ruffles around her posterior and just above her waist; she also wore a red comb in her wild, knappy [*sic*] hair and a pair of red stockings that had arrows above her ankles. Mary was bowing and giving her "howdy" to greet her kind, slow-walking pimps who were whistling weird blues songs, and frustrated whores whose baffled eyes depict the life they lead.[43]

McKinney's description of Mary embodied her as a sexual object, even though she was on South Rampart working as a cook. He described her clothes as "tight" and "short" and highlighted her buttocks. McKinney's sexualization of Mary correlated with her class status, describing her as unkempt and "wild."

For McKinney, the spectacle of the women on Rampart merged with the spectacle of the street itself. McKinney interviewed Mary Davis in an inconspicuous bar, the Suzy Q, located on South Rampart and Thalia Streets. "This happy girl," fantasized McKinney, "was the center of attraction as she arrogantly walked into the lowly Suzy Q . . . a hole in the wall 'joint' where dope fiends, murderers and thieves rub elbows and other things with each other and thirty-five cents whores whose grip on life was lost long ago."[44] McKinney was so confident of his depiction of sex and excess that he placed a literal price (thirty-five cents) on the bodies of the young women who populated the bar. In this way, he became the detached but omnipotent observer providing descriptions of South Rampart women for readers to gaze and wonder at. His representation of Rampart was overwhelmed by people described as permanent fixtures of the space: broken-down prostitutes, pimps, and drug addicts populated equally broken-down buildings. It is difficult to say if McKinney ever spent much time on Rampart Street himself, enjoying the various entertainments, outside of his work for the FWP. Nonetheless, from his black middle-class point of view, black women and girls on South Rampart Street lived in the margins, engaging in illicit sexuality. The women ("whores") with their "baffled eyes" and "frustration" suggested a dazed, confused existence. McKinney left very little room for women to enjoy the pleasures of Rampart Street without being classed as wild, a whore, or overly sexual; young women on Rampart Street were turned to sexual objects for the spectacle and pleasure of others.

As a black business and entertainment area, South Rampart housed restaurants, laundries, bars, and an electrifying nightlife. Therefore, Rampart had a thriving street life, where people searching for fun congregated.[45] Peter E. Dave Jr. described the Rampart Street of the 1940s: "They also had Camp Leroy Johnson. . . . [Soldiers] would migrate on Rampart Street because that's where all the prostitutes were and gambling joints was for black people. Canal and Rampart was a central location."[46] The image of Rampart Street as a geography of leisure has been immortalized in popular African American music such as Ida Cox's "Blues for Rampart Street" (1923) and in the jiving comedy song "Saturday Night Fish Fry" (a number one hit in 1947). Ida Cox sang of Rampart Street in various recordings during the 1920s and 1930s, claiming it for black New Orleanians:

Rampart Street in New Orleans town,
Known to everyone for miles around.
Colored music and real jazz bands,
That's the best spot in all the land.[47]

Whether or not youth were allowed to enjoy "the best spot in all the land" with or without their parents depended on their gender and class status. Tom Dent remembered his principal's directive to stay away from Rampart: "[He]

FIGURE 2.3. South Rampart. The Astoria provided hotel rooms for black patrons, and its Tick Tock Tavern was famous for jazz and nightlife. (Courtesy of Hogan Jazz Archive, Tulane University)

warn[ed] us in a voice drenched in acid: 'Stay away from South Rampart Street, or you'll end up there. A *hint* to the wise is sufficient.'"[48] But boys had much more freedom to explore the city and played on its streets frequently. Peter E. Dave Jr. often went to Rampart Street, and in the 1940s, when he was about fifteen years old, he even worked in a black dress shop located on Rampart. New Orleanian boys had "territorial rights" over streets in their neighborhoods and "throughout the city"; boys might get beat up if they entered a rival gang's territory. At nighttime Dave and his friends would play in the white playgrounds and run away if whites approached them.[49] This boldness in investigating the city and patrolling "gang"-controlled streets made boys more likely to go out and explore places like Rampart Street, even if the adults in their lives warned them away.

Many black parents worried about their children wandering the streets. Clarita Reed grew up in an uptown, middle-class family. Her father was a Pullman porter, earning enough money so that her mother could stay home. Clarita Reed's parents tried to protect her and her brother from the physical and racial violence on the city streets. They knew all too well that the streets were places where girls experienced insults, sexual violence, and street harassment. Reed was not allowed to go out, but her brother was able to bend the rules and explore the city. She recalled, "I never slept until my brother came home. . . . My brother was always out, as young people are. And you just worried until he came and knocked on my window to let him in, so my parents wouldn't know he came in that late."[50]

Typically, girls did not have the freedom that Clarita Reed's brother had. And Reed herself noted that she would never cross her parents' rules. Florence Borders, who grew up only one block from South Rampart, also noted the gendered and classed dynamics of the thoroughfare: "I imagine that Rampart Street would have a greater appeal to people who lived in a style that would not be attractive to middle-class blacks. My mother, for instance, did not go in barrooms. I don't think she called herself middle class, but she did call herself a lady. And she would not have considered it appropriate for anyone who wished to be called a lady to go into a barroom, no matter what kind of barroom it was."[51] Borders described her mother in terms of her class status and her respectability. Middle-class and striving-class blacks invested in ideologies of respectability demanded that upright young women and girls stay away from the clubs on Rampart Street. A song published in *Gumbo Ya-Ya* reflected the other side of the assumption that "ladies" did not frequent Rampart Street:

> A brown-skin gal went walkin' down Rampart Street.
> She look mighty good, but she had very bad feet.
> That gal will make you think she was some good.
> They tell me she's the worst thing in any neighborhood.
> She is a long mistreatin' rider
> Got devilment in her eyes,
> That walk she got make you think
> She's got devilment in her thighs.[52]

The song functions as an insult based on street harassment. A young woman walks down the street, presenting herself as respectable and good, but the narrator of the song suggests that she is naughty and impure. Sung from the perspective of a man watching the woman walk down the street, the song characterizes the women who frequented Rampart as erotic and sexually available.

Nonetheless, South Rampart represented much more than entertainment for the "immoral" and "low class," as the Rampart Street song would suggest. Instead, Rampart "fill[ed] the void" created by segregation. Florence Borders insisted that her mother did not think disdainfully of the people on Rampart. The street included "what they call rooming houses, because the situation at the time was that the men who ran on the railroad had time to spend in New Orleans. [They] could not check into any of the major hotels. They had to have some place to live, and many of the women who rented these

FIGURE 2.4. Dew Drop Inn, 1952. Shake dancers often performed at
New Orleans nightclubs. (Courtesy of Ralston Crawford Collection of New Orleans
Jazz Photography, Hogan Jazz Archive, Tulane University)

big houses on Rampart Street . . . to people who need[ed] a place to stay, just
considered this a business. . . . [The] segregated system did not provide for
the comfort of people."[53]

Despite Rampart Street's reputation, some girls did manage to sneak
out and enjoy black social life. Lilli Braud often went to clubs where she
enjoyed music, danced, and delighted in the excitement of black queer per-
formers, whom she considered her friends.[54] Teenager Beverly Carter also
went drinking and to the Tick Tock Tavern on South Rampart, although
her aunt (with whom she lived) strongly disapproved of her behavior,
suggesting that Beverly was out of control and did not act respectably.[55]
"Respectable" striving-class parents did not want black girls mingling with

FIGURE 2.5. Caravan Club, 1953. Albert Samuel "Junior" Garner started playing
the drums in New Orleans barrooms when he was only a preteen. Garner remembered
his nights in the mid-1940s: "I was going to elementary school and I was playing in the
Dew Drop six nights a week. I couldn't get a drink 'cause I was in elementary school. . . .
I played for all of the shows, all of the shake dancers; I was everybody's little brother."
(Courtesy of Ralston Crawford Collection of New Orleans Jazz Photography,
Hogan Jazz Archive, Tulane University)

cross-dressers, scantily clad shake-dancers, or women out enjoying the
night. They feared black nightlife on Rampart and its overt representations of sexual and bodily freedom. Figures 2.4, 2.5, and 2.6 represent
this world of black performance and nightlife that stood apart from and
challenged the staid politics of respectability. In these spaces, black per-
formers challenged geographic dislocations by inhabiting the performing
body—the reason why some mothers insisted that "ladies" did not hang

FIGURE 2.6. Female impersonator contest at the Dew Drop, 1954
(Courtesy of Ralston Crawford Collection of New Orleans Jazz Photography,
Hogan Jazz Archive, Tulane University)

out in barrooms. This, of course, is not to say that black middle-class New
Orleanians did not enjoy such entertainment. They did so, however, against
dictates of respectability, and black women thus risked being "insulted" as
improper. In such situations, we see "contests for civic space" between different groups of black New Orleanians.

Millie McClellan Charles lived only a few blocks from the Dew Drop Inn,
a club on LaSalle Street in uptown New Orleans. But like Clarita Reed and
Florence Borders, her parents restricted her movement. Not only was she
forbidden to go to the Dew Drop, she also could not go to Rampart Street or
to the Tick Tock Tavern. Charles recalled, "I'd sit down on my front porch
and look in there and wish I could [go in]. And when I got to be an adult, and
finally was on my own, . . . I went there and Frank saw me at the door. Frank
said, 'Millie, you can't come in here; I don't want your daddy getting behind
me.' And we laughed about that. . . . That was the nightclub. It was located
on LaSalle Street between Washington and Sixth. . . . See, the entertainment

was centered around Rampart Street."[56] Charles wanted to be a part of the music and club scene, but the entire neighborhood knew her father was an "almost militant," strict minister, so they looked after her, making sure she never broke the rules. Charles would walk the streets all around her neighborhood, and nobody bothered her. "They would protect me against anybody doing anything to me. . . . They knew you don't mess with Elder McClellan's daughter," explained Charles. "There was something personal in the relationship." But in explaining how she was "protected," Charles also highlighted street harassment. She was not "messed" with solely because of her father's position. Elder McClellan's concern with immorality in the neighborhood also affected how he dealt with his daughter. He did not allow her to enter clubs, nor did he allow her to dance. "My father didn't believe in dancing," she admitted; "he didn't know I danced." Charles graduated from McDonogh #35 High School in 1939 when she was only fifteen years old. But even then, her father continued to have strict control over her movement because she went to a black college in the city, Dillard University.[57]

Charles's father was not the only minister concerned with immorality on New Orleans' streets. In 1941 the *Chicago Defender*'s national edition reported on a special meeting of the city's black ministers, one that Charles's father likely attended. The meeting addressed the ministers' concerns over the sins of Rampart Street, namely the "juke joints" and gambling. The ministers talked of their attempts at "moral uplift" within the city.[58] The Interdenominational Ministerial Alliance, led by Reverend W. T. Handy of Mount Zion Methodist, conducted the meeting. According to one Dillard University student, Reverend Handy was known by some members of his congregation to "brag" and to be "too biggity and too showy . . . especially when there are visitors present. In his sermons he puts forth special effort to reveal the store of education that he has received."[59] Surely Handy's attempts at moral uplift disturbed his congregants who enjoyed a little dancing, drinking, or even gambling. At the Rampart Street meeting, Reverend Handy and the other ministers discussed the spread of debauchery from corrupt adults to innocent youths. The resolution the alliance drafted argued that gambling "contributes greatly to juvenile delinquency and an evolutionary demoralization of human character." Ministers, it seemed, found their own place on South Rampart Street.

The ministers were especially concerned with the girls who went to McDonogh #35 High School, which was located on South Rampart. They discussed five "gambling joints" on the street that were only "a stone's throw" from a police station. "Young girls and boys" from the school had to pass by the gambling establishments every day. The ministers were concerned that teenagers from #35 were exposed to immorality as they walked the street. They were most concerned about the girls, who, they claimed, "had been approached by men hanging around these joints, and in a few cases, had been lured into immoral relationships."[60] Rampart Street was indeed an area where grown men "approached" and harassed girls on the street. But girls were less likely to be "lured" into relationships than sexually harassed and abused because the men populating South Rampart Street defined teen-agers and young women as sexual objects. The "meddling" that occurred in the social space of Rampart Street marked McDonogh #35 students as women.

Black ministers who believed that McDonogh #35's location put female students' personal morality in jeopardy were certainly overreacting to the supposed dangers of the street (such as the "evolutionary demoralization" of character) and, more important, underestimating the girls' own resolve. A unique spatial dynamic existed between the McDonogh #35 girls and Rampart: the students found comfort in McDonogh #35 despite, or even because of, its location. Olga Merrick, who graduated from the school in the early 1930s, noted:

> The most striking thing, and to this day I have never forgotten, was the principal, Lucian V. Alexis. M-35 was at the corner of Rampart and Girod. And Rampart Street was a kind of hangout for our people, and Mr. Alexis had such a rapport with those people—everybody along the way protected us. All of us. And if anybody appeared like they were going to meddle any of us, some man, some colored man, always straightened them out and said, "That's an M-35 High School girl; don't bother her." And Mr. Alexis was just able to rule that street from Canal and Rampart all the way to Girod and Rampart. And nobody ever bothered us. And it was known to be a street where you could get meddled or whatever. And that was the most striking thing.[61]

Rampart was a paradoxical space where black girls experienced both safety and meddling.[62] Because McDonogh #35 was located in a black geograph-ical space, the local community could protect the girls who went to school there. Unlike the YWCA on Claiborne and Canal Street, where white boys accosted girls on their way to the building, Rampart ironically gave girls a certain type of safety, even though the school was located in a notorious gambling district where black girls and women were sexualized.

Merrick insisted that black girls and women knew Rampart Street as a site for street harassment; it was, after all, "a street where you could get meddled."[63] For black girls who suffered "insults," as Clarita Reed explained, the experience fit into a knowledge of space and place that also included a history of intraracial sexual abuse and harassment. Women who later articulated the "meddling" that happened on Rampart noted it because they wanted to clarify that they were not hanging out on Rampart Street for its unseemly entertainment. Instead, their articulations of street harassment explained the distinction between McDonogh #35 girls and other women and girls interacting on the street. This difference, in fact, often helped protect the high school girls as they traversed Rampart, whereas other black girls would not be "defended" by the black men on the street but instead would be open to abuse. These men, then, in their protection of McDonogh #35 students, defined which girls were worthy of protection based on class and educational attainments. Thus, the street harassment on Rampart constructed "worthy" middle-class and striving-class girls. M-35 girls felt as if they belonged on the geography of South Rampart because of the protection they received and so their subjectivities rotated around being schoolgirls.

For McDonogh #35 girls, the street was policed first by their principal, Lucian Alexis, and then by the men who lived or lingered on Rampart as well as by the ministers who attempted to rid the street of vice. The principal labored to control the street (he "ruled with an iron hand"), and Lucian Alexis's demeanor brooked no argument; not only were the men on the street afraid of him, so too were the students. He was an "old warrior who was very stern."[64] Female students suggested that Alexis was "eccentric" and "one of a kind," while another implied that he was unfriendly.[65] He was "a principal of a school on Rampart Street, which by any standard was a rough street," one former student described. "So he was trying to protect us as much as he was trying to protect himself. So he was a hard person to get close to. He wasn't friendly; he had this military bearing that he maintained all his life."[66] Alexis's "military bearing" helped him establish and maintain authority over the students and the geography of Rampart. He was so successful in this that girls such as Olga Merrick placed him and his authority on their mental map of Rampart Street. Alexis's concern with the safety of Rampart Street and his policing of the area revolved around gender. M-35 schoolgirls were more restricted in their movement at school than the boys. Audrey Carr Robertson graduated from M-35 in 1935. She remembered the crumbling building in relation to the neighborhood: "Our principal would let the boys go out, not the girls. We didn't go out into the streets; . . . you

FIGURE 2.7. McDonogh #35 High School (The Charles L. Franck Studio Collection at The Historic New Orleans Collection, accession no. 1979.325.1870)

brought your lunch. You sat around the building's yard. There wasn't much of a yard."[67]

Because of Alexis's iron rule, parents believed Rampart Street was safer than some of the more multiracial zones of "vice" whose location was only a few streets over from North Rampart. Storyville, the interracial prostitution zone (closed down during World War I), was located near North Rampart in the historic Treme neighborhood.[68] Despite the fact that legalized prostitution was shut down by 1930, the area was still known as a "red-light district." As a high school student in the late 1930s, Jesse Lawrence Moutan grew up in the Treme and walked to McDonogh #35. Moutan claimed that the "red-light district had not closed down then. We could not go through that area . . . to go to school. We had to walk all the way to Rampart Street, then go straight up Rampart Street. And if anybody saw you going through that district, [they would say] back to my mama, 'Why were you coming through that way?' 'Cause you just weren't supposed to. That was off-limits."[69] That parents preferred Rampart Street to some of the seedier streets only a few blocks over reveals the safety in passing through a black zone as opposed to streets where white men were known to loiter.

Black girls' movement along the entertainment district of Rampart Street illustrates the development of a gendered and classed sense of place. Furthermore, these girls' mapping of Rampart Street related directly to class status in New Orleans' black communities. Where a girl was headed as she walked along the street spoke directly to her class position. Especially in the 1930s, most black girls who could afford to attend high school rather than work to earn extra money for their families came from stable family backgrounds. They were able to go to school because someone in their family (often their parents, older siblings, or relatives) sacrificed their own hard work, money, or schooling to keep them at home. Once schoolgirls got to Rampart Street, the black men working, playing, and living on the street made the girls' class distinctions even clearer by marking their bodies as unpolluted from vice and worthy of protection. Walking along Rampart magnified the distinctions between male and female students of McDonogh #35. The girls had to be protected from meddling and policed by the school so they would not face danger or go out in search of pleasure.

But even in the moment of protection, black girls were forced to interact with men and to recognize male power on the street. Black girls' mental maps of Rampart Street included black men's power to harass a girl or to protect her. However, the geography of insults on Rampart Street would undergo a drastic change in the late 1950s and 1960s. A 1953 article in the *Chicago Defender* predicted that Rampart was to become a "ghost of days gone" as the city destroyed homes to "make way for a face lifting job which will see the construction of a modern civic center."[70] By the late 1950s, Rampart Street had already begun to change its character, dwindling from its heyday as the epicenter of New Orleans' black street life. And in September 1965, Hurricane Betsy hit New Orleans, killing dozens and causing more than one billion dollars' worth of destruction. The hurricane damaged many of the remaining homes, buildings, and businesses on Rampart Street. McDonogh #35, the local "landmark," was "ravaged to the point of total uselessness," and the school was relocated.[71] South Rampart has since become a series of parking lots, victim to the fate of many black neighborhoods leveled in the name of "progress" for city buildings, business development, and freeway construction.[72] As some critics have mourned, the history of black street life, clubs, and jazz is lost in this new mapping of New Orleans, but so too is an understanding of how black girls negotiated life in a Jim Crow city. Spaces of black leisure in New Orleans were paradoxical spaces for black girls—on the one hand, many girls found comfort in Rampart Street because they were protected, while some might have sought it out for fun. On the other hand, black girls' movements were highly controlled through street harassment and insults.

THE GEOGRAPHY OF INSULTS lays bare black girls' navigation of Jim Crow space in New Orleans. Many of these insults were never recorded. Verbal insults had a violence all their own, demonstrating the trauma of walking the streets as a black girl. But some insults descended into physical forms of violence. In 1944 a local grocery store owner insulted thirteen-year-old Hattie Louise Williams. Hattie Louise was escorting elementary school children from Joseph A. Craig School to St. Peter Claver Catholic Church for catechism. According to the *Louisiana Weekly*, "the children were walking the street in a double line" with two escorts, Hattie Louise and another student. On the way to the church, the children accidently stepped on freshly laid asphalt in front of Manuel Katz's grocery store. Katz began by insulting Hattie Louise, calling her "crazy." He then physically abused her: he slapped her face, bent her fingers back, and twisted her arms. As he assaulted her, he yelled, "Go tell it to your old black paw [*sic*]!" Hattie Louise's experience reveals the paradoxical nature of black Jim Crow space. The white grocer owned a store in the heart of the Treme—a black neighborhood, catering to black customers. Hattie Louise was "inside" the space of black New Orleans, a space that was supposed to be safe. But even here, black girls sometimes faced a hostile geography. Indeed, Hattie Louise Williams's role as a street monitor, watching over the younger children, signals the dangers of the Jim Crow geography. The *Louisiana Weekly* reported that after the attack, Hattie Williams was "at home under the care of a physician and is in a very nervous state."[73] Her "nervous state" reflected the trauma she suffered. This violence of Manuel Katz's insults would be forever etched into her mental map of Jim Crow New Orleans.

CHAPTER THREE

Defending Her Honor

Interracial Sexual Violence, Silences,
and Respectability

On Monday, February 10, 1930, Matt Piacum, a white restaurateur, called the police because his black teenage dishwasher, Hattie McCray, had been shot by Charles Guerand, a white patrolman. The police report recorded the facts of the crime: "Matt A. Piacum . . . notified the police, returning to the kitchen, Piacum asked Guerand why he shot Hattie McCray, Guerand stated that he was trying to have SEXUAL INTERCOURSE with her and that she ran at him with a knife, and he in turn shot her."[1] Charles Guerand's actions were so scandalous and the newspaper stories following the crime so melodramatic that for a moment, the silences in New Orleans' discourses of rape and race shattered. Yet over time, the history of interracial sexual violence has been lost under many layers of silence.[2]

To understand the life and death of Hattie McCray, it is crucial to understand both the politics of silence and the politics of respectability in black girls' lives. Silence, as I seek to define it, performs discursive work and has a life of its own. Silence is absence; it is stories half-told, knowing glances, and narratives and lives ignored. Histories of black girlhood and sexual violence expose the curious silences in discourses of race and sex in the Jim Crow South. Silence helps conceal what is inconvenient. Who can speak reveals systems of power, exposing who has authority over bodies. As a teenager, Amelda Betz, a black New Orleanian, worked as a nanny for the Kanton family, taking care of two small children. However, Betz's parents did not want her to work for the Kantons because, as Betz recalled in an oral history interview, "at that time my daddy and mama knew about Mr. Kanton's record." When the white interviewer asked what type of record the man had, Betz replied, "Well, he used to love colored girls, you see. . . . [His wife] didn't know, but all the colored people knew."[3] Although it was common knowledge in the South that white men abused young black girls, such information was whispered about, rumors spread quietly, or the abuse remained a public secret within local communities. These silences were necessary. Black girls in New Orleans could be punished for accusing white men of rape. In 1933, one eleven-year-old black girl, for example, was arrested after her grandmother's white employer raped her while her grandmother worked.[4]

In her memoir about growing up during the Jim Crow era, writer Endesha Holland theorizes the place of silence in the discourses of black female sexuality and black girls' subjectivities. Holland recalls her own experience with rape: a white employer, Mr. Lawrence, aided by his wife, raped Holland when she was a preteen. Holland was supposed to be babysitting their children. Unlike Amelda Betz's parents, Holland's father did not warn her about the danger of white domestic spaces or working for predatory white men. Later, Holland blamed her absent father for her vulnerability:

> I figured later that about half the girls my age in [my town]—maybe the whole Delta—lived without fathers. Out of those, maybe three quarters had been thrown by the bull like me. And we didn't have to be sitting babies or cleaning houses to fall victim to the white man's lust. We could just as easily be picking cotton or walking to the store or spending money in the white man's store when the mood would take him and he'd take us—just like that, like lightning striking.[5]

As a girl, Holland knew her school friend had experienced similar abuse while working in a white home. "Our eyes met in the mirror and we both knew; I knew she had been upstairs, and she knew I had been upstairs. It brought us together, it kept us apart," Holland explained.[6] This knowing was a secretive knowing. Their dual secrets kept them apart because they could never fully acknowledge what had happened; they could never fully define the meaning of "upstairs" in a white man's house. "Upstairs" was a metaphor for the intimate and dangerous geographies of white homes and a metaphor for their silence. After all, as Holland writes, "part of the code of having known a man was that you never talked about it openly—even with your best friend. Even girls who had lost their virginity 'naturally'—to a black boy their age, even a football star—never came right out and admitted they'd had sex. You could only let the fact be known . . . to fellow travelers who'd gone your way, through sly innuendo, knowing glances and telling silence—the way outcasts in any society identify each other."[7] This "telling silence" was one type of silence that characterized interracial sexual violence and black girls' vulnerability to white men, argues Holland. As a girl, she could not let anyone know that she had been raped because it threatened her reputation and respectability. The politics of respectability required a "long-suffering silence." Feeling like grown women and carrying women's secrets, Holland and her friend went on, jealous of "the 'children' who still acted their age."[8] As Holland describes it, her silence was that of the double bind: between the realities of Jim Crow violence and the politics of respectability.

Sexual Violence in Black and White: Silences in the White Public Imagination

White southerners considered interracial sex taboo. However, "interracial sex" most often referred to sexual contact between white women and black men. The threat of lynching hung in the air of the South for any black man in, or rumored to be in, even a consensual interracial relationship. Many people during the early twentieth century, and historians since, have discussed the terror associated with lynching.[9] Within the white public sphere, then, selective silences defined interracial sexual contact as specifically gendered: white women and black men.

At the dawn of legalized segregation in the South, gendered definitions of white and black were deployed to create and maintain new codifications of race. Thomas Dixon's novel *The Clansman: A Historical Romance of the Ku Klux Klan* (1905), along with D. W. Griffith's film version of the book, *The Birth of a Nation* (1915), revealed the importance of gender and sexuality to the southern racial project.[10] The film and book attempted to document and justify the historic rise of the Ku Klux Klan. Their narratives center on black men's supposedly insatiable lust for white women and their corresponding inability to participate in political citizenship. According to Thomas Dixon and D. W. Griffith, black men were too inexperienced and too distracted by their sexuality to properly take part in the political process; in addition, white women were too naive and weak to protect themselves or to make coherent decisions. Both the novel and film depict a respectable young white woman endangered by an oversexed black man drunk on his own political power and lust.[11] Dixon was fanatical about the impropriety and dangers of interracial sex, despite (or because of) his white father's biracial child born out of wedlock.[12] The silence here is a family secret: Thomas Dixon had a black half-brother.

As Dixon, Griffith, and others bemoaned white woman's sexual vulnerability, black women were meaningfully absent from public and cultural representations of race and rape. Their bodies became a reverse image to the white ideal of the respectable white woman as "the association between darkness and eroticism cast white women *en masse* in the role of the 'ice goddess'; upon black women were projected the fears and fascinations of female sexuality."[13] Not only were black women eroticized, but also many white commentators vilified black girlhood by sexualizing young black bodies and by denying black girls childhood innocence.[14] As Robin Bernstein explains, "White children became constructed as tender angels while black children were libeled as unfeeling, noninnocent, nonchildren."[15] For black girls, this meant that their bodies were available for white consumption.

The construction of "noninnocent, nonchildren" can even be seen in John Dollard's 1937 classic, *Caste and Class in a Southern Town*. White sociologist Dollard relates the story of a white man who had sex with black girls. "A lively woman informant" had told Dollard about a "middle-class man who was infatuated with Negro girls." As the story progresses, the age of the "girls" or young women remains unclear.[16] But Dollard continues to use the word "girl" in the passage:

> Whenever he went down-town he would not notice the white women on the street, but would follow Negro women with his eyes and then pursue them, catch them in an alley where he could talk, and ask to go home and sleep with them. Apparently he was notorious in Southerntown [Indianola, Mississippi] for this, and got a venereal disease from these girls, referred to by my informant as a "terrible disease." She said she did not understand how his wife could tolerate having him in bed with her. Finally his wife did not dare let him go into town alone, but always went with him to see that he did not follow the Negro girls. Here is to be noted the strong disapproval of the people of Southerntown which forced the white man to talk with Negro girls in alleys and which otherwise discredited him in the community.[17]

Liberal scholar John Dollard highlights here, likely by accident, how black girls' bodies were sexualized, available for white men. The white man in the story, who receives Dollard's pity, was reduced to looking for the "fears and fascinations" of sexuality in alleyways because of the rules of polite white society. What Dollard does not say is that this man chased girls, harassed them on the street, and likely made no distinction between grown women and teenage girls. For Dollard, white men were not responsible for rape and street harassment, there was no need for "consent," and black teenagers were "noninnocent, nonchildren."

The silence surrounding black girls and women as victims of sexual violence was one of many "peculiar silences" within the discourse of sexuality during the Jim Crow era. These silences reveal both the idiosyncrasies within the discourse of sexuality and the power at stake in discussions of black and white sexualities. Importantly, "like speech, the meaning of silence depends on a power differential that exists in every rhetorical situation: who can speak, who must remain silent, who listens and what those listeners can do."[18] The formation of sexuality at this time was never "subjected to dense discursive articulation"[19] because it focused specifically on those (often fictional) aspects of sexuality that supported a racist social order. In other words, white men never fully articulated white male sexual desire as it would have directly contradicted the idea of civilized white men versus unqualified black men. Meanwhile, these public discourses of sexuality also silenced white female desire, particularly that of the upper and middle classes. Therefore, a main element in the discursive formation of racialized sexuality at the time was "its strategic . . . deployment of a peculiar 'silence.' "[20]

These silences were "peculiar" in their obvious irregularity. Stories had to be half-told or rewritten and truths were hidden in order to keep racialized definitions of sexuality intact. So, white men in the public sphere associated interracial sex with black men's trespasses against white womanhood. And as white men and women routinely accused black men of raping white women or even of looking at them in the "wrong" way, whites with political power conveniently ignored the rape of black women and girls by white men. These peculiar silences regarding sexual violence were best explored by Ida B. Wells's investigative reporting. As early as 1892, Wells, in her famous *Southern Horrors: Lynch Law in All Its Phases*, challenged the idea that white men were "protecting women and children by lynching." As Wells listed towns where lynchings had occurred for consensual black male–white female relationships, she pointed out that at the same time, a white man had raped a black girl, escaping serious punishment and community censure. Wells reported: "At the very moment these civilized whites were announcing their determination to 'protect their wives and daughters,' by murdering [a black man], a white man was in the same jail for raping eight-year-old Maggie Reese, an Afro-American girl. . . . The outrage upon helpless childhood needed no avenging in this case; she was black."[21] By exposing the silences in white discourses of rape and lynching, Wells attempted to show the illogic of white supremacy and its definitions of sexual violence. Simultaneously, Wells demonstrated the way in which silence worked to uphold the racial power dynamics of segregation.

The peculiar silences around the issue of sexual violence did not remain entirely unnoticed by white activists against violence, either. A small group of southern black and white women worked together, attempting to end the horrors of lynching; these women realized that lynching was predicated on the privileges of white manhood. In the 1930s, members of the Association of Southern Women for the Prevention of Lynching attempted to use their position as white women to end the social custom of lynching. They did so by purposely complicating the southern story of race and sex.[22] The women "explore[d] the myths of black women's promiscuity and white women's purity, and noted how this split image created a society that 'considers an assault by a white man as a moral lapse upon his part, better ignored and forgotten, while an assault by a Negro against a white woman is a hideous crime punishable with death by law or lynching."[23] Nonetheless, for the majority of white southerners, the rape of black women and girls seemed impossible. The definitions of race and gender in the Jim Crow South were predicated on this very "fact." "Silence in the South," a scholar who grew up during segregation noted, "is like a shimmering mirage that hovers in the distance over a blacktop country road; it is always there, yet at the same time it is impervious to close inspection."[24]

Oral Histories and the Violence of the Ordinary: Breaking Peculiar Silences

Not only were there silences in white discourses of sexuality, but there were also silences within African American discussions of sex and sexuality, just as Endesha Holland explained. Black women did not feel comfortable talking about their inner lives or their struggle with sexual violence—especially not in the open, where white ears could hear, but also often not even with each other. Many of these silences originated in black women's desire to survive the humiliations of Jim Crow life. Rarely did black women openly discuss interracial sexual violence. For one, it was not safe to accuse white men of such a transgression, particularly powerful white men. Second, black women who were victims of sexual assault often wanted to keep the violence to themselves; being a victim of sexual violence could have been used against them by whites claiming they were sexually promiscuous.

Darlene Clark Hine has explored this type of silence, arguing that a "culture of dissemblance" kept black women from speaking about rape in order to protect their dignity and shield them from disapprobation.[25] Connected to this "culture of dissemblance" was the very real need for all black Americans to focus on survival; talking aloud about the pain and terror of segregation was not seen as a key to enduring the hardship of Jim Crow.[26] Instead of dwelling on the horrors of life, black communities encouraged each other and particularly their children to think positively of the promises of the future. Teachers told children they were talented; schools emphasized self-respect and fortitude by teaching the great African American poets (such as Paul Laurence Dunbar) and songs like "Lift Every Voice and Sing."[27] Because of all the various types of silences, the emphasis on self-respect, and the deemphasis on the struggles of everyday life, finding records of sexual violence suffered by black women in the archive is extremely difficult for historians.[28]

The sexual violence perpetrated against black girls can nonetheless be traced through both the many peculiar silences and the rare moments when these silences were interrupted. Oral histories that recount life in the Jim Crow South help to break through such silences. At some points, interviewees only hint toward a history of sexual violence and harassment, purposefully leaving holes in their stories that help maintain privacy and shield inner lives. Other times, interviewees boldly tell stories of sexual violence in order to bring to light a part of history that informed how they saw themselves and constructed their raced and gendered subjectivities in the segregated South.

The secrecy surrounding the discourse of sexual violence was made clear in an interview with Herbert Cappie and his wife, Ruth Irene Cappie, conducted in New Orleans in the 1990s. Herbert and Ruth, both teenagers in New Orleans during the 1930s, recalled events regarding sexual violence that took place in their neighborhood. Herbert Cappie began by explaining how dangerous it was for black boys and teenagers at the time: "Growing up, too, was traumatic when I was in my late teens because during those years there would be cases of rape. And if a white girl were raped, all black boys had to stay off the streets until the police had picked up one as a suspect."[29] After discussing incidents of false rape accusations, Herbert Cappie then turned to the problems young black girls and women faced when dealing with white men. Not surprisingly, as he began talking about the reverse side of interracial sexual violence (white men raping black women), his language became much more guarded. He said, "There were incidents in the black neighborhoods, the white men going with black women; yeah, it happened frequently." At first it is difficult to discern if the interracial relationships he referred to were coerced or not. But then he gave an example:

> HERBERT CAPPIE: I should let my wife tell you about this one because she is more familiar with it than I am. This bus driver would stop his bus and he would go into this woman's house and he'd spend considerable time in there. It was obvious to everybody what was going on, till a bunch of the men in the neighborhood

got together and they caught the man, and they beat the hell out of him. It was Wingy, it was another one of them I can't remember—

RUTH CAPPIE: —Francis.

HERBERT CAPPIE: Don't call his name! Don't do that. The man is dead now; let him rest in peace.[30]

The peculiar secrets in this memory abound, but the dialogue between the Cappies in the interview is particularly revealing. Herbert Cappie, when explaining the white bus driver's actions, claimed that "it was obvious to everybody what was going on." However, what might have been obvious to their community at the time of the event is not so obvious in his retelling of the story. He never clarified the relationship between the white bus driver and the black woman. It was only through the resolution of the story, when the black men in the neighborhood banded together in order to prevent the bus driver from returning, that the possibly coercive nature of the bus driver's behavior becomes clearer. To beat up a white man at this time was extremely dangerous for blacks, and they did so under the veil of anonymity. Ruth Cappie's insertion of the name Francis, one of the men who defended his neighbor, bothered Herbert Cappie, despite the fact that Francis was no longer alive.

The brief exchange between husband and wife reveals how silence in this story of possible abuse exists on several levels. First, the exact behavior of the bus driver and the neighborhood woman remains clouded in mystery. Second, not only did the victim of the assault go unnamed, but so too did the men who defended her. Indeed, the importance of this level of secrecy was confirmed by Herbert Cappie's reluctance to name the participants. And finally, it remains unclear as to why Ruth Cappie would be "more familiar" with the story than her husband. Perhaps the woman was a friend or family member of hers. Or maybe it was something the women in the community talked about at the time of the event. Either way, the Cappies left conspicuous holes in the telling of this story, leaving the entire event open to multiple interpretations.

Wanda Dell Regan also insinuated that sexual abuse and sexual harassment were common problems in the city. But like the Cappies, she did so just barely, leaving large gaps in her retelling of life during segregation. Wanda Dell Regan moved to New Orleans in 1935, when she was twenty years old, to escape the poverty of the country, exacerbated by the Great Depression.[31] She came to the city looking for job opportunities, certain that New Orleans would be a better place for her because in the country "you either did domestic work or you went into the fields. And I didn't intend to do either." By moving to New Orleans, she felt as though she would have a chance to find a more fulfilling and better paying job. Historian Michele Mitchell, the interviewer who recorded Regan's story for the Behind the Veil oral history project, asked what New Orleans was like when she arrived. Regan recalled: "Terrible. You went into the sewing factory or restaurant. And I didn't like restaurants because I didn't like the customers thinking they could get familiar with you."[32] Just as she began explaining the difficulties on the job (customers getting "familiar"), she stopped and told Mitchell to turn the tape off. Whether she finished her story by talking about the insults hurled at working black women by white men or by discussing sexual harassment by white customers, we will never know. Wanda Regan's interview further demonstrates the ways in which silence was maintained by black women to shield their inner lives. Even as she explained why New Orleans was "terrible" at first, she did so in an impersonal manner. Rather than talking about her personal experience, she distanced her language—instead of using "me," she chose the word "you," saying the customers felt they could get "familiar with you." Perhaps once the tape recorder was off, she specified her story, but it is just as likely that she continued speaking in a vague manner. What is clear from her interview is that Wanda Dell Regan did not mind sharing part of herself with the young black interviewer, but she did not want to share her inner secrets with the oral history project as a whole or to record intimate stories on tape.[33]

Not only did teenagers and young working women have to cope with sexual abuse and harassment; so too did black children. The children who experienced sexual violence often kept the incidents to themselves. At the same time, the familiarity with white violence defined their childhoods. In some oral histories, those who had been children during segregation spoke up, often breaking years of silence.

Stine George, an African American man born in 1931 in the rural South, recalled an event that happened when he was seven. One Sunday in 1938, George, his five-year-old brother, and his nine-year-old sister were on their way to see their cousins. A young white man whom the Stine children knew stopped them. The man took Stine's sister into a house and raped her. The young boys were left outside, wondering what would happen to their sister. Frightened, they ran into the woods for safety. Stine George was sixty-three at the time of his interview. As he began to narrate his memory, George said, "I shall never forget this, and this is something nobody ever knew because we don't tell it. I wouldn't tell it now because it's painful, it will be painful to even tell it, but with what you are doing, I'll tell it."[34] The trauma caused by his sister's rape left a scar on Stine George. And as he talked to the interviewer, he emphasized that this memory had been silenced within him. He attempted to stress to the interviewer that the story was (and is) never told, and by using the present tense, he emphasized how the silence traveled through the past straight into the present: "we don't tell it," he said. According to George, the reason for the silence was twofold: they did not have the power to accuse even a white teen of raping a black girl, and the story was simply too painful to recount.[35]

It is especially significant that witnessing the rape of his sister was part of his childhood memories. As he told the story he continually emphasized their ages: "All of us, under ten. . . . Like I said, my sister was but nine or ten."[36] His repetition of their ages suggests that Stine could not completely comprehend the sexual abuse as it happened, for they were all less than ten years old. It also suggests a trace of guilt—by reiterating his age and youth, he reminded himself and his listener of his helplessness.[37]

Ferdie Walker, born in 1928 and growing up in the urban streets of Atlanta, was also haunted by the memory of sexual assault. In her interview for the Behind the Veil oral history project, she said, "I'll tell you this one thing that really sticks in my mind, one really harassing kind of thing that I went through at the time. I was eleven years old, and I will never forget it."[38] Every week, Ferdie waited for the bus at her local stop, where two white policemen would regularly drive by and expose themselves to her. As an adult retelling this story, she attempted to emphasize the type of trauma that this form of sexual violence had on her. She said, "I had a morbid fear of policemen all my life and it has not completely gone away yet."[39] Walker's memories reveal the intense feeling of insecurity that many young girls experienced during Jim Crow. Ferdie Walker knew she was vulnerable and realized that she could not trust whites, something made painfully obvious because the police, who were supposed to protect children, would not protect her. At eleven years old, Ferdie Walker was forced to become aware that her body was seen as a sexual object. Her encounter with the policemen became a moment of embodiment, of "becoming a body in social space."[40]

The encounter highlighted her status in society as a black girl and was part of the sexual socialization of girls in the segregated South. White violence was outside the bounds of the law. The abuse mapped her body as part of an unprotected minority: "That was really bad," she recalled, "and it was bad for *all black girls*, you know."[41] By asserting that *all* black girls suffered sexual assault from white men, Walker portrayed black girlhood as a community that encountered the intersection of racial and sexual violence. By doing so, she insisted that black girls who came of age during segregation had common experiences with white violence and thus a common identity.

In these accounts of sexual violence, the children coped by trying to hide from whites, retreating to spaces where they could disappear. This hiding represents another form of silence within the experience of sexual violence. For, as children hid, they vanished from the space of segregation, silencing their very existence and their experience. Stine George hid in the woods with his brother.[42] Ferdie Walker stepped back from the curb and withdrew from view while waiting for the bus. That both interviewees remembered hiding signals the intensity of trying to disappear from the white gaze (and in Walker's case, the white male gaze intent on sexualizing her body). Young Endesha Holland also made use of geographic disappearance: "One time [Mr. Lawrence] almost came into the kitchen. . . . He didn't notice me, perhaps because I stood way back, making myself invisible. At ten I had already learned the secret of invisibility all black folks knew."[43] The act of vanishing was to protect one's self. Black children knew that to survive in the Jim Crow world, they had to walk the streets carefully. In part, the effect of disappearing meant withdrawing from the streets and society, silencing one's physical self. Abdul JanMohamed, in his discussion of "racialized sexuality," appropriates Foucault's rule of "the cycle of prohibition" to express the double bind of a raced (and I would add here *gendered*) subject in the Jim Crow era: "renounce yourself or suffer the penalty of being suppressed; do not appear if you do not want to disappear. Your existence will be maintained only at the cost of your nullification."[44] For children, the act of disappearance was important for their very survival.

Ferdie Walker admitted to the interviewer that she never told her mother what happened. Her experience with the police officers was kept within— her own secret. She said, "If I had gone home, my mother would have made me stay."[45] She explained that the bus driver knew she would be at that particular stop, so he always stopped, regardless of whether she was visible or not. Thus, by hiding and keeping secrets, she refused to cede the streets as white ground. At age eleven, she resisted by remaining on the city streets, even if that meant she had to vanish.

Fear is also a central theme in these remembrances. Walker described her lifelong fear of policemen as "morbid." Stine George continuously talked about his and his brother's fear: they were scared, they did not know what was happening, they did not know what to do, and they did not know where to go. This type of sexual terrorism focused particularly on children; the fear it caused stayed with Stine George and Ferdie Walker their entire lives.[46] As scared and confused as Stine George and his brother were, their sister must have been not only physically hurt but also terrified. She was taken from her brothers, assaulted, and then left to find her way back home alone. How might Stine George's sister and Ferdie Walker have understood their experience? What was their framework for understanding white violence toward their bodies and their selves?

Hattie McCray's death offers a different avenue for understanding sexual violence. Unlike oral histories, the McCray case provides the wider cultural framework for grappling with the issue of sexual violence by bringing the state concretely into the narrative and by revealing a parallel discourse about sexual purity that existed in the black press. By reconstructing the discourse surrounding Guerand's attack on her, meanings associated with black girlhood—and particularly with black girls' sexuality—become clear.

Hattie McCray and Charles Guerand: Murder as a Sexualized Crime

Hattie McCray, a black fourteen-year-old, from uptown New Orleans, worked as a waitress only three blocks from her home. Her workplace was a familiar, yet treacherous geography. On February 10, 1930, an off-duty white police officer, Charles Guerand, attempted to rape her.[47] According to one report, fearing for her safety, McCray had fled to the kitchen. After announcing to all those around that he would "kill that God Damned Nigger wench," Guerand followed Hattie. In the kitchen, "an argument concerning the girl's chastity ensued." After the dispute, Charles Guerand proceeded to shoot and kill Hattie McCray.[48]

After the crime, the police quickly arrested Guerand, and much to the surprise of New Orleanians, in April 1930 he was found guilty of murder and sentenced to death by an all-white male jury.[49] The guilty verdict was reported as a triumph in both the black and white papers; it was the first time in New Orleans history that such a verdict had been given to a white man for killing a black girl. There was no denying that the case brought white men's sexual contact with black girls into the courtroom and the newspapers. The case was understood as a sexual crime. One black teenager and McDonogh #35 student, Althea Hart, wrote to W. E. B. Du Bois at the NAACP about McCray's death. Hart argued that "far too many of our people have suffered the same injustices as this girl and the same thing will continue if our people doesn't stand behind us." Hart acknowledged that "the victim was but a child and had been annoyed by this man for some time. He insulted the girl."[50] Hart placed Hattie McCray's experience within a wide framework of black girlhood under Jim Crow. Black girls, as we have seen, were constantly "annoyed" and "insulted." Hart, by using the word "insult," emphasized both the sexual violence and street harassment experienced by McCray and other black girls in the segregated South. Hart's letter also demonstrates how black school girls thought and talked about the case. Her emphasis on childhood highlighted the need to fight constructions of "noninnocent, nonchildren." McCray's death would have deeply affected other girls her age as they thought about their place in Jim Crow New Orleans.

Both because McCray was killed and because of the sensational nature of Guerand's crime, the silence regarding the sexual abuse of black girls by white men was made public. However, the silence was broken only for a moment, as the white press and judicial system attempted to bring order back to the sexual discourses of race and place. Although the newspapers had varying interpretations of the crime, certain things were clear: this was a sexualized murder, and Charles Guerand killed Hattie McCray because he was denied access to her body. According to Guerand's statement to the police, he had been "fooling" with the "Negro girl" all morning.[51] Hattie's white boss stated that Guerand could not "make her," and so he killed her.[52] Guerand was infuriated because he assumed that this body would be available to him, and he acted on his sexual fantasy through violence. The hubris displayed, particularly in announcing his intentions to those around him, suggests that he believed the murder of a black girl a prerogative of his whiteness.

Despite New Orleans' infamous reputation as a city with frequent color line crossings and interracial sex, Louisiana, like other southern states, had become increasingly concerned with regulating the boundaries between white and black.[53] The process that solidified Jim Crow laws in New Orleans also ended some of the city's more renowned interracial contact.[54] In fact, interracial marriage was outlawed in 1894, and interracial concubinage was declared illegal (at least on paper) in 1907.[55] And white New Orleanians interpreted, at least in part, *Plessy v. Ferguson* as an attempt to separate the races physically because of fears of interracial sexual contact. A white New Orleanian who supported segregation suggested as much, saying, "A man [who] would be horrified at the idea of his wife or daughter seated by the side of a burly negro in the parlor of a hotel or at a restaurant cannot see her occupying a crowded seat in a car next to a negro without the same feeling of disgust."[56] This man's hypothetical example of the "horror" of integration only worked because whiteness was represented by a genteel white woman, while blackness was represented by a "burly negro" man. White-black touching in this context was sexualized, yet the fear displayed by white men was directed toward sexual contact between black men and white women only. Thus, by 1930, what was so striking about Guerand's conviction is that it brought men's sexual exploitation of black girls out from the shadows.

Interpretations of Murder and Sexuality in the White Press

Neither New Orleans' history of interracial sex nor its relatively recent prohibitions against it prepared the white press for Guerand's shocking behavior. As the facts of the case and trial unfolded, the white press did not initially support Guerand, but reporters treaded carefully so as to protect the reputation of whiteness. And although they condemned the murder, New Orleans' white newspapers downplayed Guerand's crossing of the color line, treating it as something best ignored or politely glossed over. They were therefore not concerned with the life or person of Hattie McCray. Too much talk of Guerand's horrifying actions would bring attention to white men's culpability in interracial sex and interracial sexual abuse.

Therefore, the white press attempted to preserve a silence—that of interracial sexual desire on the part of Guerand. Reporters for the white press never failed to mention that Guerand was "threatened" physically by McCray at the time of the killing, thus implicitly suggesting self-defense rather than a sexualized crime. They did this despite the fact that Guerand was nearly a foot taller and seventy pounds heavier than McCray.[57] For example, the *Times-Picayune*'s first story on the murder, under the subtitle "Threatened with Knife," noted, "Going into the rear of the place . . . the policeman made advances to the girl and an argument ensued. According to Assistant District Attorneys Culligan and Granzin, to whom Guerand made a verbal statement, the girl reached for a knife, threatening to kill him."[58] Another paper alleged, "Guerand, according to the police report, made an indecent proposal to the negro girl. . . . She refused to accede to his wishes, the report said, and an argument ensued. . . . [T]he girl reached for a knife and threatened to kill him."[59] Although the papers referred to the "indecent" overtures made by Guerand, they always figured the killing as one of self-defense rather than one of sexual desire and control.

There was little evidence that the five-foot-one, 115-pound McCray even had a knife at the time of her murder except for Guerand's own statement to the police. At the crime scene, the investigators found no weapon beside her body.[60] And further, by naming Guerand's sexual actions as "advances" or "indecent proposals," the white press suggested that he asked for sex rather than demanded it. Such a suggestion epitomized the idea that an adolescent black girl might want to have sex with a grown white man, casting black girls as smaller versions of black jezebels. Although the *Times-Picayune* continued to report on Guerand's court battles for the next five years, it mentioned Guerand's sexual intentions only once more, at the time of his conviction.

The white press spoke so little of interracial sex and desire because Guerand's actions embodied the abject. His crime blurred essential definitions that helped order and classify Jim Crow society.[61] The abject is unacceptable, disgusting, and frightening as it makes ordinary understandings of life confusing. In this case, Guerand's crime confused definitions fundamental to white supremacy because his actions, when fully articulated, disturbed classifications of white versus black manhood and white female purity versus black female immorality. Thus, the crime could not be told in its entirety; silences were necessary. Furthermore, that Guerand was a police officer was especially troubling. As a white man he was supposed to be a calm, controlled citizen. As a patrolman, Guerand was a member of the white working class, but in his job he represented the rationality of white rule in New Orleans. When narrated clearly, Charles Guerand's crime disturbed the definitions of white manhood and in turn white identity. The truth of the crime had the potential to collapse racial meanings or to expose the fallacies upon which they were based.[62]

Furthermore, the white press's troubling narrative of the crime disavowed Hattie McCray's pain. As one feminist scholar explains, "Pain is what divided white childhood from black childhood in U.S. popular culture."[63] The denial of Hattie's pain by the white press was a disowning of a psychic realm of interiority.[64] She was not granted a self that could be terrified, hurt, or injured, so even as papers like the *New Orleans Times* reported on the event, they denied McCray full personhood. They marked her as nothing but a body, absent of any interior emotions. Further, by suggesting that she initiated the violence, the press ignored the more likely scenario that she felt fear. Instead, she was cast as a rebellious, possibly even dangerous working girl. Certainly, McCray, staring at a potential rapist who had the power to arrest her or injure her physically, must have been petrified. The writers in the white press denied Hattie McCray an interior self by ignoring the actual event that led to the killing—an attempted rape. And thus the murder was not placed in its proper context. The white press disregarded how McCray's personhood/girlhood was denied at the moment Guerand assumed she was sexually available.

In April 1930, after the jury declared Guerand guilty, the *New Orleans States* mentioned again the reason for the crime, this time clearly calling Guerand's act "immoral." In so doing, the paper suggested that Guerand's interracial encounter prior to the killing was inappropriate and *not* community-sanctioned. It gave credit to McCray's white male boss for protecting the young girl: "It was shown that the policeman had pursued the girl with immoral intentions and had been twice repulsed by her. On the evening of the murder he had repeated his attempt . . . [but] had been prevented from attacking her by her employer and then deliberately shot her down."[65] If the paper was making allusions to interracial sex between white men and black women, it did so carefully. By insisting that McCray's boss, rather than her own resistance, protected her from assault, it suggested that although there was inappropriate behavior on the part of Guerand, white manhood en masse and its morality were not called into question.

Not only did the *States* praise the white boss, but it also gave credit to the all-male white jury, declaring the jurors' decision "just." "This verdict of an unusually courageous jury," argued the paper, "ought to have a repressive effect on men like this policeman who believe that persons of color have no rights they are required to respect. It means that in this city the Negro can and does get justice and protection in our criminal courts."[66] The editors of the paper fully distanced themselves from Guerand's actions. In opposition to Guerand's errant manhood, the members of the jury were described as proper, civilized men ("courageous"). By closing the case, silence regarding the issue of sexual abuse was restored for the white community because, as the verdict seemed to demonstrate, "the Negro" got justice and white men were "courageous." However, the author of this article failed to see the contradictions in his or her argument. The paper claimed that African Americans were given justice and protection in court, but it is clear that they were not safe on the streets of New Orleans. Guerand was a police officer and thus himself a part of the criminal justice system. And although his actions were not sanctioned by the police department, black New Orleanians knew there were many other officers who used their power to harass black girls and boys.[67] Guerand's belief that he had power over Hattie suggested how elusive safety and protection were for black girls in Jim Crow New Orleans.

Girlhood, Sexuality, and Respectability in the Black Press

The black press strategically used Hattie McCray's tragic, untimely death to break the peculiar silence about sexuality and race in the Jim Crow South. The case illustrated the fallacy of stereotypes of whiteness and blackness. By placing the case in the headlines, the press attempted to prove that white men (not black men) were capable of being sexual "beasts" and full of "lust." And at the same time, the newspapers challenged white definitions of black girlhood as sexually advanced and promiscuous. In so doing, they disproved the adage "that not only was there no such thing as a chaste Negro woman— but that a Negro woman could not be assaulted, that it was never against her will."[68] The black press seized the opportunity to define black girlhood as pure, good, and virginal. Consequently, Hattie McCray's *respectability* became the most important element of her tragic story.

From the very first glance at black newspapers, African American readers never doubted the sexual nature of Hattie McCray's murder. The black press focused directly on the sexual aspect of the encounter and portrayed the murder itself as a sexual crime. The *Louisiana Weekly*'s first article on the murder announced "Girl Refused Advances of White Beast" on the front page.[69] It introduced the case to its readers by calling Guerand a "lust crazed murderer" guilty of a "wanton killing."[70] The black press purposely and explicitly turned the dominant language of race and rape on its head. By employing the language of a sexually "crazed," lustful beast, the *Weekly* drew on a discourse most often deployed by the white press to describe black men.[71] By March, the *Chicago Defender* also ran an article on Hattie McCray's murder. Because of its distance from Guerand's transgression and, more important, from the South, the paper was extremely bold and straightforward in reporting the crime, claiming that the "policeman became attracted to her."[72] And in April, the African American newspaper the *Pittsburgh Courier* ran an article on McCray.[73]

Afro-American and Afro-Creole newspapers had a long history in New Orleans. The *Louisiana Weekly* had been founded in 1925 by a middle-class black Creole family and was deeply concerned with the politics of respectability.[74] The paper promoted "proper" behavior for blacks by publishing articles that urged black Americans to act tastefully and featured photographs of respectable striving-class women.[75] The paper's emphasis on self-respect and the rights of citizenship despite America's racist society made "respectability" more than a moral code—it was political.

Women and men who aligned themselves with such a philosophy "contested racist discourses and rejected white America's depiction of black

FIGURE 3.1. *Louisiana Weekly* headline regarding Hattie McCray, February 22, 1930
(Courtesy of the *Louisiana Weekly*)

women as immoral, childlike, and unworthy of respect or protection."[76] But just as respectability symbolized a political stance, it was also a mode of self-presentation. For many middle-class and striving-class black New Orleanians, respectability required "proper conduct" and appearance in order for African Americans to remain clean, pure, and ready for citizenship.[77] At the turn of the century and into the 1920s, there was a concern among some middle-class African Americans over the possibility that lower-class and working black women were sexually degenerate, particularly those exposed to the dangers and seductions of the bustling modern city.[78] Middle-class and striving-class black Americans who were obsessed with "morality" made girls and young women responsible for their own respectability. They assumed lower-class girls had undesirable personalities and shockingly bad or outdated ethics. The politics of respectability was concerned with girls' ethics and sexuality—yet these discourses often ignored the possibility of unwanted sexual contact.

For black New Orleanians, Hattie McCray's resolve to fight Guerand proved that black women were not sexually promiscuous. The *Weekly* advertised her purity in big letters, highlighting the respectability of McCray. The NAACP and the Federated Civic League of Louisiana raised funds from the black community to help the state prosecute Guerand. A resolution published in the *Weekly* by the Federated Civic League highlighted the sexual nature of the crime and Hattie McCray's purity, therefore revealing the politics of respectability at play in the local discourse: "Hattie McCray, a colored girl, of but 14 years has been ruthlessly murdered by a white police officer, not in the discharge of his duty, but in an effort to appease his bestial lust. . . . [W]hereas the said Hattie McCray did give her life in defense of her honor, therefore be it resolved that . . ."[79] It is clear that honor required *defending*, that respectability was a girl's responsibility.

The language in the resolution and in the paper following the crime exposed the double bind presented in the discourse of rape in the local black press. Young girls faced a difficult choice: be "ruined" by white men or face possible death or imprisonment. Another case reported by the *Weekly* some years later carried a similar message; a black girl successfully fought off her white attacker only to be jailed in a Louisiana state penitentiary.[80]

The public celebration of Hattie's virtue by the NAACP, the *Louisiana Weekly*, and the *Chicago Defender* reminded readers that respectable womanhood and girlhood was the ideal image for "the race" as a whole. Pretty, innocent girlhood symbolized a dignity and morality absent from mainstream white discourses of black Americans.[81] The NAACP magazine the

Crisis represented the wholesomeness of the race in its pages. Under the leadership of W. E. B. Du Bois, the *Crisis* presented a "eugenic family album, a visual and literary blueprint for the ideal, modern black individual."[82] Of course for young girls this meant that they were from the "better classes" and that they were moral and good.[83] Throughout the 1930s and 1940s, the majority of *Crisis* covers were graced by a proper, beautiful young woman or cute girls.[84] In the 1930s, the *Crisis* also briefly tried to promote children's art and writing in the "Youth Pages," and the *Chicago Defender* had a special section for children, "The Children's Greats Weekly." Thus, children were an important part of the respectable black family. They were the future and represented the progress and promise of the race. Indeed, the *Louisiana Weekly* emphasized McCray's girlhood. The first paper covering the crime juxtaposed McCray's murder with a photograph of another teenage black girl—a music prodigy (Figure 3.1). This juxtaposition gave readers a visual image of responsible black girlhood to go along with McCray's tragic story.

It was in this context that Hattie McCray became the poster child for virginal girlhood. The reverence for the purity of McCray was at its zenith when the *Louisiana Weekly* published the poem "Defending Her Honor." Printed a couple of weeks after the murder, the poem paid tribute to Hattie McCray's respectability:

> Defending her honor,
>   Protecting her name,
> She fell, bullet wounded—
>   Thank God but not in Shame!
>
> She fell warding off
>   A beastly attack,
> A sterling young woman,
>   Even though she was black.
>
> Defending her honor,
>   Protecting her name,
> She fought for her virtue,
>   And died for the same.[85]

Written by Ivy Lenoir, "Defending Her Honor" was published on the readers' page—the section of the paper that featured letters to the editor and editorials from guest writers. At the time she wrote about McCray's death, Lenoir was a thirty-six-year-old mother from a highly respected family and a graduate of Xavier University.[86] In part, this poem can be read as an example of how the cultural narratives of honor surrounding McCray's death "encouraged women to articulate publicly a new sexual subjectivity."[87] Lenoir outlined a sexual subjectivity for black girls (and even perhaps for herself) that included honor and dignity. She constructed this subjectivity around notions of purity. One of the most compelling lines, "even though she was black," points directly to the dominant culture's opposition of blackness and purity. Yet Lenoir's work attempts to break down this opposition, inscribing dignity onto McCray's body. The poem was a praise song for the virtuous body, even as it glorified the death of Hattie McCray.

That Hattie McCray died for her virtue was understandably important to the black community. The *Louisiana Weekly* and Ivy Lenoir certainly recognized that crimes committed by white men against black girls were fueled by the idea that black girls were licentious and not innocent children. The irony here, of course, is that black children were not quite children and that black women and men were not quite adults.

However, the language displayed in "Defending Her Honor" placed black girlhood on a pedestal. The discourse was saturated with expectations that were unattainable for many black girls and young women. Consequently, Lenoir's poem could lead readers to believe that being abused was shameful; she suggested that Hattie McCray would have lost her virtue had Guerand succeeded in raping her. The language in the poem and the papers valued McCray only for a presumed purity, implying that a black girl's acceptance and belonging within the aspiring black community—and her value in the fight for racial justice—hinged on her respectability. The responsibility placed on Hattie McCray to defend her honor was enormous. What type of pain might this language have caused for a reader who had been sexually abused by a white man but who had chosen to live rather than to fight?

The emphasis on bodily purity continued at Charles Guerand's trial, where both blacks and whites testified to McCray's good character.[88] The Louisiana papers and the *Chicago Defender* all noted the argument over Hattie McCray's "chastity," and though they did not comment on it, the "argument" was cited as the reason for the killing. At the very core of the crime was the fact that this white police officer did not believe Hattie could be a "pure" girl—he believed her body, her color, marked her as unchaste and unworthy of protection. Understandably then, central to the story in the black press and to Guerand's trial and conviction was that Hattie McCray was the perfect picture of virginal girlhood. The *Defender* reported frankly, "After the slaying the coroner examined her and found she was a virgin."[89] The paper offered no commentary on this violation of McCray's body.

That the coroner may have testified to this in court is probable. However, this information is not in the official coroner's report in the case file.[90] It is unclear whether Hattie McCray would have been happy that her virtue was defended by the state in such a personal way. There was little respect for her body, even after her death; the only way the white justice system could suggest that she was not shameless and deserving of murder was if she was indeed a virgin. Purity was not written on her body, her age was not sufficient evidence, and it was not enough that she was killed in cold blood; the court had to medically prove that Hattie McCray was still an innocent girl.

In April 1930, the black community and the *Louisiana Weekly* celebrated the death verdict by the white jurors. As late as 1945, the paper was still commenting on the "infamous" crime and trial of Charles Guerand, who was convicted and sentenced to death for the murder of Hattie McCray.[91] The NAACP also celebrated the verdict, calling it "a 'single victory' for the African American race."[92] The *Chicago Defender* wrote an extended article on the trial, praising Hattie for her purity, explaining the case and witnesses in detail, and highlighting the politics of rape. The paper reported that "the McCray child was murdered on February 10th, when she resisted what is said to have been an effort at rape by Guerand."[93] The *Defender* concluded the article by insisting on Hattie McCray's respectability: she "was only fourteen years of age and had left school only two weeks previous to her murder in order to work in the restaurant and help her family." In both articles on the case, the Chicago paper reported that Hattie had been working for only two weeks, thus explaining her absence from school.[94] This was a clear attempt by the paper to represent Hattie as a member of the "aspiring," striving class of African Americans, depicting her as not only self-conscious about her chastity but also hopeful for a better education.

The Color of Crime and Innocence

Although Guerand was found guilty of his crime and sentenced to death, his attorney, A. J. Hollander, continued to fight the verdict, which the black papers noted, "violated tradition."[95] Following the death sentence, white newspapers began to refer to Guerand not as a murderer but as an "ex-cop," and if they mentioned Hattie McCray at all, she was simply a "negro serving girl."[96] This language clearly exposed the power differential that existed between Guerand and McCray and revealed the ways in which that differential would inform how they would be remembered. After failed appeals, including at the level of the state supreme court, Guerand's attorney continued to submit motions declaring that his client was insane. Hollander grounded Guerand's insanity on three facts: a blow to the head several years prior to the crime, a family history of insanity and disease, and Guerand's own attempted suicide six years before the killing of Hattie McCray.[97] By claiming insanity, Guerand was able to save his life and eventually regain his freedom. Guerand passed back and forth between sanity and insanity, diseased and goodness, ultimately returning squarely back into white manhood.

Hollander's attempt to prove his client's insanity by history of disease represented a blurring of racial boundaries. In the early twentieth century, many white doctors, reformers, and city planners defined disease in racial terms. Progressive Era whites worked tirelessly to define the black body as contaminated and degenerate. In 1908, for example, Rosa Lowe argued that African Americans "are naturally prone to disease by heredity . . . and by reason of their prevalent mode of life. . . . They are markedly subject to certain special diseases, which may also be called racial."[98] At the turn of the century, there was vigorous debate in both the white and black community about the health of black Americans. It was taken for granted by both groups that the African American death rate exceeded the birth rate, leading to the possibility that the race would not survive "natural selection."[99]

Guerand's defense attempted to prove that his genes were at fault for his insanity when he submitted records to the court: his first cousin suffered from mental illness and was an "imbecile," and his father died from complications of "cerebro spinal syphilis arthritis."[100] That he called upon genetics (and thus eugenics) to prove mental illness was highly ironic. For the previous ten years, syphilis had been painted as a black American disease. In 1928 one researcher, concerned with the healthfulness of African Americans, claimed "syphilis" was a "common scourge with the American Negro."[101] Another spoke of the "ravages of syphilis" on the black community and suggested that "this disease is a tremendous factor in the high Negro death rate, not only for this venereal infection, but for the 'degenerative diseases' which it super-induces. In fact, syphilis and its sequelae account very largely for the great excess of the Negro death rate today over that for the whites. Among the latter, the general trend for syphilis has been downward during the last two decades. Among the colored, the picture is a very different one."[102] These experts painted syphilis as a "black" disease, whereas educated whites were no longer affected by it. Nevertheless, Guerand's attorney argued, "such disease is hereditary, and counsel verily believes the brain of your petitioner has been affected."[103] This defense proved to be much more palatable than Guerand's initial defense, which centered on his alleged drunkenness. By claiming that his crime was induced by insanity, a madness associated with African Americans and the lower classes, the public as well as the judges could feel detached from the crime. The crime no longer was associated with the failures and prejudices of the Jim Crow South; instead it was a crime of faulty genetics perpetrated not by an upstanding white officer but by the lower social orders. The crime was placed in its correct context.

In April 1930 Judge A. D. Henriques denied the motion for a new trial on the basis of insanity because "the code of criminal procedure makes it mandatory that when insanity is pleaded as a defense *it must be pleaded prior to the trial*."[104] But despite his verdict, the judge appointed a "sanity commission" that would determine the defendant's "present" sanity. The three doctors concluded that Guerand was indeed insane, and he was placed in an asylum. Five years later, in 1935, it was medically determined that Guerand had been insane at the time of the murder. On the advice of Guerand's doctors, the judge decided to grant him a new trial despite his previous decision regarding the defendant's motion. But in order to fairly stand a new trial, Guerand would have to be declared sane enough to stand before court.

The very basis of his defense, insanity, would have to be vacated in order for Guerand to stand a new trial and take a plea. This did not prove to be too difficult. The judge heard the testimony of the doctors, who decided once again in Guerand's favor: he was now sane. The doctors "had Guerand under constant observation from the time of his commitment, and they declared that he had recovered his reason, and was sane and responsible. Upon which declaration the Court granted the defendant a new trial."[105]

That Guerand was so easily able to cross the boundaries of insanity and sanity speaks to his whiteness. Despite having been convicted of murder and despite the genetic evidence submitted that he was not mentally stable, the defense was able to prove that Guerand had passed back into the threshold of sanity. The court arguably wished to paint Guerand's crime as a nonwhite crime (or a crime that had no relation to race). The state was able to reinstate meaning where meaning had once collapsed. By defining the crime as one of insanity and disease, the state of Louisiana was able to distance itself from the more unmentionable issues of interracial sex and sexual violence. The court was able to silence the argument regarding Hattie McCray's chastity before the murder and to forget Guerand's words yelled in the restaurant: "that God Damned Nigger wench." The NAACP realized that Guerand would not be fully held accountable for his actions. "The authorities have decided that five years confinement is enough for killing a Negro girl, even under the most outrageous circumstance," wrote Charles Houston.[106]

After several delays, Guerand's new trial took place on March 2, 1937. And, the court noted that "on this day, the defendant, through his counsel, offered to the State a plea of guilty of manslaughter, which was acceptable to the District Attorney and so ordered recorded by the court."[107] The court once again silenced the issue of black girls as victims of interracial sexual violence. The *Louisiana Weekly* did not so easily forget the memory of Hattie McCray. After Guerand was given a new trial, it was the only paper to republish the facts of the case, to call on the "Negro child's" virtue, and to reprint Guerand's guilty words yelled in the restaurant.[108]

After Guerand's guilty plea with the caveat of mental insanity, the judge concluded that his penalty should not be too harsh, one to three additional years. The court recorded, "In passing sentence the court took into consideration the defendant's prior good reputation, his mental condition at the time of the killing, the fact that he had been in the Insane Asylum for almost six years and when returned from that institution had been incarcerated in the Parish Prison for fully eighteen months."[109] Indeed, the court fully ignored the crime for which Guerand was initially indicted and sentenced, and in reference to why such a minor punishment might be passed, it referenced Guerand's color: "The defendant is a *white man*, aged 34 years, born February 11, 1903, and prior to the time of his trouble bore a *good reputation*."[110] It was important to fix the meaning of white manhood as good, since the crime itself was abject, threatening the boundaries of race and gender. The crime had the possibility to destroy the meaning of white manhood. For whites, ignoring the horror of the actual crime, murder, and guilty words was crucial; for, as Iris Marion Young has written, "the abject provokes fear and loathing because it exposes the border between self and other as constituted and fragile; and because it threatens to dissolve the subject by dissolving the border."[111] Guerand was able to pass fully back not only into a secure position of "sanity" but also into whiteness, where his color bore his innocence and inherent goodness. In an editorial, "Justice Mocked," the *Louisiana Weekly* decried the miscarriage of justice for Hattie McCray and the eventual fate of the "child-killer" Guerand.[112]

The court's decision to free Guerand so soon proved that although the initial trial was regarded as a fair and "just" one by white and black New Orleanians alike, his crime could not fully be acknowledged within the framework of Jim Crow. So instead of receiving the death sentence, Guerand served most of his time in a state insane asylum and was eventually released as a free man in 1938 by virtue of an official pardon.[113] In the end, Guerand was not even "guilty by reason of insanity." At this time, the NAACP said,

"This case alone is an [awakening] to the public that the only recourse to such [injustice] is vigilant and consistent fighting."[114] Recognizing Guerand's crime required acknowledging white abuse toward black girls and thus upset definitions of black and white femininity and black and white girlhood.

HATTIE MCCRAY'S SUBJECTIVITY AND experience is impossible to recover. Her words and thoughts can be gleaned only from others' words, each with their own agenda. Was she a member of a striving class of African Americans attempting to reach above their current status? Did she dream of returning to school or of getting married? Had she internalized the discourses of respectability and responsibility? Certainly her encounters with Guerand embodied her as a black woman. In those moments she was clearly aware of her body: aware of the areas where Guerand attempted to grope and touch, areas to which he made crude references. Perhaps his behavior toward her was something with which she was familiar. Hattie McCray knew that Charles Guerand, a white police officer, believed she was a prostitute. He did not see her as a girl, as her family did, but as a sexually available woman: this much was clear to her. In that moment, her notion of self was in conflict with white racist constructions of black bodies. Her worldview and his were irreconcilable; she refused to give in.

We may never know Hattie McCray, but her case gives us insight into other girls' experiences. What was the framework for black victims of sexual violence to understand their experience? Here, Hattie's case provides an entry into the language used to describe abuse and into the silences in the discourses regarding the abuse of children. Even though the African American press insisted that Hattie McCray had been sexually propositioned by Guerand, the discourses surrounding her death in the black papers reinforced the politics of respectability that required girls and young women to protect their bodies from contamination. The politics of respectability created a double bind for young women. While reading the accounts of Hattie McCray's trial, girls who had been abused may have felt proud or perceived a sisterhood with this singular "star" of their group. But many may have also believed that they had not lived up to middle-class African American standards of morality and may have felt ashamed. The story would have enforced the fear and anxiety that so many of them experienced.

CHAPTER FOUR

The Geography of Niceness
Morality, Anxiety, and Black Girlhood

People living in the Seventh Ward and the Treme (bounded by Esplanade to St. Louis Streets and Rampart to Broad Streets), two overlapping neighborhoods in downtown New Orleans, encountered a world of excitement. Residents frequented black-owned businesses such as the Pecan Grove Dairy and Peete's Pharmacy, social clubs such as the Autocrat Social and Pleasure Club, and sandwich stands and restaurants such as Dooky Chase. Black children growing up in downtown New Orleans came of age in an area of the city that lived up to its reputation for interracial fraternizing. As two of the most diverse neighborhoods in the city, the Treme and Seventh Ward were home to black and white Creoles, African Americans, Italians, German Americans, and other ethnic whites.[1] One resident of the Treme recalled, "The community I grew up in was white and black."[2] Another, Louise Bouise, remembered the Seventh Ward in the same way: "More or less, the Creole people moved into the Seventh Ward. . . . It was a totally integrated neighborhood. . . . Then we played with the white children, white and colored. Though the colored children I played with more or less looked like white children. . . . In the neighborhood we played together, but everything else we did separately."[3] For Louise Bouise, the neighborhood stood apart from the segregated city. Bouise remembered the geography of her childhood as a thrilling, integrated space. But the stories of two teenage girls growing up in the midst of the Great Depression, Jeanne Manuel and Ellen Hill, tell a more complicated narrative of downtown New Orleans neighborhoods.

In 1938 Jeanne Manuel lived in the heart of the Seventh Ward. Her black Creole family held a secure position in the neighborhood and owned their home—a traditional shotgun-style house with a total of four rooms. Her father worked as a plasterer, a profession noted for skill and craftsmanship— and also a profession dominated by black Creoles. Manuel's mother stayed at home with her children, although she sometimes helped the family by working as a seamstress. Like Jeanne Manuel, Ellen Hill also grew up in

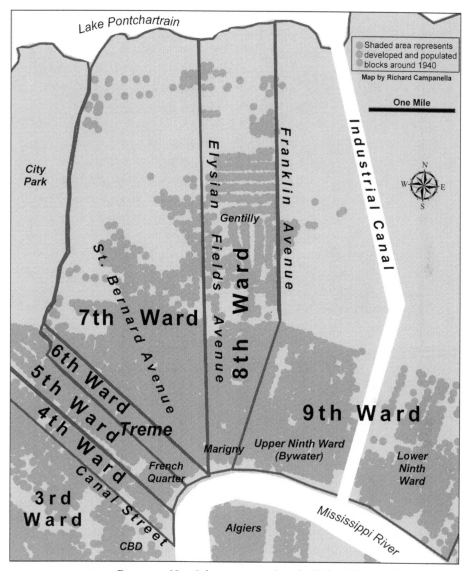

FIGURE 4.1. Downtown New Orleans, ca. 1940 (map by Richard Campanella)

downtown New Orleans. During 1937 to 1939, Hill lived in both the Treme and in the Seventh Ward. Unlike Manuel, Hill did not have a secure position in the neighborhood; she lived with her mother and six siblings in a "lower-class tenement,"[4] a one-room apartment with a communal bathroom down the hall. She was American black in a neighborhood dominated by black Creoles. Her father, an alcoholic, had left the family; her mother worked as a domestic for a white family for a few dollars a week and then sought help from the New Deal, going on "direct relief." Despite their differences, both Jeanne Manuel and Ellen Hill were considered "nice" girls, and both were afraid of losing this respectable designation. Jeanne Manuel's and Ellen Hill's relationships to the category of niceness highlights tensions specific to New Orleans relating to geography, skin color, ethnicity, and class.

Hill's and Manuel's life histories were collected by the government-sponsored Negro Youth Study (NYS), which sought to examine the character and personality of black children and analyzed the "abnormal position" of black youth in U.S. society.[5] The American Youth Commission (AYC) had funded the Negro Youth Study. In 1935 the AYC of the American Council of Education began an examination of the problems of America's youth. During the Great Depression, scholars, politicians, and reformers alike were concerned that both black *and* white youth were becoming disenchanted with American mores and democracy; they worried that excessive idle time might ruin the country's children. The AYC studied the "characteristics" of youth and analyzed the goals of education in relation to the social, political, and economic problems of the depression years.[6] In 1936 the AYC decided to sponsor studies on America's black youth through the NYS. The NYS publications were at the forefront of what came to be known as personality development research.[7] For the scholars of the NYS, "personality" referred to an "individual's traits, habits, and attitudes which determine his social role."[8] They investigated both "healthy" and "unhealthy" social and psychological development.

The NYS culminated in the publication of four books by central figures in the sociology of race. Two of these books examined black youth in the South: *Growing up in the Black Belt: Negro Youth in the Rural South* was written by famed African American sociologist Charles S. Johnson, and *Children of Bondage: The Personality Development of Negro Youth in the Urban South*, focusing on children in New Orleans, was written by Allison Davis and John Dollard.[9] Of the four books, *Children of Bondage* was the most popular, in its fifth printing by 1947;[10] a group of sociologists even wrote a follow-up to the study for its twenty-year anniversary.[11] To write *Children of Bondage*, Davis and Dollard, along with their team of researchers, interviewed children attending New Orleans junior high and high schools during 1938.[12] The interviews with Jeanne Manuel and Ellen Hill, collected over the course of nearly half a year, allow extraordinary access into these two girls' daily lives.[13]

The interviews reveal the centrality of geography to the girls' subjectivities. When talking about her junior high school, Ellen Hill explained that the girls "are Creoles and downtown, and I think they're nicer and refined and cleaner too."[14] By insisting that the girls at her school were "nicer," Ellen Hill was articulating her own conception of girlhood respectability. This respectability was closely aligned with geographical location and ethnicity. Perhaps because she was not Creole, Hill found it important to continually emphasize her own niceness. For Ellen, the neighborhood she lived in marked her as respectable—she was surrounded by "nice" Creole girls, so she must be nice too.

In the 1930s, at the very center of the ideology of respectability was the moral imperative to be a "nice" or "good" girl. Parents, teachers, pastors and priests, and black social reformers policed the behavior of teenage girls to make sure they remained "nice." Nice was a polite euphemism for sexually and morally wholesome. The protection of girls' sexuality was of utmost importance to elite, intellectual, and striving-class African Americans during the early twentieth century.[15] Historian Stephanie Shaw describes black parents who "emphasized the importance of disproving the sexual myths and stereotypes and insisted on sexual self-control and . . . respectability."[16] Another historian notes how black social reformers "frequently promoted 'respectable reproductive sexuality within the safe confines of marriage' as a viable means of uplifting the masses and working toward black progress."[17] Children of all class backgrounds did indeed hear the messages parents and reformers sent to them. The girls' voices from the NYS illustrate the consequences of the black middle class's project of uplift and racial betterment and make evident the ways in which black girls internalized the politics of respectability.

Allison Davis and John Dollard used the language of "respectability" specifically; for example, they noted which girls in their study were "respectable" or "nice" and which were not. And the girls themselves used this language as well, sometimes referring to "respectable" people but more often using "nice" or "good." Beverly Carter, another teen interviewed for the NYS in New Orleans, talked about the importance of respectability in her world in an essay she wrote for her interviewer. "I try hard to be part of the best kind of people. When I went to [Hoffman Junior High School] I did not like the crowd of children[;] most of them seem to be somewhat in the low class of people," Carter explained. She also noted her resolve to remain part of the "respectable" group, despite what others, including her teacher and aunt, said about her. "There are so many people that expect me to be good and to prove it, while there on the other hand are people that are waiting for my downfall," she wrote, "but I am determined."[18]

The girls interviewed by Johnson, Davis, and Dollard spoke clearly about the set of moral standards by which they lived, influenced by a language of respectability intertwined with the politics of sexuality. Beverly Carter noted this dilemma when discussing her own desires to be part of the "best kind of people." In another life story she wrote about trying to remain sexually pure while also attempting to maintain her respectable reputation, but she constantly felt frustrated. She explained, "I try to be good and you will see what will happen to you. People will talk about you and it [will] make no difference how good or how bad you are."[19] While trying to satisfy her boyfriend and the expectations for respectability, she asked her interviewer, "What would you do?"

In New Orleans, the ways in which black girls thought about respectability related directly to their location in the city. Beverly Carter, for example, felt as if the girls at the uptown junior high school, Hoffman, were not the best kind of people; Ellen Hill agreed with her. Niceness, then, had a geography. This is not to say that "nice" girls were not located on both sides of Canal Street—they were. Instead, I want to suggest that in each neighborhood, there were particular geographies of respectability. These geographies of niceness were also aligned with geographies of fear. Respectable girls were often afraid and anxious of what might turn them from "nice" to "bad." They always worried, as Beverly Carter did, about their potential "downfall." In Jim Crow New Orleans, there were many experiences that might challenge a girl's respectability: racial violence and street harassment, police harassment, poverty, or pleasurable sexual experiences.

Scholars and the Race Problem: Making *Children of Bondage*

Although the interviews with Ellen Hill and Jeanne Manuel provide an opportunity to understand sexuality and the gendered geography of New Orleans, the girls were restrained in what they could say and how they could voice their opinions. Additionally, while some of the interviews were transcribed verbatim during the conversations, others were reconstructed from the field researchers' notes just after the interviews took place. Historian Stephanie Shaw's work on the Works Progress Administration interviews with former slaves offers suggestions for reading such complex sources. Shaw found that in response to 1930s WPA oral history interviews, elderly "freedpeople's responses were routinely more sophisticated than what the questions, on the surface, seemed designed to elicit."[20] It is crucial, then, to read the NYS interviews for the complexity and concerns black girls brought to the conversation, even when the questions asked seem straightforward, simple, or obsessed with the scholars' interests in psychoanalysis or class.

Allison Davis, John Dollard, and their researchers spent months with their interviewees and amassed pages of reports, including not only the interviews but also the children's school reports, health records, interviews with family members, and sometimes essays written by the interviewees. The sociologists' methods of interviewing created an intimate pseudo-psychological atmosphere in which the interviewers encouraged the girls to confess their dreams, sexual desires, and fears. In many ways, Jeanne Manuel and Ellen Hill constructed life narratives—a sort of autobiography—through their interviews. In *Reading Autobiography*, Sidonie Smith and Julia Watson argue that individuals and institutions "coax" life narratives from their tellers, creating moments of "confession."[21] Other scholars of life narratives have called this the "interpersonal" aspect of personal narratives.[22] Chad Heap has argued that the interpersonal aspects of interviewing especially affected social scientists of the 1930s whose methods and approach "bordered on exploitation and voyeurism by positioning the sociologist as an unquestionably normative, all-knowing interpreter of the supposed peculiarities and abnormalities of particular urban populations."[23] Historians and cultural theorists have cautioned scholars against using life narratives as direct evidence of the past.[24] Although Ellen Hill's and Jeanne Manuel's interviews cannot be read as direct evidence of their sex lives or their anxieties, the interviews demonstrate how these girls defined niceness within the double bind.[25] Allison Davis and John Dollard's academic interests and personal ambitions are also evident in the interviews.

African American scholar Allison Davis was born in Washington, D.C., in 1902. Although he came of age during segregation and in a Jim Crow city, Davis had access to an excellent education. He attended Dunbar High School, the most prestigious segregated public high school for African Americans in the country.[26] His father worked in a secure job for the government, and his family lifestyle could easily be defined as part of the elite black class in Washington. During the time in which Davis grew up, the city was famous for its large number of college-educated, successful African Americans. After graduating from high school, Davis left D.C. to attend Williams College, becoming the valedictorian of his class. In 1925 he earned his first master's degree in English from Harvard University. Afterward, he taught English literature at Hampton Institute, an industrial school for minorities in Hampton, Virginia.[27] "Teaching in the standard manner made no sense to these poor and poorly schooled rural blacks. I decided that I didn't know anything to teach them since our backgrounds were so different, yet I wanted to do something to affect such students," explained Davis of his time at Hampton.[28]

Next, Davis returned to Harvard to begin studying anthropology. As a graduate student, Davis would attend Yale and the London School of Economics and would conduct interviews (along with his wife, Elizabeth Davis) in Natchez, Mississippi, for a book on racial caste: *Deep South: A Social Anthropological Study of Caste and Class*. Once that research was completed, Davis moved to New Orleans to teach at Dillard University. He lived, worked, and researched in New Orleans for nearly five years. It was while he was there that he and his wife conducted interviews and collected data with New Orleans children and their families for the NYS.

Elizabeth Stubbs Davis first interviewed female participants for her husband in Mississippi. Elizabeth Davis's interviewing was also an important part of the research for *Children of Bondage*.[29] Not only did she interview and spend nearly six months with Ellen Hill, but she also conducted a few interviews with Jeanne Manuel. In the introduction to *Children of Bondage*, Davis recognized his wife's skill as a researcher and interviewer: "To my wife," he said, "I am indebted not only for gathering life histories, but also for her constant aid in the analysis of the Negro class modes of behavior, a work she began with me in 1933 in the social anthropological study of [Natchez, Mississippi]."[30]

In 1940 Allison Davis accepted a professorship at the University of Chicago, and in 1947 he became the first tenured African American on the faculty.[31] During the early twentieth century, the University of Chicago became known as a powerhouse for sociological studies, especially for studies in the emerging field of "urban sociology" and for research on black communities. Lloyd Warner (Davis's thesis advisor), Ernest Burgess, and Robert Park were a few of the most famous scholars associated with the Chicago School. NYS scholars E. Franklin Frazier and Charles S. Johnson, along with Allison Davis, were the most prominent African American scholars associated with the methods of the Chicago School.[32]

This diverse and rich educational history, Davis's elite background, and his mentor Lloyd Warner influenced Allison Davis's interdisciplinary method. Indeed, of all the books in the NYS, *Children of Bondage* was the most inspired by Warner's theories of overlapping social class/racial caste systems, which was sometimes at odds with the work of other sociologists of race, such as E. Franklin Frazier, who looked toward institutions and structures.[33] In his work, Allison Davis melded sociological and economic data with in-depth, qualitative interviewing and psychoanalysis. For Davis, young children's sexuality and sexual training was of extreme importance to his psychoanalytic and class-based approach. This meant that Davis's line of questioning in interviews focused not only on the sexual lives of adolescents but also on their infantile sexual history: masturbation as a child, suckling (on their mother's breast, on their thumbs, and on pacifiers), toilet training, and the physical punishments they received for their inability to learn societal norms.[34] For a variety of reasons, many contemporaneous readers did not approve of the psychoanalytic aspects of *Children of Bondage*. One child development psychologist argued that Freudianism "failed to improve the product. The data supplied by Davis and Dollard do not provide any critical tests of psychoanalytic or behaviorist hypotheses, nor are these hypotheses well-enough substantiated to provide a dependable interpretation of life history data."[35]

White psychologist John Dollard was born in Wisconsin in 1900 and described his ancestors as "Famine Irish."[36] Like Davis, Dollard was also influenced by the Chicago School of research—he received his Ph.D. in sociology from Chicago in 1931. In 1932 he began researching at the Yale University Institute of Human Relations.[37] He also studied psychoanalysis at the Berlin Sociological Institute.[38]

In 1935 John Dollard researched racial relations in the South, spending five months in Indianola, Mississippi, for his now classic book *Caste and Class in a Southern Town*.[39] Dollard later recalled in a 1970s interview that he got the idea for the research and its emphasis on racially formed castes from Allison Davis, Lloyd Warner, and Burleigh Gardner (the coauthors of *Deep South*). At this time, all of these scholars were working together, visiting one another at their research sites, and exchanging theoretical concepts. Dollard noted the connections between *Deep South* and his *Caste and Class*: "I was certainly influenced by their work. What I brought to my study that they didn't have was a strong basis in Freudian analysis. Without the Freudian analysis, the study was structured without content. To get a complete sense of the southerner, I had to show him loving and hating, laughing and breathing. In this way, Freud is unparalleled in describing human life. . . . Theirs should be read for the caste analysis and mine should be read for the intimations of emotional structures of feeling and hatred."[40] Dollard's use of class and caste was informed by the Freudian concepts of drive (natural instincts toward free sexual relations and uncontrolled aggression) and civilization (the restrictions placed on people by the modern social order). According to Dollard, what made southern lower-class African Americans notable was that they were segregated out of society, thus placing them outside of the bounds of modern civilization.

Dollard believed, therefore, that southern blacks were free to follow their natural instincts. These "natural" instincts were toward freer (promiscuous) sexuality. Even in the 1970s, he explained his theories in a manner that exposed a troubling notion of race and sexuality:

> It is saddening to think that when all those Negroes are properly socialized, as will occur very rapidly, they are probably going to have a lot less fun. They will be under the powerful example of the culture as a whole to change and approximate themselves to the white middle-class norm of society. Middle-class life is really limiting and restrictive, with its concern for time, cleanliness, and morality. There is no philosophical device by which I could ever see how one would compare the relative sexual and aggressive freedom that lower-class Negroes used to have and still have with the satisfaction of mastery, social position, and prestige that the middle- and upper-class whites have. All we know is that if people get a chance, they will approximate themselves to the middle-class white model.[41]

Dollard believed that African Americans following their natural drives were sexually promiscuous. He would never expect poor black girls to be concerned with cleanliness, moral questions, or sexual respectability. In the 1930s, anthropologist Hortense Powdermaker, simultaneously working in Indianola, Mississippi, for her book *After Freedom*, fundamentally disagreed with Dollard's interpretations of black fun and sexual freedom. She argued, "It is often felt and said that the Negro is more free with himself and other people. The popular conception of the Negro as a 'child,' a 'spontaneous creature,' unrestrained and living fully in the moment, implies an inner freedom that comes from lack of conflict and inhibition. . . . Our material contradicts it repeatedly."[42] Even in the 1930s, then, Dollard's views on race and sexuality were challenged by feminist interpretations.

The racist/classist implications of Dollard's theory are self-evident. Dollard believed that if lower-class black girls were not "properly socialized" and thus free to follow their base instincts, then they would naturally choose to be promiscuous. Dollard would have been incredibly surprised to find a lower-class black girl who did not want to experiment sexually or who resisted the sexual advances of white men. In *Children of Bondage* Davis and Dollard obsessed over girls' class status and sexual respectability or disrespectability. Reviewers of NYS publications noticed this focus on sexual mores. One reviewer of *Children of Bondage* favorably noted, "The authors skillfully dissect raw data in which the reader may find full explanation of the degraded mores which caste has produced and defiantly maintains."[43] To Dollard's credit, though, he believed that lower-class whites had lower sexual standards than middle-class whites, and these standards, he believed, approached (though were not identical to) the freedom lower-class blacks experienced.[44]

Despite its controversial use of psychoanalysis, Davis and Dollard's *Children of Bondage* was reviewed positively by a wide variety of scholars. Allison Davis explained, "[Our] book is a study of personality, and is presented in a manner so as to reach a large public. The whole organization of the book, as well as the style, has been planned from the first page to make the book lucid and perspicuous for this audience."[45] By structuring each chapter around the particular life narrative of one child, Davis and Dollard's writing style exposed a "harsh realism" that necessarily spoke of their objectivity and education.[46] One scholar noted the book's style when reviewing E. Franklin Frazier's work against Davis and Dollard's NYS studies. The way that *Children of Bondage* read, he argued, made the reader feel as if he stepped into the actual world of the child. "If one wanted to run the risk of oversimplification, he might say that *Negro Youth at the Crossways* [by Frazier] represents a more intellectual experience of the problem while *Children of Bondage* yields more of a direct aesthetic, emphatic experience," the reviewer observed.[47] Davis and Dollard unceasingly presented what they saw as the "realities" of youths' lives.

By delving into the intricacies of the sex lives of individual children, Davis and Dollard believed they portrayed an otherworldly life of the "lower-class" street and the inside world of the social controls and the restrained sexual fantasies of the upwardly mobile. This could be done only with what literary critic Marlon Ross describes as the "cool perspective."[48] Davis and Dollard had to present sex talk in the disinterested voice of the expert. Even then, however, readers might question their methods. On reading a draft of the manuscript, Mordecai Johnson, president of the historically black college Howard University, worried, "In two or three places the authors have made record of sexual passes or 'impertinences' of students in relation to the investigators." He believed that the manuscript would be "improved if these references were deleted and the investigators were kept in the position of detached observation."[49] Extraordinarily, Johnson thought that by merely deleting evidence of sex talk and flirtations, pure objectivity could, indeed would, be restored. His objections to the discussions of sexuality reveal how sex talk could make readers feel uncomfortable and also question the overall objective value of the research.

The Gender of Anxiety: Davis and Dollard (Mis)interpreting Girls' Fears

The girls interviewed for the Negro Youth Study attempted to express their anxieties, many associated specifically with sexuality and geographies of respectability. But NYS anthropologists and sociologists held gendered notions of what constituted rational fear. For adolescent boys, the NYS scholars clearly understood some experiences that caused anxiety: lynching, police brutality, and other violent encounters with whites. In *Growing Up in the Black Belt*, for instance, Charles Johnson dedicated a subheading of a chapter called "Relations with Whites" to the subject of lynching. In so doing, he pointed directly to the adverse psychological effect of white violence, arguing that lynchings "left a vivid imprint on the minds of youth." He gave an example of one young man who experienced "deep scars of horror, fear, and dismay."[50] In the same chapter, however, Johnson failed to mention experiences of interracial sexual violence or sexual harassment or the ways in which girls might fear white men for different reasons than boys did. Charles Johnson's omission demonstrates what researchers believed constituted "rational," understandable, or observable fears. In *Children of Bondage*, Davis and Dollard reported the "bitter experiences" of one teenage boy. A white man had placed a gun to the boy's back and threatened to shoot him because he had cheered Joe Louis's victory over a white boxer. Davis and Dollard explained, "Such a fear experience would leave any boy more intimidated for future dealings with white people."[51] The scholars listened carefully for boys' expressions and narratives of fear and anxiety; meanwhile, Allison Davis, John Dollard, and Charles Johnson did not clearly hear the girls' articulations—some of the girls' anxieties the experts labeled as irrational, while others remained silences that would never fully be expressed. The scholars' definition of "irrational" fears often related to black girls' sexual worlds.

Julia Wilson, for example, was a sixteen-year-old high school student in New Orleans when she was interviewed for *Children of Bondage*. Julia was living with her mother and father, even though she was recently married (she disliked her husband).[52] Davis and Dollard narrated Wilson's story in "Frightened Amazon," the first personality study in the book meant to be emblematic of the harsh underworld of a lower-class girl. Davis and Dollard defined Wilson's behavior as dominated by both violent rage and irrational fears. Children like Julia Wilson, who were deemed violent by the sociologists, were thought to be "driven by strange and unpredictable animosities and by equally mysterious and uncontrollable fears"; they were "the children of wrath and self-love."[53] They continued, "We know . . . that Julia is subject to chronic irrational fears."[54] By labeling her fear as "chronic," Davis and Dollard suggested that her fear was pathological and a sign of her thwarted, unhealthy personality. Nonetheless, her fear of sexual violence rings loud, even if Davis and Dollard did not notice.[55]

Julia's greatest anxiety was the fear of bodily exposure. She was terrified to go to the doctor for fear that he might see her naked and presumably (although not explicit in Davis and Dollard's text) would have to touch her. Instead of going to the doctor when she mistakenly thought she was pregnant, she chose to marry young. Julia admitted, "I was scared. And I didn't want to go to a doctor, I told [my boyfriend], 'cause I didn't like to let [the doctor] look at me. So I married him. When I found that I wasn't going to have a baby, I got mad at him, and I ain't like him no more."[56] The authors of *Children of Bondage* found Julia's fear of bodily exposure to be "unexpected," particularly because they thought she was promiscuous and interested in relationships with men. Unfortunately, Julia's original interviews are not contained in the archive, so the dynamic between Julia and her interviewers is lost. So too are the more complex words and ideas she may have tried to express.

Nonetheless, when sexual violence is highlighted in Julia's story, her fears appear rational. According to Davis and Dollard, Julia often dreamed of being assaulted by men.[57] Possibly believing the stories were fictitious, Davis and Dollard did not attempt to explain the source of these fears; however, they were certain that Julia demonstrated a "definite fear of penetration."[58] They quickly defined her dreams and fears of sexual attack as a "puzzling" aspect of Julia's personality.[59] The dreams that Julia experienced are not as puzzling if one reads them in the wider context of the Jim Crow South and with the other NYS interviews. Both Ellen Hill and Jeanne Manuel also experienced similar dreams. Jeanne dreamed of street harassment and the danger of a neighborhood man "meddling" her sister. Jeanne told her interviewer, "I dreamed [my sister] and I were riding on a train and you were working on the train. . . . I was sitting with [my sister] sewing, then there was an old man who I see all the time and he came up and he meddled [my sister]. I called you and you put him out. I was just screaming when he meddled [her]."[60] Ellen Hill also dreamed of street harassment—of being chased by an old man who intended to molest her. She explained, "I didn't want him to know I knew he was following me and I just kept walking faster and faster and faster and so did he and I kept trying to wake myself up. . . . He was an old man with whiskers."[61] That Davis and Dollard did not find Jeanne's and Ellen's dreams "puzzling" is noteworthy. They assumed that because Manuel and Hill were from respectable or striving-class families and because they were both virgins, the fear of sexual violence was not unusual. But if Manuel's and Hill's dreams along with Wilson's anxieties are read as a fear of sexual violence and the ever-present street harassment, they appear to be completely rational, given the culture of violence in which they all lived.

The only explanation Davis and Dollard could give for Julia Wilson's behavior was that she had "a grudge against life itself" because she was born into lower-class society without a chance for advancement. She was "rejected" from the world, which led to frustration; she responded with "aggression."[62] Their analysis could not take into account sexual violence as a reason for Julia's fears. They also found that her "deep animosity toward people stem[med] from the hostile demands and the abrupt, traumatic training which she received from her mother and oldest sister."[63] In other words, Davis and Dollard claimed that the early instruction (feeding, toilet and pacifier training) the women of the family gave to Julia caused her to be overly aggressive and frightened when it came to sexuality. However, Davis and Dollard ignored Julia's relationship with the men around her as she was growing up. Davis and Dollard briefly mentioned that Julia's father was a bootlegger whose clients gave Julia drinks when she was as young as ten.[64] In addition, Julia's family rented one of their rooms to male lodgers.[65] Because the records no longer exist, it is unclear if the interviewers ever followed up on these questions. Was Julia sexually abused by any of the many men in her life—the lodgers, her father's customers, or one of her doctors? What is known is that Julia did attempt to articulate her fear of sexual violence to the interviewers. But the fear that was reflected in "Frightened Amazon" reads not only as "irrational" but also as imagined.

Evidence of black girls' fear and anxiety reveals the everyday implications of sexual, racial, and spatial politics in their lives. Historian Joanna Bourke explains, "Emotions lead to a negotiation of the boundaries between self and other or one community and another. They align individuals with communities. . . . Fear is a form of 'emotional labour' that endows 'objects and others with meaning and power.'"[66] Bourke emphasizes the role that emotions such as fear and anxiety play in constructing subjectivity. Black girls' fears demonstrate what was important in maintaining a girls' sense of self and what put that sense of self in jeopardy. Their feelings, such as pain, fear, and anxiety, make abstract words like "power" more meaning-ful: Who had the power to make black girls fearful? What produced their anxieties? Answers to these questions expose the flow of power in the Jim Crow South. Yet more important, an appreciation of the intensity of the emotions themselves allows for a somatic understanding of the implications of power. Those crippled by fear—girls constantly threatened, ignored, or attacked by the state—are often outside the bounds of full citizenship. So, black girls' emotions make tangible complex networks of power within com-munities. Barbara Rosenwein has suggested that historians of emotion ana-lyze "systems of feeling" in "emotional communities" or, more precisely, the emotional ties in social communities.[67] Black girls' emotional communities in the 1930s consisted of relationships with their parents, churches, teachers, schools, and neighborhoods. They also had intimate relationships with boys and girls of their same age. Through an analysis of these relationships, we see not only who played important roles in girls' lives but also how girls felt about those around them. Additionally, the various communities of which girls were a part each had set values determining what was good or bad, right or wrong, and helped define what was safe or dangerous and what and whom was to be feared. These social communities assuaged some of their fears (those associated with segregation, for example), while the community sometimes instigated other anxieties (those associated with sexuality and loss of respectability). Through the examination of fear and anxiety, then, black girls' lives within the double bind becomes clearer.

Niceness on the Margins: Ellen Hill

Ellen Hill was a fourteen-year-old living in poverty in New Orleans at the time of her interviews. According to Elizabeth Davis, Hill was a nervous, frail girl with light brown skin and frizzy black hair.[68] Because her mother worked long hours during the day, Ellen learned her code of ethics from her grandmother, her church, and extensive reading of books and newspapers. The discourse of respectability and proper conduct permeated her world. When interviewer Elizabeth Davis gave Ellen a copy of Arna Bontemps's *Sad-Faced Boy* as a gift, Ellen excitedly opened the book but then stopped and said, "I read in *Manners of the Moment* that you shouldn't pick up a book and read it when you're visiting. Is that right?"[69] The question revealed an intimacy between interviewer and interviewee. Ellen Hill viewed her ses-sions with Elizabeth Davis as "visiting"—time spent between friends. But

Hill's question also illuminates her preoccupation with right conduct and respectability. Throughout her interviews, Hill stressed a girlhood respectability defined by being a "nice" girl. Ellen believed that niceness would eventually lead to an education, a respectable occupation, and high standing in the black community. Ellen wished to be a "credit to her race."

For Ellen Hill, niceness also corresponded to space: the geography of the neighborhood, domestic geographies, and geographies of the body all influenced girls' moral standing. The places where girls lived and hung out could mark them as either nice or promiscuous. During an interview at her school, Wicker Junior High, Ellen Hill pointed out a fellow classmate to Elizabeth Davis: "You saw that girl in white that spoke to me this morning? There is a scandal about her. She's always hanging 'round beer parlors and nightclubs and she's got lots of money too. She's supposed to be going with a white man!"[70] For Ellen, the extra money and presence of white men were evidence that this student was a prostitute, exchanging sex for money. Her body and her performance of race, femininity, and sexuality marked her as disrespectable and discredited. That the "girl in white" was involved in a "scandal" suggested that the entire school community defined her behavior as disgraceful.

The girl in white's time at beer gardens was further evidence of moral offense for Ellen Hill. The respectable black community in New Orleans continually voiced concerns that beer gardens and dance halls were sinful spaces. Girls who frequented forbidden geographies fascinated NYS scholars Allison Davis, John Dollard, and Charles Johnson. Their curiosity about the extracurricular activities of black youth was connected to a larger uplift mission. Youth congregating in dance halls threatened respectability because dance halls were associated with immoral behavior, physical closeness between youth, and improper sexual activity.[71] For example, in 1939 the *Louisiana Weekly* reported, "For many months we have lamented the fact that beer parlors and so-called entertainment establishments cater so largely to minors, and have urged civic and religious organizations to protest to proprietors and city authorities."[72] And as late as 1954, sociologist Robert M. Frumkin studied black girls who were spending too much time at dance halls. Frumkin attempted to assuage the anxieties of parents who thought that their girls were involved in licentious behavior.[73] The gossip concerning the girl in white mirrored the "respectable" communities' concern over beer parlors' reputation as a corrupting geography.

Ellen Hill's school functioned as an important marker of respectability. Hill believed that the girl in white was an outlier and that most girls in her school were nice. Ellen told Elizabeth Davis, "There's plenty of girls like that at Hoffman [Junior High School], but most of the children at Wicker are Creoles and downtown, and I think they're nicer and refined and cleaner too. These uptown people aren't Creoles and they don't care how they dress or look, and come to school anyway."[74] Ellen clearly believed that there was a geography of niceness. She identified as a downtown girl—a girl with refined sensibilities. On the other hand, she mapped the girl in white as like "uptown people," as careless of bodily appearance or propriety. Ellen Hill believed a stereotype that uptown girls were not Creole, nor were they clean. Of course, Ellen was not Creole either. This presented a major problem for her personal articulation of niceness. She was always afraid that she might be mistaken for just a common black girl instead of for what she had worked hard to maintain—the image of a nice, educated, clean girl. Respectability, as Ellen defined it, in the city and neighborhood in which she lived was closely aligned with categories that Ellen did not neatly fit into: Creole, light in color, financially 'well off' (at least well off enough so that her mother would not have to work as a domestic).

Because Ellen struggled to fulfill the role of respectable girl in her neighborhood and school, she dreamed of moving to Alabama for college. Elizabeth Davis asked Ellen if she wanted to move to the North, away from the constraints and violence of the South. Ellen responded, "That is alright with me, but I want to go to Tuskegee first. That's Booker T. Washington's school. And then I'll go to the other places. New Orleans ain't a good place for colored; we ain't got nothing here. That's why I want to go away. You jus' can't get to be nothing."[75] She continually mentioned her desire to go to Tuskegee and emulate Booker T. Washington. Ellen believed she could escape Jim Crow life in New Orleans if only she could get to Tuskegee. In this way, we see the mundane effects of the psychic violence of segregation. It was not segregation specifically that Ellen blamed for her problems but rather the inability to reach her dream of a respectable life. Ellen wanted to go to college and become a credit to her race; yet she believed this could not be done in New Orleans. She insisted, "We ain't got nothing here," despite the presence of two black colleges within the city limits. Indeed, Elizabeth Davis's husband taught at one of those colleges, a fact of which Ellen was aware. Ellen Hill could also look in her own neighborhood to see examples of black New Orleanians who were a "credit to their race." She could look at her school and see children from families who represented the black elite in New Orleans. But because Ellen did not come from a family securely respectable, or maybe even because she lived as an outsider on the outskirts of the more stable black Creole downtown neighborhood, Ellen could not see how she could achieve permanent respectability and success in New Orleans.

Ellen's goal of being a Tuskegee graduate and a "credit to her race" revealed her profound concern with niceness. At the very core of Ellen's identity sat purity and respectability. Her anxiety, fear, and worry stemmed from her inability to reach these goals. For Ellen, the horror of Jim Crow was not just the daily insults that black New Orleanians faced; it was that and more: the inability to live a life of niceness and success devastated her hopes for a future in New Orleans and her sense of self.

Ellen Hill articulated a connection between class and niceness. So too did Davis and Dollard. In *Children of Bondage*, the two scholars defined "nice" strictly through a "caste" system. For them, "nice" corresponded with a morality that emulated white middle-class standards of self-control and cleanliness.[76] When Allison Davis and John Dollard explained differences between black New Orleanians based on class, they reported a "chasm" between classes, one that could be explained by behavior. The difference, they argued, "lies between the stimuli and goals of the 'respectable,' status-bound lower-middle class and those of the recalcitrant, impulsive, physically aggressive lower class."[77] Here, they defined "respectable" as exactly what they believed lower-class black New Orleanians were not: sexually pure, controlled in bodily desires, and suitably mannered. For the NYS scholars, class, social respectability, and niceness overlapped. Davis and Dollard placed Ellen Hill in the " 'respectable,' status-bound lower-middle class," or what some historians would call the aspiring or striving class.

But the relationship between class and niceness in black New Orleans was not as clear-cut as Davis and Dollard (or even Ellen Hill) made it out to be. For the girls themselves, niceness often did not neatly correspond to class status. Even some girls who were not reaching for a higher social position attempted to attain certain standards of niceness. For them, being "nice" meant that they did not go running around with boys, they usually were still in school, and they held to high moral standards—as well as refrained from sex, fights, alcohol, and hanging around with boys alone. Consequently, nice girls could come from any neighborhood or class background in New Orleans, if they followed these simple rules. There was a certain cachet, a self-respect, afforded to nice girls, which provided a positive self-identity where one was not always available. To be a nice black girl meant retaining dignity in a segregated world.

Certainly, girls from lower-class backgrounds had a much more difficult time adhering to the moral standard of niceness. Geographies of the home were difficult spaces for lower-class girls: girls who stayed home unsupervised because their mothers worked had to be careful with whom they hung around after school. In addition, older girls whose families fell upon financial difficulties (like Hattie McCray's family, for example) often had to quit school and work. Ellen Hill's oldest sister was in this situation; she had wanted to continue her education but was forced to quit high school to help the family.[78] Ellen Hill's mother, Juanita Hill, was clear about the way in which class and respectability intertwined in her girls' lives. She said her daughters' friends were "nice children with nice houses," emphasizing the geography of domestic spaces.[79] Niceness in this context referred not only to proper behavior but also to high standards of cleanliness and the properness of the home (her girls took a bath at least once a day despite their decrepit surroundings and shared bathing facility). Indeed, Juanita Hill deplored the geography of her home—the cramped spaces and insufficient bathroom made her apologetic.

Davis and Dollard used another teen's life history, fifteen-year-old Mary Hopkins's, as emblematic of lower-class life. Mary Hopkins's family, like Ellen's, was on governmental relief. Davis and Dollard explained: "The family is secure also in having ready and unhindered access to the basic goals: food, shelter, clothes, sex and aggressive responses can all be made; these goal responses in turn reinforce the Hopkins' lower-class folkways. There is no bothersome goal of high status to lure them into anxious days and wakeful nights. Mary shares in this confident atmosphere."[80] Even still, the language of respectability colored the way Mary Hopkins saw the world, although she was not of the striving class; Hopkins's niceness seemed to dismay the scholars. First, Davis and Dollard classified Mary's friends by their respectability: "Three of Mary's seven girl friends are called 'real nice' meaning that they do not permit sexual approaches from boy friends and that they approach middle-class standards. One girl is known to have intercourse with her boy friend and she is teased about it but not rejected in any other way."[81]

Davis and Dollard used "nice" to suggest that three of the friends were of the striving class. Indeed, here niceness and class status collapsed, becoming synonyms of each other. But like those friends, Mary did not engage in sexual activity. Davis and Dollard defined Mary's insistence on chastity as "puzzling" for someone of her class level, even though her mother had clearly instructed her not to let sex ruin her life, nor to let boys in the house while she was alone. Mary explained, "I don't never let them inside the house unless someone is home. Even if you don't do nothin', people talk about you, and my mother says to keep 'em out."[82] Davis and Dollard speculated that

Mary did not become sexually active because she was "not a good looking girl," did not have the ability to tease boys, or did not have any physical traits that might "lure" them to her.[83] But instead of seeing Mary Hopkins's chastity as an unfortunate byproduct of ugliness, as Davis and Dollard explicitly did, one might consider it much more likely that she had made a conscious choice to forgo sexual relations. And, boys had propositioned her in the past.[84] Hopkins believed she was from a "nice" family regardless of her mother's job as a domestic worker. Mary Hopkins attempted to live up to standards of niceness, and for her, this choice had nothing to do with her class position or social ambition. Hopkins's very claim on "niceness" complicates Davis and Dollard's more narrow assumptions.

The "dilemma of the lower-class girl with regard to sex," suggested Davis and Dollard, "is that there is no one to police her a good part of time."[85] They understood "policing" strictly as parental supervision. Davis and Dollard did not understand that girls' behavior was not merely constrained by the watchful eyes of parents. The discourse of moral purity came not only from parents but also from newspapers, school, and church. Girls who took these lessons seriously often policed their own behavior, as Mary Hopkins and Ellen Hill did.

Ellen Hill learned about respectability in her Baptist church, which clearly outlined behavioral standards for congregants: dancing and card playing were sins—sins that Hill admitted enjoying.[86] Hill explained to Elizabeth Davis that although she was baptized, she did not take communion. When Davis asked why, Hill responded thoughtfully, "I don't feel worthy. I am good enough, I guess, [but] I don't think it's right." Ellen felt that if she disrespected church standards, then she, as a sinner, could not stand before God and the church. She said that her friends all took communion without seriously considering the consequences. "They don't think nothing about it," she said, "they just goes on up—cause they're members—but I don't think you should do like that."[87]

Ellen Hill's use of "worthy" here is significant. "Worthiness" was the language by which Hill expressed her anxieties. Her decision to give up spiritual chastity—by dancing against the wishes of her church—caused her to question her self-worth. Although she said "I am good enough," her internal conflict was made clear by her addition, "I guess." It was not just that Ellen was sinning by playing cards or that dancing made her feel unworthy; she also felt that maybe card playing, at her age, was not wrong. She suggested that when she was twenty-five she might be ready for communion, saying, "So by the time I'm twenty five I will have had enough of 'em and then I can give them up and take communion. But I don't think they're sins now, so it's not right to take communion."[88] Even for Ellen, a girl obsessed with niceness, definitions of right and wrong were nuanced. But clearly, worthiness was a complicated matter. To be worthy before God meant being in line with church teachings. Although she justified dancing and card playing for herself and at her current age, she did not question the authority of the church. Hill's thoughtfulness and articulations conveyed her worries. Mary Hopkins, like Ellen Hill, also held back when it came to her participation in church. Mary Hopkins's family was Baptist as well, but she too enjoyed dancing and so she would not officially join the church.[89]

Ellen Hill's notion of worth was also directly tied to her mother; many "respectable" people in the black community believed mothers instilled "nice" behavior in girls through proper parenting.[90] And so a daughter's behavior was seen as a reflection of her mother's and vice versa. If a mother's respectability was in question, girls feared that their reputation might also be ruined. Psycho-sociological scholars such as Charles Johnson and John Dollard often blamed maladjusted male citizens on maternal failure.[91] This generation of scholars suggested that "because all too many black women did not mother successfully, they failed to raise sons equipped to resist racial prejudice."[92] Ellen Hill's interview demonstrated that a mother's ignorance was a horrible thing for a child, boy or girl. Ellen explained this with a concrete example: "One little colored boy, his mamma is ignorant and doesn't know nothing," she explained. "He's always calling somebody 'nigger' and using bad words. Look like anybody would teach him better, huh?"[93]

Ellen Hill's own mother's behavior came to the forefront during the course of the interviews. During seventh grade, Ellen's school performance plummeted; she went from one of the top students to one of the worst students in her school. Her grades dropped so low that she was in danger of failure and demotion. Anxiety occupied Ellen's thoughts and was written on her body. When Elizabeth Davis first met Ellen, she observed that Ellen "seemed quite nervous" and underweight.[94] And when Ellen went to the doctor, he noted that her hands and fingers shook.[95]

At first, Elizabeth Davis did not understand Ellen's poor health and school performance. Only after interviewing Ellen's mother and grandmother did Davis discover the reason for Ellen's poor grades and high anxiety. As it turned out, Ellen's mother was pregnant despite the absence of a man in the home; the pregnancy coincided with Ellen's mysterious behavior at school.[96] Ellen Hill was worried about her mother's behavior and sexual respectability.

Her mother's pregnancy was not the only thing Ellen concealed from Elizabeth Davis when discussing her life story; she also lied about the location of her home and how many siblings she had. Ellen began opening up only months after the initial interview. Ellen finally admitted that she had been worrying about the pregnancy "plenty." Even after her mother began showing, Ellen and her sisters "didn't know she was going to have a baby. Me and Velma used to talk about it most every day and we'd say she looked like she was going to have a baby. Amie would say, 'no, she didn't believe she was.' So we'd just go on talking about it." [97] The uncertainty concerning their mother's pregnancy caused serious concern for all the girls.

The family's reputation was at stake. Despite their constant worry, the sisters never asked their mother if she was pregnant. "None of us had nerve to do that," Ellen explained. The girls did not ask their mother because they feared an illegitimate birth. And in their curiosity they did not dare accuse their mother of impropriety. When Elizabeth Davis asked if the father of the baby was someone other than the older children's father, Ellen vigorously defended her mother. "Oh no! 'Cause me and Velma counted up. . . . [M]y daddy left in September and she begun to look funny about February so that would be all right," she said.[98] Even in defending her mother, Ellen exposed the reason for her anxieties. The sisters were indeed worried that their mother's pregnancy was the result of sex outside of marriage. The girls spent the months before the birth anxiously "counting up." Additionally, Ellen's defense also exposed a moral discourse of right and wrong. Ellen noted that after counting the months, the sisters determined that the pregnancy was "all right."

Ellen's grandmother Miriam Greene was surprised to learn that Ellen had tried to hide her mother's pregnancy from Elizabeth Davis.[99] But Greene quickly interpreted her granddaughters' discomfort: "Children really are funny, now ain't they? But you know—there's no telling what [the girls are] thinking. I guess [Ellen's] ashamed. . . . Seven children [her mother's] got now, and with the father away; I guess [the girls] thought it ain't right, but she was that way when [their dad] left her."[100] Miriam Greene articulated the girls' main fear—that the pregnancy was not "right." In doing so, she used a word that both her granddaughter and daughter would repeat throughout their interviews: ashamed.

Juanita Hill, like her own mother, used a language of shame to articulate her daughters' fears. Moreover, Hill felt partially responsible for her girls' anxieties. Ellen's mother knew that because she worked, her daughters could easily get in trouble—particularly in trouble with boys. She implied that it was miraculous that none of them had become pregnant. Juanita Hill was especially saddened because she could not provide a respectable home for her daughters. "They ain't bad girls, none of 'em," she explained to Elizabeth Davis, "and with me working all the time and the father being drunk, it's a wonder something doesn't happen to them, I'm telling you. But they always say where they're going, and they don't have no bad friends. . . . [T]hey oughtn't have to be 'shamed of their house and their father."[101] Because of the absence of her husband, Juanita Hill was solely responsible for the girls' behavior and upkeep. She did not want them to feel ashamed of the house; instead, she too wanted her daughters to be able to make claims to niceness. But because she was working, she could not always be there for them. She clearly loved her children and wished to keep them in school as long as possible, but the Great Depression on top of segregation's already limited opportunities made this a difficult task for her.

Ellen Hill's articulation of shame centered on the geography of the home and her family life. Although the drunkenness of the father certainly caused some dishonor to the family's standing, the girls were much more concerned with their mother's behavior. Once the father left the house, so too did the shame Ellen felt about his alcoholism. He was no longer a reflection of her character. But the embarrassment that Ellen felt over the lack of a respectable home and the possibility of having a promiscuous mother mortified her. She did not want the light-skinned, proper professor's wife, Elizabeth Davis, to see her home, find out about the large number of children there, or even talk to her mother. Ellen worried that her mother's social position would keep Elizabeth Davis from viewing her as a nice girl, and she was visibly distressed after she found out that Davis had visited her home. It was only after Davis talked to Juanita Hill and learned of the new baby that Ellen was honest about these embarrassments. Indeed, Ellen had even lied in her first interview about her mother's job. Ellen claimed her mother was a "nurse," not a domestic worker for a white family.[102] The lies and concealment helped Ellen control the interview and construct an ideal life narrative. The lies themselves reveal Ellen's hopes, just as they reveal her fears. She presented the self and story that she wanted Elizabeth Davis to know. Perhaps this story would have never been questioned but for the long duration of the interviews and Elizabeth Davis's visits with Ellen's grandmother and mother.

But even as Ellen attempted to hide her family from the gaze of the interviewer, her embarrassment about her family's social status was clear from the beginning. Early in the series of interviews, before Ellen started to discuss her mother's pregnancy openly, Elizabeth Davis asked Ellen if she was ashamed of being black or of her skin color. But Ellen consistently defined her humiliation around her family situation and not because of her color. When Davis inquired about what Ellen thought of her looks, Ellen responded:

ELLEN: No, I ain't proud of them but I'm not 'shamed.
ELIZABETH DAVIS: Of your color?
ELLEN: It's all right, too. Only where we live I'm 'shamed and when my father was drunk.[103]

In this conversation, Davis attempted to begin a discussion specifically about race and skin color. But Ellen refused to discuss her anxieties regarding race. Instead, she voluntarily brought the conversation back to a discussion of respectability.

Ellen rarely articulated anxiety over race or color, and she seldom mentioned Jim Crow. Those particular anxieties were incredibly difficult for children to express in words. More often, these fears are expressed in oral histories or memoirs, as adults narrate their past and make sense of their coming-of-age.[104] Instead, Ellen insisted, "I wouldn't want to be nothing but Colored." And she unfailingly expressed the sentiment, "I don't want to look white either."[105] For Ellen, "colored" did not primarily signify second-class citizenship or automatically denote promiscuity or vulgarity. Instead, in Ellen's conversations with Elizabeth Davis, racial subjectivity played out in terms of respectability. None of the stereotypes defining black Americans as second-class citizens applied *if* you were the type of "colored" person who lived in the right neighborhood and proper house and who lived an educated, clean life. Ellen saw examples of black New Orleanians in her own neighborhood who would fit this description. In some of her first interviews, Ellen articulated these feelings fairly clearly. In one, she told Davis, "I want to be famous and a credit to my race."[106] Ellen said this even as she was struggling to pass her classes in school.

In Ellen's set of interviews, her frustration with Jim Crow might also be read as a frustration with the ways in which segregation constrained opportunities for black advancement. Although there were educated black New Orleanians all around Ellen, there were still limited opportunities for those who did graduate from college. Good jobs were simply not given to blacks. Those who did succeed despite these circumstances were often, although not always, Creole or light in color. And still, although attending a local college might seem in reach for Ellen, making it through high school was extremely difficult—if not impossible—for most black girls in the depths of the depression, even those with the desire, drive, and support from family members.

For Ellen, and for other girls coming up during Jim Crow, articulating fears relating to racial violence was incredibly difficult. Throughout the course of the interviews, Ellen was unable to talk about racial violence explicitly, with one notable exception. Toward the end of the interview process, when Elizabeth Davis and Ellen Hill were close friends, Davis asked Ellen if she had read about the recent lynchings in the black newspaper. Ellen's response exposed her feelings about the complexity of the relationship between white and black in the segregated South:

> Colored people ought to start not taking so much. All the good colored people ought to get together and get some guns. Don't let them low class ones know 'cause they'll tell the white folks[,] and then when they get ready to lynch somebody, they ought to start shooting. That's what they ought to do. Get up in trees and just shoot every white person you can. They ought to practice shooting so that they could get at least half [a] dozen whites and then if you die, it won't make no difference. Six for one, that's good. That's worth dying for.[107]

Ellen Hill's response to the local lynching suggests that racial violence affected her psyche. Even as she said she would never want to be "nothing but colored," she noted that it would "make no difference" to die, if one was to die shooting whites. In one breath she is fine being "colored" in American society, and in another she is willing to give her life. That she believes killing racist whites is worth a life reveals the true psychic cost of living with racial violence in the Jim Crow South.

The violent reaction she had to the newspaper story also exposes her anger toward her social station. But even as Ellen Hill discussed the possibility of fighting white racism, she continued to describe black New Orleanians in terms of class. In her estimation, only "good colored people" would make worthy fighters. On the other hand, "low class" colored people would be untrustworthy and unaware of their political stake in self-defense. As Ellen Hill thought about the possibility of a better, safer future, she saw a "good" or "nice" class of black Americans invested in the progress of the race. Even in her imagined world, Ellen wanted to be classed with the "good" black people. She couched her fantasy in such a way that allowed her to further distance herself from ignorant "low class" black New Orleanians.

Ellen dreamed of getting an education and remaining respectable. Yet still, she was always anxious that someone might not view her as a nice girl, that she might one day lose that designation, or that she might not become someone important. Her fears were not completely unfounded. In a study that followed up on *Children of Bondage* twenty years later, Ellen Hill was still trying to graduate from college. She had moved north, married a police officer, given birth to six children, and worked part-time as she went to school. Of her job, Hill noted, "It's a waste of time, not a career or profession like teaching."[108]

A Good Creole Girl: Jeanne Manuel

Jeanne's parents taught her much about her place in New Orleans' segregated society, including about her Creole heritage, which included her obligation to her "group" and her obligation to be a nice, respectable girl. Jeanne Manuel identified with the category "nice girl" differently than Ellen Hill. For Ellen, remaining nice was a constant battle. But for Jeanne Manuel, everyone already viewed her as a nice Creole girl from a nice downtown neighborhood, including her interviewer and Davis and Dollard. Indeed, the NYS scholars feared that she might be too nice, that she might have taken the message of respectability too far. For Jeanne, niceness corresponded to neighborhood geographies as well as to geographies of the body—its color and comportment. Despite being secure in her identity of a nice girl, Jeanne Manuel also had fears associated with niceness.

"When I was about twelve years old and in grammar school, a little girl asked me if I wanted to see a book of some pictures," Jeanne told her interviewer Claude Haydel. "I told her yes. It was a picture of a man and a woman. One of 'em had clothes on. . . . [T]hey were doing something awful."[109] Jeanne constantly described her fear of bodily exposure and of sex. She insisted that sex, even in marriage, was "awful." She said, "I don't like the action, I don't like the idea of not having no clothes on, and I don't see why your husband should look at you when you don't have no clothes on, and I don't like the idea of looking at him when he ain't got no clothes on, I think they should have a substitute for having babies."[110] Jeanne Manuel's distress when it came to the subject of sex reveals the ways in which the message of "respectability" intertwined with her daily life and was a source of anxiety. In the text of *Children of Bondage*, Allison Davis and John Dollard suggested, "Perhaps [her parents] have trained her too well."[111]

Jeanne Manuel's articulations of "awful" sex exposed the crises of the adolescent moment—a moment of development when she was forced to think about, confront, and consider engaging in sexual intercourse. Jeanne was truly afraid of engaging in sex play and confused about what sexual inter-course entailed. In *Children of Bondage* Davis and Dollard correctly con-cluded, "Some of her sex fears are expressed in the record, but undoubtedly many are not. She looks on the sex act as one with no possibility of pleasure for her, but rather as submission to a kind of assault."[112]

A twenty-one-year-old Dillard University student named Claude Haydel interviewed Manuel.[113] Like Jeanne, Haydel was also from a downtown Creole New Orleans family; he was the ultimate insider, the youngest son of Seventh Ward elite and local activist C. C. Haydel.[114] At the beginning of his report, Claude Haydel noted that Jeanne "cooperated without any hesitancy. She too felt free to talk to me about color, passing for white . . . because we were both Creoles."[115] Haydel knew the other girls and families in Jeanne's downtown neighborhood. Their shared community reveals Jeanne Manuel's centrality in the downtown community and neighborhood, whereas Ellen Hill's obscurity shows her marginality in the same community. One inter-view illustrated Jeanne Manuel and Claude Haydel's interrelated histo-ries when Haydel asked Jeanne about a girl in her class. Jeanne said, "You ought to know, you are friendly with her" and "she is going [out] with your cousin."[116] As Jeanne and Claude Haydel discussed her experiences with sex play and fears of sexual intercourse, the way in which she viewed her own place in New Orleans society became clear.

Jeanne built a moral code based on an understanding of right and wrong informed by Creole culture, which enforced a particular type of politics of respectability. More than anything, "Creole" signified an ethnic identity in Louisiana. Black Creoles in New Orleans were a tight-knit group of friends, families, and extended kin networks, segregated from white society by Jim Crow laws that defined them clearly as "colored" and also segregated from American blacks living in New Orleans by culture, history, class, and some-times biases. They placed a high premium on their cultural experiences as a multiracial and multiethnic people, on Catholicism, and on their con-nection to French culture.[117] Although black Creoles lived throughout New Orleans, Creole families and black Creole culture dominated downtown New Orleans. Jeanne explained her racial and ethnic identity to Haydel by suggesting that "there should be three classes of people, white, Creoles, and Colored. It wouldn't matter if they had some dark ones in the Creole group as long as they were nice, but I wouldn't care to go around with them."[118] This comment exposes the way in which Jeanne understood Creoleness mainly by class and comportment. For Jeanne, "niceness," even more so than skin color, defined her Creole racial/ethnic identity. To be Creole also meant to be nice and respectable. For her, "Creole" defined niceness, whereas "colored" signified the opposite. This racial/ethnic component to niceness was not unlike Ellen Hill's understanding of "nice girls" at Wicker who were "Creole" and therefore cleaner and more refined. Both girls' understanding of Creoleness also illustrates the complex interrelation of class, color, and ethnicity in New Orleans, although Jeanne's insistence that she would not hang out with the "dark ones" also suggests that it was more difficult for girls with dark skin to be seen as nice, respectable girls.

Jeanne's identity as a downtown Creole girl made her feel valued, despite the humiliation of Jim Crow. According to Jeanne, she did not wish to be white, nor did she look up to or respect whites for their social position. When Jeanne was asked if she liked whites, she responded, "No they've got too many conveniences. They've got pools to swim in, parks to play in, nice theaters. They've got everything, and anyhow they don't like us so why should I like them?"[119] And when Jeanne referred to the whites living in her neighborhood, she told Elizabeth Davis, "There's plenty ole cheap pecks around."[120] In her neighborhood, Jeanne saw whites who were not superior to her, at least in her opinion. For Jeanne, class and respectability were important components of identity. To emphasize respectability meant that although one might be defined as "colored" by white society, one's family, neighborhood, and local community were worth more than that. For Jeanne, then, low-class whites were no better than her. In fact, they were much worse. One of the reasons they were worse was their inability to live nice, clean lives.

Jeanne defined herself as a deeply spiritual person, and thus, for her, Catholicism and niceness were closely aligned. Jeanne's sisters teased her about her religious devotion. But Jeanne said proudly, "My sisters are not as religious as me. I am the most religious one out of the children."[121] Jeanne defined church as a place of reflection, prayer, and hushed devotion. "I like the silence in church. You can pray in silence," she said. Haydel pressed Jeanne by suggesting that she was merely a strict Catholic who simply followed the rules. But Jeanne was insistent; she knew exactly why she loved church: "I told you, I like church because of the silence in church. I like to be around where it's quiet sometimes. I don't like to be where there is always noise." Jeanne's prayers, in the silence of church, were for things she wanted, for the dead who could not pray for themselves, and "to make sacrifice to God." Jeanne also regularly attended church so that she could have the courage to "live right."[122]

Despite her devotion as a strict Catholic, Jeanne was also a staunch critic of the sexual politics of the church. She had thought deeply about church policy and questions of religion, sexuality, and morality. When Claude Haydel asked Jeanne's opinion of the priests in her parish, Jeanne responded,

> I don't think priests should like the ladies. After twelve years in the seminary they should have decided whether they were willing to give up the ladies or not. Maybe some of 'em wait until they get old to like the ladies, huh? I know one girl they said the priest liked, and she liked him, but she went away. Another girl the people said liked a priest but she said she was going to be a nun. She is in the convent now. Some of those priests don't do nothing but run around. Some stay out until eleven o'clock at night. Some stay out later since they be around the dances the church give. . . . There should be some changes made. For instance the priest shouldn't be allowed to go out much. They should stay in like the nuns unless they got some place in particular to go. They shouldn't drink so much and fool around [with] ladies and they shouldn't be allowed to live so kingly.[123]

Jeanne was certain in her opposition to priests "liking the ladies." She felt it was their duty to live a life of strict devotion, excluding not only sex but also alcohol, dancing, and other worldly things. Her critique of the priests' role in her culture hinged on an analysis of the sexual and gender politics of the church. She saw diverging standards for nuns and priests. She also believed that the priests often were guilty of what she was supposed to refrain from: staying out late and involvement in sexual relationships.

Jeanne's complex moral code was completely logical and consistent to her. When Claude Haydel asked if she saw anything immoral about sexual intercourse, Jeanne responded, "I don't see anything in it, in the first place, and I do think it's wrong. People will talk about you if it ever got around. They will say you are indecent and a whole lot of stuff. The girl will be talked about."[124] Jeanne clearly articulated community sanctions against nice girls having sexual intercourse. Nice girls had to face community gossip, which Jeanne Manuel often participated in.

Jeanne Manuel, like Ellen Hill and Beverly Carter, discussed the politics of gossip in her interview. When talking about her clique of friends she said, "Our bunch has a paper now called *Gossip Times* . . . that's just a little paper we write. Every time we know something about somebody we put it in the paper and things like that." All the girls in her clique read and helped write the paper. The boys were not allowed to read the paper because they did not take it seriously (they would rip it up) and because, just as often, they were the subjects of the columns. The girls would "just sit and read it and laugh."[125]

The girls of Jeanne's group circulated stories not only about outside girls and boys but about those of their group as well. Thus, the *Gossip Times* policed their clique's behavior as much as the behavior of other youths. By making fun of the offenders of niceness, they clearly defined appropriate behavior for themselves. Additionally, if any girl stepped outside of the bounds of respectable behavior, she knew she would be the subject of ridicule—most likely in the *Gossip Times*.

Even as she discussed community sanctions against premarital sex, Jeanne Manuel also truly believed sex was immoral. When asked about sex after marriage, she further clarified her position regarding the morality of sex. Jeanne pointedly questioned the contradictions in the discourse of sexual intercourse: "That's what I don't like about it. It's so wonderful after you are married but it is looked upon as so wrong if you do it before you are married. It should be the same in both cases."[126] To relieve this contradiction, Jeanne stuck to her belief that sex was "awful" in all situations and under every circumstance.

Because of Jeanne's closeness to Claude Haydel, she felt free to ask him questions about sex that had previously preoccupied her. Her questions reveal an underlying anxiety that sex itself was something to fear. During one interview Jeanne asked, "Do you know what 'paw' means?" When Haydel did not quite understand the question, Jeanne clarified:

> JEANNE: Well, I was reading in a magazine that a movie star said she couldn't stand her husband "pawing her."
> HAYDEL: Did that have an effect on you?
> JEANNE: Sure, if she couldn't stand it after marriage she must have thought it was awful, and so I thought it was awful too.[127]

Jeanne's knowledge of sex was heavily influenced by popular culture. Her question reveals that she did not understand the meaning of "pawing," but the context in which she read it led her to believe that it was "awful," and she may have thought that the "pawing" act of sex was violent. Her question further exposed that Jeanne's fear of sex came from different angles— popular culture, church, home—but also proved that sex was something she had thought a lot about.

Unlike Ellen Hill, who refused to date boys because she despised them, Jeanne had boyfriends; so although Jeanne disliked the idea of sex play, she was obligated to put up with boys.[128] Her clique was composed of both girls and boys who dated one another. It was assumed that pretty Creole girls would grow up and marry Creole boys from their same downtown neighborhood, because downtown Creole society placed a high premium on marrying a Creole boy from a nice family. Marriage might not come right away, if a girl was destined for college at Xavier University, but it was expected nonetheless.[129] Accordingly, heterosexual boy-girl relationships were exceedingly important in Jeanne's social world. She explained to Haydel her relationship with her boyfriends: "I used to let them sit close to me and kiss them now and then, but they always wanted to and I didn't; so it was best that they leave me alone. I don't believe in that very much and surely not all the time like they wanted to."[130] That Jeanne did not believe in kissing "very much" illustrated her moral uncertainty concerning sex play; kissing was something she struggled with. At the same time, it is clear that she did not want to be as physical as the boys did. Jeanne repeated twice the boys' intense interest in kissing: "they always wanted to" and "all the time," which made clear the boys' intentions. When Haydel asked if she ever went further with her boyfriend, she was adamant: "You mean if I ever gave him too many liberties? . . . No I didn't."[131]

Claude Haydel's relationship with Jeanne Manuel bordered on the inappropriate; at least for a girl like Jeanne, intimate sex talk was extremely provocative, particularly with a college-aged man. She was open with him while he continually prodded her about her sexual fantasies. She expressed her anxieties around sex and sexuality, and those anxieties extended to her relationship with Haydel. The incendiary nature of the relationship was evident when Jeanne discussed with Haydel a dream she had about him: "One evening you were holding me in your arms and asking me for too many liberties and I told you no. Then you kissed me and I disappeared." The dream had come after Haydel and Jeanne had discussed getting undressed in front of one's husband. Jeanne believed she had the dream because she had been preoccupied by their conversation when she got home that night. Jeanne found herself in a profound moral quandary. She confessed, "I thought about how awful it was and maybe we shouldn't have talked about that."[132]

In an interview a few days after Jeanne revealed her dream to Haydel, they revisited the subject. Jeanne admitted that their conversation about sex "was too deep."[133] But in that same interview, Haydel continued to push her regarding her view of sex. Haydel suggested that sex was pleasurable in marriage—that two people in love had sex willingly. When Haydel had suggested there was enjoyment in sex, Jeanne exclaimed, "Pleasure! Out of something as awful as that? I thought people did that just to have children. Well I guess I'd just have to divorce my husband [if he wanted to have sex]. . . . [I]f he loves me he wouldn't want to do me that [way]."[134]

At the same time that the sexual nature of the conversation with Haydel truly troubled Jeanne, they maintained a unique relationship throughout the interviews. Haydel, Davis, and Dollard all believed that Jeanne had a crush on Haydel. Haydel did not discourage those feelings. As a downtown Creole, Haydel knew the other girls and families in the neighborhood. Even as he teased Jeanne, he did not ask leading questions; usually, he asked the question in the opposite direction of what he was sure she would say. For instance, knowing her family background as very light (nearly white-looking) Creoles, and being from a similar family background himself, Haydel knew that Jeanne would not want to date a dark-skinned boy. But he asked Jeanne, "Probably you like a sort of dark boy [to date]?" Jeanne responded passionately, "Who? No indeed! I don't like no dark boys. They are all right, but I don't like 'em for myself."[135] Ultimately, her comfort with (or crush on) Haydel was expressed by her willingness to discuss boys and sex with him despite his teasing, her sex dreams, and the provocative nature of the topics they discussed.

In *Children of Bondage*, Davis and Dollard concluded that Jeanne's sexuality was repressed because of the social controls of her class status, claiming that she had been trained "too well." They argued, "Jeanne is strongly suppressing her womanly feelings, but they are there nonetheless, otherwise she would not be afraid of them. It is surely no accident that her dreams show a marked preoccupation with sexual themes, and seem to illustrate quite clearly the punishments for sexual actions. Granted that Jeanne's parents want her to be a virtuous girl, they probably do not want her to shun marriage and parenthood altogether."[136] Surely, however, some of these sex dreams were provoked by the interview situation itself, which often dwelled on the possible pleasures of sex. In Davis and Dollard's analysis, her fear of sexuality was concrete and comprehensible given her social "caste." Unlike other girls in the study (such as Julia Wilson) whose fear of sexuality seemed both bizarre and mysterious to the researchers, Jeanne Manuel's fears appeared to derive strictly from childhood training—the training of her parents, church, and class. In their view, her intense dreams stemmed from her frustrated and repressed sexual impulses.

But Jeanne Manuel's fears tell a much more complicated story; her anxiety concerning sex reveals her social development as a teenage girl in the Jim Crow era while also exposing the way in which girls' subjectivity changed over time. Jeanne's subjectivity was built on ethical grounds. She came to understand herself and her self-worth through her adherence to a moral code that included religiosity, purity, niceness, and a Creole heritage. For

Jeanne, these things intersected. Once Jeanne was old enough to have to confront sex and sex play, she found the components of her identity wavering. Her fear of sex revealed how unstable certain aspects of her subjectivity were at the moment of adolescence. It also showed how, at a moment of crisis, such as experiencing sexual violence, Jeanne's view of herself might be completely altered. It is also impossible to know just how Jeanne's subjectivity shifted once she reached the next phase in her life as a sexually active teenager or adult. However, it is clear that as a teenage girl living in New Orleans, sexual purity was a crucial component to her subjectivity as a black Creole girl.

Twenty years after her interview with Claude Haydel, the authors of *The Eighth Generation Grows Up* found Jeanne Manuel, a woman in her thirties, married to a Creole man from New Orleans. As children, they grew up in the same neighborhood and knew each other as third graders. Manuel had two children and lived as a housewife on the West Coast.

THE TREME AND THE Seventh Ward, the downtown neighborhoods that Ellen Hill and Jeanne Manuel called home, underwent a significant transformation in the post–World War II era, as did the moral geographies associated with these spaces. Like many urban neighborhoods, the area experienced decline as New Orleans suburbs were developed.[137] In the 1950s, many residents of downtown New Orleans moved to brand-new developments toward Lake Pontchartrain, including Gentilly and black neighborhoods of New Orleans East such as Pine Village and Plum Orchard. These neighborhoods represented a new possibility for modern living. Other residents moved away from the Jim Crow South completely, leaving for Chicago or California, as Ellen Hill and Jeanne Manuel did. Those who moved out of the Treme and the Seventh Ward—to the suburbs or out of the Jim Crow South—did so with a sense of hope, looking for geographies of freedom and equality.

In 1954, further hastening the changes to the older sections of the Treme and the Seventh Ward, the city of New Orleans made plans for a new highway construction that would make use of Claiborne Avenue to shuttle suburbanites—white and black—to the French Quarter and Central Business District. Claiborne Avenue had long functioned as a business quarter and gathering space for residents of the Treme and the Seventh Ward. By 1956, the interstate plan was confirmed with the aid of the Interstate Highway Act. Construction began in 1966. One of the most important streets in the Seventh Ward and the Treme, Claiborne Avenue, turned into the corridor for Interstate 10. One black New Orleans resident and Claiborne business owner recalled, "You can't fight things like that. It was modernization that made this a ghetto, and nothing we could do would have made a bit of difference."[138] These series of changes forever altered the contours of the geography of niceness. The Treme and the Seventh Ward were no longer the "respectable" neighborhoods of the past.

Some former residents look back to that "nice" neighborhood with a sense of nostalgia, remembering the black community that, in some ways, thrived in the area. Darrlyn Smith wrote a Seventh Ward "nostalgia dictionary" to capture a world vanished and to honor "the nostalgia of hundreds of people—those who grew up in the Seventh Ward and those who wished they did; those who left, those who remained and all who want to remember the ambiance."[139] Beverly Anderson wrote in her memoir, *Cherished Memories*, "There are several reasons for writing this book as I soothe a part of my nostalgic soul in an attempt to recapture the blissful years in New Orleans. . . . The culture for me was rooted in close family ties, hard work, creativity, self-pride, high expectations, independence, the Gold Rule, Catholicism . . . and a shared sense of belonging to the unique Seventh Ward."[140] These memories of the Seventh Ward and the Treme seem surprising in their memorializing of black communities that existed alongside the everyday violence of Jim Crow. When traveling back to the post-Katrina Mississippi Gulf Coast, poet Natasha Trethewey was "stunned" to find similar "fond memories of a segregated Gulfport."[141] But as she stopped and reflected, she realized that the nostalgia is not so much about the past but about the present: a reminder of the unevenness in what some people have lost and gained in the post–civil rights, post-Katrina Gulf Coast. Trethewey argues that the "nostalgia about the days of Jim Crow implies that the alternative hasn't always benefited poor and low-income people equally and that reforms that should help all members of a society still privilege some people over others." There have also been "nuances of what some people lost."[142] Jeanne Manuel and other Creole girls, in leaving and losing the Seventh Ward, lost a space, neighborhood, and community that helped underscore their worth as valuable human beings; Manuel would have lost her geography of niceness even as she gained new freedoms (as well as new struggles) in California. Perhaps Ellen Hill and other girls who were not so centrally part of the geography of niceness, girls who were not Creole and not Catholic, may not have missed the old neighborhood in the same ways. Because as Ellen Hill believed of New Orleans, "You jus' can't get to be nothing."

CHAPTER FIVE

Relationships
Unbecoming of a Girl Her Age

Sexual Delinquency and the House
of the Good Shepherd

Behind the high brick walls, shut away from the bustle and pulsating life of the
city stands the old established House of the Good Shepherd, a holy retreat for
many world worn girls and women who find there with the good sisters quiet
for their souls, work for their hands and consolation for their bruised spirits.
—*Mrs. Joseph E. Freund,* New Orleans Times-Picayune *(1937)*

The bulky brick building of the House of the Good Shepherd sat in downtown New Orleans on the corner of Bienville and North Broad. A concrete
wall, cracked from age and adorned with ironwork, separated the convent
from its neighbors. At the entrance the name "Good Shepherd" announced
the building to the surrounding community, visitors, and passersby. At the
heart of the convent stood the chapel; all guests were funneled through its
doors. Inside, white nuns worked to rehabilitate the "world worn girls" of
New Orleans—both black and white.[1] The building was an imposing site of
church, municipal, and parental authority in downtown New Orleans. The
convent's centrality in the black community and the visibility of the building
ensured that all girls noticed its presence.

Many black women who grew up in New Orleans in the first half of the
twentieth century remember the House of the Good Shepherd, although the
actual building was demolished decades ago. Some recall that their parents
regularly threatened to send them to the convent.[2] This threat was so ubiquitous that it was featured in Darrlyn Smith's *New Orleans 7th Ward: Nostalgia
Dictionary, 1938–1965.* Under the entry "House of the Good Shepherd" Smith
wrote, "Institution for wayward girls located on Bienville and Broad. Parents
threatened to enroll girls who misbehaved."[3] While some women remember
the threat of being sent to the House of the Good Shepherd, others distinctly
recall the coercive force suggested by the physical structure. Uptowner Lilli

Braud remembered seeing girls peer out of the second-story windows. From her vantage point, the girls looked trapped inside, as if they were in a jail. Braud believed that if she behaved badly enough, she too would be locked inside the brick building that held sorrow-filled faces.[4]

The enclosed structure of the building, along with the nuns and girls cloistered inside, created a grim aura. Although many women recall the House of the Good Shepherd, very few remember the Sisters or why girls were actually sent there; the convent, though familiar, remains a mystery. Most women, thinking back, suspected that the girls were either in trouble with their parents or pregnant or both. The mystery of the House of the Good Shepherd was not singular to black New Orleans; white New Orleanians also recall the convent. Furthermore, postwar homes for delinquent girls and maternity homes throughout the country were, as one historian has noted, "gothic attic[s] obscured from the community by the closed curtains of gentility and high spiked fences."[5] The physical structure, its geography, and the mystery and threat of the House of the Good Shepherd worked to discipline the girls of New Orleans. Its very existence signified and confirmed a dividing line between "nice" and "bad" girls.

The House of the Good Shepherd's story is deeply tied to the racial politics of the South, as well as to the particularities of New Orleans. It was one of very few biracial reform homes in the South.[6] The facility was biracial, rather than integrated, because within its walls wards were segregated by race. The Sisters took in girls and young women from all class levels, religions, races, and ethnicities, but they were especially indispensable to the black community.[7] Like other southern cities, New Orleans did not have a publicly funded delinquency home for black girls even into the 1950s.[8] In most southern cities, therefore, black girls picked up by the authorities were often sent to jail with adult criminals. In New Orleans, however, girls might also be sent to the House of the Good Shepherd or to other smaller orphanages and asylums that accepted black children. Each year the Sisters of the Good Shepherd took in about 180 girls.[9] Approximately 50 black girls and a slightly higher number of white girls occupied the convent at any time.

To reconstruct the world of the House of the Good Shepherd, I have gathered a variety of sources detailing the secretive institution: photographs, census data, reports on the methods of the Sisters of the Good Shepherd, court documents, newspaper articles, and monographs on the subject of female delinquency. These sources come from different years, even different decades, each divulging only a tiny portion of the whole story. Nonetheless, from these sources the world of the House of the Good Shepherd emerges, and it provides a striking contrast to the world inhabited by "nice" girls.

Tracing the Roots of the Good Shepherd

At first glance, the mysterious building seems without context—separate from the city surrounding it. Yet the convent's development closely mirrored the period in which it was founded. The Order of the Good Shepherd traced back to a seventeenth-century community of cloistered nuns in Angers, France, the Sisters of Our Lady of Charity of the Refuge. Reorganized in 1835, they became the Sisters of the Good Shepherd; some of these Sisters were silent and cloistered, constantly praying for fallen women, while others worked in the world, devoting their time to wayward girls. Soon, Houses of the Good Shepherd were established throughout the United States. The order opened a convent in New Orleans in 1859, just prior to the start of the Civil War.[10]

The first three vows of all Catholic women's religious orders are poverty, chastity, and obedience. After these, the Sisters of the Good Shepherd pledged "to labor for the salvation of souls."[11] They toiled for girls' souls by vowing to reform those who had fallen into sin. In 1866, Mother Superior Mary of St. Terese begged the New Orleans community for donations, promising to continue "rescuing fallen women from the mire of sin and awakening her soul once more to a consciousness of virtue of God and of heavenly hope."[12] In the same year, the Sisters of the Good Shepherd moved their walled convent to the corner of Bienville and Broad in downtown New Orleans. They would remain in that location for nearly a century. Charitable contributions and public funds from the city chest of New Orleans supported the convent financially; later, the Associated Catholic Charities (ACC) of Orleans Parish contributed funds.[13]

The House of the Good Shepherd further expanded its reach during the Progressive Era (1890s–1920s). Progressive moral reform movements such as the Woman's Christian Temperance Union sought governmental regulation of morality.[14] White Progressive activists expressed deep concern for working-class white girls and young women who inhabited the dangerous modern city.[15] These white purity activists launched a national campaign to raise age of consent laws to align with new notions of childhood, adolescence, and virginal innocence.[16] In Louisiana the age of consent rose from twelve years in 1885 to eighteen by 1920.[17] Simultaneously, among middle-class and aspiring-class black activists, there existed a similar "moral panic" over poorer black female migrants coming into large, dangerous cities from rural areas.[18] White and black activists both believed fallen women were victims of vicious men, poor moral educations, and substandard living conditions in the modern city.

It was during this period of reform that the House of the Good Shepherd began receiving more girls from the city—girls who had been through the newly powerful local court system. Previously, black and white girls had been placed in the convent by their parents or guardians. But during the early twentieth century, girls were sent to the convent by the courts for sexual delinquency. In the late 1920s the ACC was established. Its office oversaw the children and youth sent to the House of the Good Shepherd and other Catholic charitable organizations.[19] Although understaffed (in the 1940s it had only one social worker), this move represented the professionalization impulse of charities during the Progressive Era. However, the House of the Good Shepherd remained an outlier—although the ACC brought access to a social worker, religious women without professional training in social work, psychology, or health ran the convent. And unlike many other Progressive reform homes, the House of the Good Shepherd continued to rely on religious moral instruction as the primary mode of rehabilitation.

By the 1930s, therefore, the House of the Good Shepherd operated with a complex notion of sin and piety influenced by definitions of immorality from different decades. This makes tracing the Good Shepherd's methods all the more complicated. On the one hand, the growing professionalization of the Progressive Era penetrated the walls of the convent through the city courts, the children's bureau, and the ACC. But on the other hand, descriptions about life behind the walls from the early 1900s and into the 1940s tell overlapping and similar stories that reveal the Sisters' unyielding commitment to older ideals of industry, confession, and penance. This is not to say the Sisters' methods did not change over time, but that the Sisters embraced change only reluctantly.

Beginning in 1939, the Sisters at the convent struggled with a newly appointed Jewish judge to the juvenile court, Anna Veters Levy. The politicking that ensued centered on who would have ultimate authority over the girls' bodies—the state or the Sisters. Judge Levy objected to what she saw as the convent's antiquated methods of dealing with juvenile delinquents. Furthermore, the basis of her concern stemmed from an important philosophical debate over the role of professionalization and religion in reforming girls. Levy insisted that her job required that she "remove children from such institution when the care and discipline of children committed to such institution is found to be unsatisfactory."[20] She believed the convent was just that sort of institution.

The House of the Good Shepherd operated on a program of authoritarian domesticity.[21] In essence, the Sisters became the parental authority of the wards and wielded this power to ensure the girls behaved. The Sisters believed their power came from above, from God through the auspices of the Catholic Church. Once Judge Levy stepped in, however, she challenged the Sisters' influence. Levy's authoritarian hand became mightier than that of the Sisters. Judge Levy believed the House of the Good Shepherd should be an auxiliary of state authority—and nothing more.[22] She protested the fact that parents might actually send their children to the convent without governmental approval. She told the Sisters, "Girls should not be accepted in institutions unless placed there by the juvenile courts of this state. . . . In no event should a girl be accepted directly from her parents, relations, guardians . . . unless placement is approved by a juvenile court."[23] In her court, municipal authority trumped that of the church.

The Sisters complained to Bishop Joseph Rummel about Judge Levy and her attempts to limit their authority over the girls. The Sisters believed that Levy talked "disparagingly" about the nuns, their religious program, and their medical services in open court and in conferences with parents.[24] When a sixteen-year-old white girl told Judge Levy she wished to stay at the convent rather than go to the all-white state institution in Alexandria because Sister Madeleine had told her she would not be able to practice Catholicism at Alexandria, Levy became upset. Allegedly, Levy told the girl, "You can tell Sister Madeleine for me that she is guilty of Contempt of Court and I'll certainty tell her myself when this hearing is over."[25]

Levy's education (bachelor's, master's, and law degrees from local all-white universities) as well as her professional standing gave her the authority to "objectively" critique the Sisters' work. In juvenile justice, "there is no punishment to be weighed and no need for show of power or authority in dealing with children," Levy argued in a book she published about her years in the juvenile court.[26] To improve the House of the Good Shepherd, Levy suggested that the convent hire professionals, such as lay teachers, social workers, and especially nurses, and end compulsory work requirements. Levy also objected to the space of the convent: the wall enclosing the structure and the mixing of girls of different ages in rooms together.[27] The Sisters fiercely resisted the changes Levy proposed, partially because they did not have the money to radically reform the space of the convent or hire professionals but also because they resisted the idea that hard work and industry harmed the girls in their care. Nonetheless, by the mid-1950s, the Sisters began readjusting the ways in which they approached redemption. And in 1955 they began raising funds for a building that would take into account new methods for dealing with delinquent girls.[28]

Bad Girls: Delinquency, Stigma, and Race

During the decades that the House of the Good Shepherd served New Orleans, the nuns identified the girls by the stigmatized categories of "fallen," "wayward," or "delinquent." However, by 1908, the state of Louisiana established separate laws and a juvenile court that would provide for "neglected and delinquent children."[29] Delinquency, then, was the criminal label for girls accused of improper sexuality in the 1930s. The stigmatized category "delinquent" contrasted with "niceness" because stigma always works in relation to a set of ideological norms.[30] As was explored in the previous chapter, black New Orleanians used a language of niceness to identify proper girlhood. Nice girls wore their cleanliness; they had tidy clothes and well-kept hair. Furthermore, sexual purity denoted nice behavior: a nice girl's body was not only clean but also innocent. Not surprisingly, then, "delinquent" girls were identified by a filth and impurity of the body.

Historians of childhood and youth have noted the ways in which scholars, activists, and the popular press emphasized the various "girl problem[s]" and "youth problem[s]" of the 1910s to 1930s.[31] Notions of delinquency overlapped with fears that boys and girls were developing improper or dangerous masculinity and femininity. In the 1930s and 1940s, delinquent black girls were defined as unclean. Their bodies and tattered clothing and the poverty surrounding them became stigma signs—markers of their supposed abnormality and failure to live up to standards of proper girlhood.[32] Of course, access to clothing, proper washing facilities, and a well-kept home environment were class-specific. Girls who lived in poorer families were much more likely to be blamed for delinquency. Sociologist Allison Davis, for example, invoked a classed notion of respectability versus delinquency: "When one observes the aberrant sexual, educational, and 'legal' behavior of a large portion of Negro adolescents . . . the first thing one learns is that there are major differences of behavior within the Negro group, according to economic levels."[33]

Journalists, researchers, and reformers declared that filthy living spaces created unclean bodies, which, in turn, led to immorality. A 1937 article published in the *Louisiana Weekly*, "Youth, Crime, and Squalid Homes," clearly linked filth with juvenile crime. The author addressed children living in "sub-standard homes" and "squalor," arguing that poverty, located primarily in the slums, created immoral youth that might eventually rot the whole "super-structure of society." In this view, the immorality of poor black urban youth had the potential to destroy American society and culture. The author of "Youth, Crime, and Squalid Homes" argued for more resources and reform directed to poor black neighborhoods in American cities, believing that the only cure for delinquency was a "proper environment," such as a clean home and pure living. This lesson in physical and moral cleanliness, the piece maintained, was crucial for community building.[34] Delinquency, then, was defined in black communities as specifically an urban (slum) problem.[35] In this way, poor black children were often stigmatized as delinquent, problem children.

These connections between poverty, filthy environments, and immorality coalesced in the medical and sociological literature on diseased black bodies. Diseased African Americans were already stigmatized, assumed by doctors, reformers, and researchers to have failed to live up to a proper mode of living and thus deserving of their fate in sickness. The Urban League's southern director, Nelson Jackson, blamed black girls for the spread of venereal diseases among southern African Americans: "It is the teen-age girl who furnishes much of the [sexual] activity. These girls quite often live in communities which do not offer sufficient group work and recreation facilities or other normal outlets for expression. Their recreational outlets frequently take the form of nightly visits to taverns and 'juke-joints' where men in uniform congregate. From there they are taken by soldiers to cheap hotels and rooming houses by taxi cab drivers or wander off to dark places where illicit sexual activity occurs."[36] Jackson defined these "promiscuous," diseased girls in opposition to girls who engaged in "normal" behavior. A revealing linguistic slip occurs in his narrative: Jackson seems to blame all black girls, rather than just aberrant girls, for the spread of disease. He argues that it is "the teen-age girl" who is responsible for sexual activity without mentioning the men with whom the girls are partying or sleeping. To Jackson, the men are blameless victims while the girls are unclean: they go to "dark," inappropriate places and have unclean, diseased bodies.

The association between unclean spaces, "unclean" bodies, and immorality may at first seem an odd one. Yet the coupling of moral health and physical cleanliness had a long history in American life. From the 1880s to the 1920s, euthenics—inspired by eugenics—argued that clean home spaces promoted moral health for children.[37] In this mode of thought, the physical body is a boundary, the only thing separating the outside (a filthy home, for example) from the interior of an individual (one's moral core, such as the soul). The bodily boundary is always fragile. The outside and inside are connected through pores, mouths, and sex organs; dirt, dust, and disease from the outside can make their way inside. In 1944 an article in the African American newspaper the *New York Amsterdam News* explored the ways in which the filth of the "ghettoes" of New York infiltrated the bodies of black children living there:

> The average Harlem home . . . is filthy, insanitary and unfit for the
> normal life of youth. Water-soaked and foul-smelling apartments,
> basements, infested by bugs, roaches and other vermin . . . are the
> homes in which too many Negro children must spend long hours
> or parade through the streets and expose themselves to other kinds
> of unhealthy conditions. . . . There, five occupy a single room in
> which they cook, wash, eat, dance, drink hard liquor and engage in
> debauchery before the very eyes of their children.[38]

This discussion of delinquency exposed the fragile boundary between inside and outside. According to the article, in "filth" poor residents ingested insanitary food and drink, washed their bodies with the dirt that surrounded them, and danced and had sex, resulting in sweaty bodies inside the home. In this narrative, even actions normally defined as positive—such as cleaning the body—were corrupted. The size of the home also became an issue; in crowded space, bodies touched and overlapped, as did social activities. Such discussions of delinquency marked poor children as predestined for a life of immorality and criminal behavior while (sometimes unintentionally) blaming delinquency on the messiness of the home rather than on structural and economic inequality.

A 1951 article in the *Louisiana Weekly* echoed similar concerns. In a special two-part report, the newspaper followed two recently hired African American juvenile officers who worked with the city's black juvenile delinquents. The officers explained that while parents were away, youth went to "sordid places" and made contact with "questionable characters." The first article centered on delinquent girls' sexuality. The officers claimed, "Girls, especially, who have been the victims of carnal knowledge are invariably from broken homes whose fathers and mothers are carrying on illicit relationships with companions before the children. . . . In many cases such girls have practically no relationship with boys of their own age levels and want none."[39] The article implied that these "delinquent" girls hung out in distasteful, dirty places and, therefore, were sexually impure. The girls picked up by the police officers were arrested, sent to the House of the Good Shepherd, and labeled "sexually delinquent."

The "filth" written on poor girls' bodies identified them as members of an urban lower class and as social outcasts. Uncleanliness became a stigma symbol for reformers—a mark of debasement, leading the juvenile courts, officers, judges, or nuns to see young women as immoral and incapable of caring for themselves.[40] Written on poor girls' bodies, then, was the unseemly femininity and immorality that was a sexualized product, "bred" in the "slums" of urban America.[41]

Coming to the Convent: Girls and Sexualized Crime

Between 1930 and 1954, black girls came to the Sisters for a wide array of sins. Parents might send their children to the Sisters if they misbehaved or were "ungovernable." And the juvenile courts sent girls who were caught stealing, drinking, or disturbing the peace.[42] Despite local myths to the contrary, the convent did not accept girls who were pregnant.[43] In 1942 the executive director of the Associated Catholic Charities wrote to the bishop and included a review of cases that went before New Orleans' juvenile courts. Most of these summaries do not mention the girls' race, but they do provide clues into how Good Shepherd girls came to be confined at the convent while revealing the ways in which disease was used by the Sisters and the court to mark all the girls in their care as sexually delinquent. Although girls came for a variety of reasons, over half were accused of improper sexual activity. Even more were marked as sexually promiscuous once they entered.[44]

In the available documents, improper sexuality was usually recorded in relation to "carnal knowledge" charges brought up on the girls' adult male abusers or partners. But girls were also accused of being entertainers in a "night club of ill repute," married to or living with men of whom parents disapproved, or simply "in need of medical attention," which the girl and parents ignored.[45]

As soon as a girl was admitted to the House of the Good Shepherd, the convent nurse gave her a medical exam. The records constantly referred to the girls' medical status: one with a "four plus Wassermann report" would remain "in the Convent of the Good Shepherd because of need of medical treatment," as would a "girl in need of medical treatment which parents ignore."[46] A Wasserman test determined whether or not a ward was afflicted with syphilis, a sexually transmitted disease. This test was commonly used on prostitutes, delinquent girls, and black men, despite its notorious unreliability.[47] According to the criminal courts, reformers, and doctors, syphilis and gonorrhea were two venereal diseases that denoted immorality and criminality in women.[48]

The comments in the House of the Good Shepherd case files referring to the girls' medical diagnoses illustrate the ways in which the ACC and the Sisters believed that measuring disease likewise measured immorality. For them, sin was written on the body. In one record the Sisters noted, "The judge was inclined to allow girl to go home before medical information was brought out."[49] In other words, the nuns wanted to use the "medical information" in court as a reason for further detaining the young woman at the convent. In such cases, the Sisters knew (with physical, somatic proof) that the House of the Good Shepherd girls were guilty of immoral activity, and this medical proof seemed reason enough for them to keep a girl interned inside the convent. Accordingly, the transgression of premarital sex—even in the case of rape— was written on the body of the wards. The sin of improper sexuality was a crime of action; the sinful act was caught in the body through a wicked disease.

Black women and teens, however, were already always defined as promiscuous and were thus less likely to be blamed for prostitution—their regular sexuality was dangerous enough. The medical establishment viewed their bodies, like that those of black men, as sexually immoral and diseased.[50] The eugenics movement, which lasted into the 1930s, and the Tuskegee experiment (1932–72) medically defined African Americans in particular, but also poor whites, as licentious and contaminated. Such definitions were so popular that an educated white respondent in a 1930s survey argued against interracial marriage on the grounds that "we [whites] would have more venereal disease because the Negro is full of it."[51] Even among progressive white and black scholars and researchers, there remained a close association between poor black women and sexual promiscuity.

The stories of three black girls sent to the House of the Good Shepherd— Ramona Cruz, Dorothy Jackson, and Vivian Thomas[52]—demonstrate how sexual delinquency was used to discredit black girls. The girls had wildly different paths to the House of the Good Shepherd, yet their stories reveal a Jim Crow culture that led juvenile courts to define black girls as "delinquent." At the same time, their stories are potent reminders of the existence of the double bind in these girls' lives. Although some of the girls sent to the House of the Good Shepherd lived outside the bounds of niceness, they still contended with the racism of Jim Crow and the expectation of purity of the middle and professional black classes, along with expectations for purity from religious leaders.

Ramona Cruz: Stigmatized Sexuality

Disease as proof of guilt and sin resonated throughout the limited case files for the House of the Good Shepherd. One ACC record contained the story of two teenage black girls living in New Orleans. The short narrative of the girls' troubles makes the nexus of disease, class, race, and guilt all the more clear:

> Mable, age thirteen, lived with her fourteen-year-old sibling, Ramona. Their parents were divorced and the father resided in Memphis, Tennessee. He had remarried, but sent a check each month to his first wife for the support of the children. [Their mother] had left the children in the home alone, but she came to pay rent and would visit them every two or three weeks.
>
> These adolescent girls lived in a one-room apartment behind a house. It was upstairs and there were six families living in this rear house which had one community toilet. . . . The room was furnished with only bare necessities and always appeared to be untidy. There was only one bed. Cooking, eating, sleeping, bathing and other activities were carried on in this one room.
>
> Mable and Ramona had a poor relationship. Ramona was aggressive and bossy. She forced Mable to do all household chores. Mable sometimes refused and Ramona beat her. The mother was aware of Ramona's hostile, antagonistic attitude and openly abused her when she visited the home. . . . Neighbors often told [the mother] about Ramona's boyfriend and of her sexual behavior in the community yard.
>
> . . . Both girls were attending school irregularly. The teacher . . . was unable to get the cooperation she needed from the home. She referred them to court because of poor school attendance, neglect and delinquency. She knew their environment was conducive to delinquency. A medical examination revealed that Ramona was sexually delinquent.[53]

Ramona Cruz was sent to the House of the Good Shepherd, while Mable Cruz was sent to Saint John Bercham's Home for Neglected Girls. In this narrative, the girls' troubles began with lack of parental supervision, but the case file also made a strong connection between the uncleanness of the home and immorality. According to the social workers, the home was "conducive to delinquency"; they thought that the small, poor housing led to filth, which led to immorality. That the girls cooked, ate, slept, and washed themselves in only one room—their only living space—further exacerbated the "untidiness." Ramona Cruz's class status made it more likely that she would be accused of delinquency and promiscuity. In the eyes of social workers, the unclean home and crowded surroundings stigmatized the girls as immoral.

The untidiness of the home proved problematic for the girls, but a medical exam verified Ramona's sexual delinquency; either a broken hymen or a sexually transmitted disease medically proved Ramona's sin. Her punishment for such delinquency was to be sent to the convent. Ramona's "crime" was an intimate relationship with what the neighbors called a "boyfriend"; the record did not mention any prostitution or widespread promiscuity. And although her violence toward her sister remained an integral part of the story, the file charged her with nothing more than truancy and sexual immorality. Ramona Cruz failed to live up to standards of proper femininity and normal girlhood. Her teacher and the juvenile justice system marked her as a discredited individual—one who could not care for herself. She was stigmatized by both her poverty and her sexuality.

The Cruz family's story, however, is much more complicated than what the social workers recorded inside the case file. Ramona's mother did not live with her children, but she provided them with food and rent and even attempted to discipline them. She cared for her family but could not be there with them. It is possible that she worked away from home, perhaps living with and caring for a white family. Thus, what is defined in the ACC case record as "neglect" and "sexual delinquency" could have also been narrated as a story about the inherent inequalities of racialized domestic work.

Ramona's sense of self developed within this larger context of race, class, and sexuality. Within her family, she had some measure of authority. She was the older child, and it was her job to care for her little sister. This was an enormous responsibility. She had to get herself and her sister to school, figure out what they would eat, and try to keep the apartment clean. Ramona may not have taken on this role willingly nor taken her responsibilities seriously. After all, she skipped school, and the home was "untidy." But at the same time, it appears that Ramona put at least some effort into her role as the family nurturer. She and her sister were enrolled in school, their absence was noted, and Ramona attempted to delegate chores to her younger sister. Ramona's subjectivity probably fluctuated—in her life she was somewhere between a child and a woman on her own. She lived her life in this middle space, between a caretaker with all the responsibility and a dependent who needed help from others. If she did see herself as some type of caretaker, being sent to the House of the Good Shepherd was a sign that she had failed in that role for herself and for her sister. Now, she would be taken care of and watched over by the Sisters, while her sister would be outside of her reach.

What is clear from the record is that Ramona was largely alone. Her father and mother were gone. Ramona most likely came to understand her role as a black woman in society through this lens. Not only did the absence of caretaking affect Ramona's sense of self, so too did violence. Her mother's discipline was harsh. Ramona passed on this discipline to her little sister. Perhaps Ramona found her solace and pleasure in her relationship with her boyfriend. But the confluence of Ramona Cruz's race, class, and sexuality in Jim Crow New Orleans led her to the doors of the House of the Good Shepherd.

Dorothy Jackson: Race, Intraracial Crime, and Jim Crow Justice

Dorothy Jackson, a black sixteen-year-old, lived in uptown New Orleans with her eight siblings, mother, and father. Dorothy's father would beat her, tie her to a bed, and threaten to kill her. In June 1946, Dorothy ran away from home. Angered, her father, Arnold Jackson, searched for her. He carefully watched the home of twenty-six-year-old Ione Washington, who lived only a mile and half from their house. Jackson believed his daughter was hiding at Washington's home because her brother, who served in the military, and his daughter were friends. After observing the home from afar but without a sighting of his daughter, Jackson began questioning the women inside: Ione Washington and her nineteen-year-old sister Lillian Washington. The sisters claimed they did not know where Dorothy had gone. Infuriated, Jackson shot and killed Ione Washington and critically injured Lillian. After three days on the run, Jackson surrendered to the police. With plenty of witnesses and evidence, the assistant district attorney Guy Johnson believed not only would Jackson be found guilty but that the city could also seek the death penalty.[54]

The *Louisiana Weekly* closely followed the sensationalized courtroom drama. The police located the state's star witness, Dorothy Jackson, just before the trial began. The *Weekly* wrote, "Miss Jackson, a pretty sixteen-year-old, testified on the stand that she loved her father although she admitted that he had threatened to kill her."[55] In addition to Dorothy's appearance in court, the judge also ordered the all-white jury to the scene of the crime in the uptown neighborhood.

Despite the seemingly insurmountable evidence, Arnold Jackson was acquitted. The *Weekly* noted this injustice a year later: "A year ago the name of Arnold Jackson was on the lips of every Negro in New Orleans and most fair minded whites of the city."[56] Once Jackson was released from jail, the authorities picked up Dorothy Jackson for "relationships unbecoming to a girl of her age with the opposite sex."[57] She was sent to the House of the Good Shepherd.

Dorothy Jackson's story highlights the indifference of the white justice system; it did not protect black women and girls from abusive fathers and husbands. Arnold Jackson, who beat his children and murdered a black woman in cold blood, was released from jail. Those in the black community in New Orleans complained that they did not receive proper protection from the police or from the courts. Intraracial crime plagued the black community just as interracial crime did. In January 1949, the *Louisiana Weekly* published a cartoon, labeled "A Gentleman's Agreement," illustrating this problem with the justice system (Figure 5.1). A black man who had killed other black citizens stands before the Jim Crow court begging for mercy. The cartoon features the Grim Reaper whispering, "Let him go, he'll kill more for us 'cause he knows we won't punish him" to a white male judge symbolizing the "Southern Courts." The cartoon represented white supremacy's hold on the state governing system. White jurors and courts rendered black lives and suffering unimportant.

The inefficiency of the Jim Crow justice system comes to light when we ask, as the *Weekly* did in 1947, "What's become of Arnold Jackson and trial for attempted murder?" Not only was he released by 1947, as the *Louisiana Weekly* reported, he also continued to wreak havoc on his family. Tragically, nearly five years after Ione Washington's death, Arnold Jackson killed again. In June 1951, his "common law" wife left him. Enraged, Jackson hacked her head and arms with a meat cleaver, killing her instantly. He then set her home afire. The fire not only seriously burned his three young step-grand-children but also led to Arnold Jackson's own death. At the hospital he admitted to the murders and also implicated himself in the murder of a previous girlfriend.[58]

But what became of Dorothy Jackson? Her life after her father's earlier acquittal is not recorded in any of the newspaper accounts. However, we do know that she was sent to the House of the Good Shepherd shortly after his release. Perhaps her fate was not accidental—the convent's high walls not only kept "delinquent" girls inside but also worked to keep abusive men like

FIGURE 5.1. "A Gentleman's Agreement," January 1, 1949
(Courtesy of the *Louisiana Weekly*)

Arnold Jackson out. Indeed, Dorothy Jackson's stay at the convent opens the question of how such a place could become a refuge for girls who had run away from home looking for safety. The convent's seclusion, high walls, and all-female space made it the safest space for girls who had been abused by the men in their lives, especially given that the Jim Crow court system would not protect black girls. Arnold Jackson shot two black women looking for his daughter, but he could not challenge the authority of the white nuns protecting Dorothy after he was released from jail. Still, the police may have sent Dorothy Jackson to the convent for reasons other than protection from her father. A stay at the House of the Good Shepherd, no matter what the reason, would be deeply discrediting to Dorothy's reputation. Furthermore, the newspaper reported that she had engaged in "relationships unbecoming of a girl her age." Readers of the *Louisiana Weekly* could easily identify Dorothy Jackson as a sexually delinquent young woman with a deranged father.

Like Dorothy Jackson, many of the girls held within the walls of the convent had lived in poverty and experienced sexual or physical abuse at the hands of family members or friends. The Sisters often noted if the wards came from "immoral" or even dangerous home environments.[59] Brenda, a white ward, for example, lived in "deplorable" conditions. Her mother left her father and her eight siblings in a single-room apartment. Brenda blamed her mother for leaving and for (unnamed) "sordid" experiences. Because of these experiences, "she was very definitely in need of the protection . . . which the Convent could give her."[60] A black ward, Viola, was placed in the convent after being picked up by the police for stealing; her case was connected to a "carnal knowledge" charge against two men with whom she was arrested.[61] In another case, a sixteen-year-old "begged" the judge to commit her to the convent for at least one year. Not only did she have a venereal disease, but her case also included a carnal knowledge charge against an older man who lived in her home.[62] And, a black eleven-year-old who was raped by her grandmother's white employer was arrested and sent to House of the Good Shepherd. *The Weekly* reported that "they subjected the young miss" to an "examination which revealed" that she had venereal disease.[63] It is clear that the Sisters of the Good Shepherd saw themselves as these girls' protectors. However, it is not clear to what extent the Sisters blamed the girls themselves for their experience with sexual or physical abuse, nor is it clear how they navigated the injustices of the Jim Crow judicial system.

Dorothy Jackson's subjectivity developed within a culture of violence. Not only did she contend with Jim Crow violence, but she also had to face her father's wrath. Surely, her relationship with her father was complex. She expressed love for him on the witness stand, but she also ran away from him to save her life. The documents that shed light on Dorothy's life do not come from her point of view; her life is recorded only briefly in newspaper articles and glossed over in police records. But it is clear that the sixteen-year-old had multilayered experiences in relation to her physical body. As a child and teenager she suffered severe physical abuse. At the same time, she found support and possibly love from the Washington family and from an older boyfriend. Although she may have enjoyed physical pleasure with her boyfriend, Dorothy Jackson was then sent to the House of the Good Shepherd, where she would have learned new lessons about her body, morality, and self-restraint. These contradictory experiences around her body must have led to a sense of self defined by the embodiment of paradoxical feelings of pleasure and pain.

Vivian Thomas: Youth, Punishment, and Interracial Mixing

Although many girls who ended up in the House of the Good Shepherd struggled with poverty and domestic violence, some girls sent to the convent came from the black middle class or striving class—as did fifteen-year-old Vivian Thomas. On Saturday, February 5, 1949, a large group of college students gathered for a party at the home of a local New Orleans resident on Orleans Street in the French Quarter. Students wandered in and out of the party. They drank soda and beer and ate hot dogs while listening to a singer performing ballads. The students chatted with one another; some danced. None of this was unusual. Social gatherings in the French Quarter on a Saturday night were common. What made this particular party noteworthy, however, was the presence of students from the local white colleges, Tulane University and Newcomb College (the coordinate women's college of Tulane), along with students from the local black colleges, Dillard and Xavier Universities.[64] The party on Orleans Street disrupted New Orleans' Jim Crow politics of space. The ethic of segregation insisted that "nice" young white men and women, like those attending Tulane and Newcomb, abide by the rules of racial separation.

Orleans Street in the French Quarter represented a "front of town" area, where mostly whites lived. The neighborhood where the interracial party was held was less than 10 percent black (but down the street from St. Mary's Academy).[65] Indeed, as the party progressed, a white neighbor noticed black men entering the house. Alarmed, he called the police. Later, he testified, "The laughter of Negroes is louder than the laughter of other people, and that made the party disturbing."[66] The neighbor provocatively suggested that "such goings on" happened every night.[67] After a series of harassing visits by the local police, sixty-four people were arrested.

Although many in attendance were college students, the people arrested ranged in age from fifteen to thirty-three. Those over eighteen years old were sent to jail, found guilty of "disturbing the peace," and fined five dollars or five days in jail. Meanwhile, the only juvenile picked up at the party was a fifteen-year-old black teenager, Vivian Thomas. Vivian was sent to the House of the Good Shepherd.

Students in the New Orleans Young Progressives (sometimes referred to as Young Progressives of America), a former subsidiary of the Progressive Party, had hosted the interracial party. The Progressive Party had supported

Henry Wallace, a socialist, for president in 1948, and Young Progressives across the country in the late 1940s organized around issues of racial equality and interracial unity.[68] The local narratives of the New Orleans party and subsequent arrests intertwined the issue of improper racial mixing with suspected communism. One newspaper informant, a sociology student who was purportedly only "observing" the party, suggested that the other students in attendance were "definitely pink bordering on the red side." The white newspaper quickly pointed out in the subheading to its article that the party was "sponsored by junior size Wallace organization."[69]

Of the people arrested, twenty-two were white students from Tulane University or Newcomb College, and twelve were black college students from Xavier and Dillard Universities (but there were also housewives, and two "maids" nineteen and twenty-two years old).[70] The investigation by Tulane's administration into the interracial gathering found that although there were "idealist" students attending, it was not hosted by or associated with the Communist Party.[71]

From the beginning, the police did not emphasize the students' politics or their "outsider" status. The lawyers for the students noted that when the police first responded to the prying neighbor's phone call, they entered the party saying, "Who are these n——gg——rs? [sic] Were they invited here?" They also taunted, "You ain't got no civil rights here yet. It's against the law to have a mixed party. Break it up."[72] Clearly, the police were less interested in the political leanings of the students than in their use of space. The students responded to the police by insisting on their right to hold the party. And, indeed, New Orleans statutes did not prevent their gathering. The youth of the Young Progressives deliberately reworked the segregated space of New Orleans in order to challenge the intertwined raced, gendered, and classed politics of the Jim Crow order. By holding the party in the apartment of a white student who lived in a "front of town" neighborhood, the Young Progressives were taunting the Jim Crow order of New Orleans. A similar party in the home of a black (or white) student living in the Treme, for example, might not have attracted such notice.

After returning to the party several times to harass the students, the police finally rounded up all the attendees, separated the men from the women, searched the partygoers for weapons, and took them to the local jail. The racial slurs and insults continued after the arrests. As the police threw the black women into a cell, one said, "If I had a five gallon can of gasoline, I'd throw it in the cell and burn up all them n——gg——rs." One cop accosted a white female student with, "What's a nice girl like you doing at a party with n——gg——rs?"[73] By recognizing her as a "nice girl" he was recognizing her place in New Orleans society rather than coloring her as an "outside element" or a lower-class white New Orleanian. The students were then ushered to night court, where a marathon session relayed the details of the party and the students' transgressions of Jim Crow ethics.[74] According to the students' attorney, one officer's very first statement to the court was, "When I walked into the apartment, I saw NEGRO MEN and WHITE WOMEN dancing." The students' attorney argued that he said this "in a loud voice, so that everyone in the courtroom would be sure to hear."[75]

The insinuation by the police, of course, was that more than just "partying" was going on at the interracial gathering. The police wanted to draw attention to improper sexuality activity. According to the local black newspaper, the *Louisiana Weekly*, the police officer testified that he did not want the judge to ask probing questions because "he did not wish to embarrass anyone by having to state exactly what they were doing."[76] The police officer thus suggested that the students were engaged in interracial sexual activities. Their presence at the party, together, was insinuation enough for those southerners who equated interracialism with amalgamation.[77] After further questioning, the police officer could not recall any one person who was not "dancing, talking or merely walking through the house." But to further discredit those in attendance, the officer consistently referred to the black young women and men as "niggers."[78]

Vivian Thomas had attended the party with her parents. After her arrest, the police department released her to go home while her parents remained in custody. According to lawyers' documents, the police officers assigned to take her home decided instead to send her to the House of the Good Shepherd. By placing Vivian in the House of the Good Shepherd, the police were sending a message. And if the Sisters followed procedure, Vivian would have been given an invasive "medical exam" on entrance to find out if she was "sexually delinquent." Because the police insinuated to the court that the partygoers were engaging in immoral and "embarrassing" activities, it is logical to assume that they told this to the Sisters as well. Yet, we cannot know how the nuns balanced their calling to work with wayward girls with the pressures put on them by local police to help control behavior disruptive to the Jim Crow order.[79] Whether or not the Sisters fully cooperated, the police's decision to send Vivian Thomas to the House of the Good Shepherd demonstrates how municipal authority used the convent to control girls and uphold segregation. Gwendolyn Midlo Hall—a student activist in the Young Progressives—could not remember Vivian Thomas as she thought about the incident over sixty years later, but she recalled, "All [young] girls were terrified by threats that they would be sent there."[80]

In the confrontation between the Young Progressives and police, Vivian Thomas developed a political subjectivity. In her activism, she may have seen herself as an active agent in the fight for racial equality. At the same time, however, she experienced state authority: local law enforcement had the power to police and control her body. The police determined, in part, how Vivian would interact in the space of the Jim Crow city. But they also had the ability to police the more intimate spaces of her body: the medical exam at the House of the Good Shepherd represented a form of state violence.

Vivian, unlike Ramona Cruz, was from a middle-class family and had a community of support. Her attendance at a party organized by college students heavily interested in politics (and attended by middle-class African Americans) suggests that she was in the "aspiring class" of black Americans that looked upon education as a means to bettering one's position in society and as a way to help strengthen the race as a whole. Indeed, Vivian Thomas would later graduate from high school and attend Xavier University. The House of the Good Shepherd, then, took in girls from all classes, even if they more routinely worked with girls from the working class. Vivian's story complicates the Sisters' work, showing that they not only dealt with girls who were defined as delinquent because of poverty, sexuality, and abuse but also worked with girls who were deemed delinquent because they were a political threat to the Jim Crow order.

Bad Girls Made New: Catholicism and Life inside the Convent

Once a girl entered their walls, the Sisters of the Good Shepherd worked to rehabilitate her. The nuns tried to turn stigmatized girls into pious, solemn women who could become housewives, mothers, and nurturers. The House of the Good Shepherd used institutional and municipal authority in fashioning selves. Moral weakness, the stigma sign of entering girls, was deemed a problem of the inner self—the soul. Therefore, the Sisters of the Good Shepherd attempted to teach what we might call a Christian—or more specifically, a Catholic—subjectivity.[81] The Sisters controlled the wards by rewriting their past, remaking their bodies, encouraging confession, and providing penance. Ideally, this remade Christian subject canceled out the evils of juvenile delinquency. It is impossible to know if the Sisters "successfully" turned the wards into Catholic subjects or how (and to what extent) girls resisted the changes in self sought by the nuns. However, investigating the Sisters' methods provides a picture of how the House of the Good

Shepherd contained and monitored the sexualities and bodies of the wards in their care.

Girls of all religions were committed to the convent, either by parents or the courts, and entered with their own religious histories. By 1940, nearly one-third of the black population in New Orleans was Catholic.[82] Unlike black Protestant girls, black Catholic girls placed in the House of the Good Shepherd were familiar with Catholic doctrine, rituals, and white Catholic authority figures. They knew what it meant to be a subject of religious authority and had a familiarity with Catholic discourses of sin and sexuality. Nuns, for example, taught girls who were educated in Catholic schools; both white and black nuns taught black children in New Orleans, depending on the school. In her memoir, *A Light Will Rise in Darkness: Growing Up Black and Catholic in New Orleans*, Jo Anne Tardy writes about life as a black Catholic girl in the 1940s. She remembers cleaning the nunnery for the Sisters of the Holy Family, a black order of nuns. Inside hung a series of photographs, including pictures of the Holy Family founder, Henriette Delille; Pope Pius XII; and "the ubiquitous image of the current Archbishop of New Orleans, Joseph Francis Rummel."[83] The images of white father figures reinforced for black Catholic girls a church hierarchy while simultaneously teaching a lesson about race.[84] All whites were not to be feared—some looked over you, although with a judging eye, and as confessors, others held your deepest secrets. After all, black Catholic girls had regular interactions with the white priests in their parish.[85]

Jo Anne Tardy fondly remembered Father Walsh, the priest who had taught her catechism and heard her confessions. The moral training she received from him reached farther than the church building. While Tardy was in junior high school, the priest stopped Jo Anne and her friend while they were crossing the street, headed for a group of older kids. Father Walsh said to them, "Don't go over there, Jo Anne. . . . Don't associate with trash. Stay over here. They don't care anything about their immortal souls!"[86] Jo Anne then realized the older teens were taking turns making out. Father Walsh's presence in Jo Anne Tardy's coming-of-age story signals the interrelatedness of Catholic doctrine, white father figures, and lessons about sexuality for the girls who grew up in the city. At that moment, Father Walsh taught an important lesson about improper sexuality, sin, and one's soul—a lesson she never forgot.

Thus, black Catholic girls knew, perhaps better than their Protestant counterparts, what to expect from the religious training offered by the Sisters of the Good Shepherd. At the same time, however, New Orleans was a

Catholic city. Black girls of all religions knew enough to fear the House of the Good Shepherd. And black Protestants engaged in some Catholic rituals and celebrated Catholic holidays. Millie McClellan Charles explained, "Our lives were dominated by the Catholic religion, even though we were Protestant."[87] Nonetheless, the New Orleans black community was divided along the lines of religion: some black New Orleanians even claimed that black Catholic girls were less likely to befriend black Protestant girls.[88] Yet once inside the House of the Good Shepherd, Protestant and Catholic girls found themselves living, learning, working, and worshiping together.

To affect a Catholic subjectivity, the first step of the Sisters of the Good Shepherd was to throw away the ward's past and then renew her—just as nuns did when entering the convent. This helped the girls forge new identities inside the walls of the home. The Sisters advised the delinquent girl to "keep the story of her former life secret, telling it only to the mother in charge who [would] guide, direct and console her."[89] The original purpose of this secrecy was to protect the identity of the wayward girl, so that the outside world might never know she had been a ward of the Sisters of the Good Shepherd—itself a stigma and mark of sin.[90] But refusing to allow the past to enter the walls of the convent also created a space of rebirth; girls could become whomever they chose. The girls' identities were also "thoroughly protected" by their new religious name—"such as 'Catherine' or 'Mary'"—thereby protecting the family name and the ward's future. No one inside of the convent, except the Mother Superior and the particular Sister charged with a girl's care, would know the young woman's birth name.[91] In the process of renaming, a girl received the opportunity to construct and enact a completely new self.[92]

Not only were girls given new names, but all of the wards of the Good Shepherd were called "children" by the nuns, regardless of religion or age (the girls ranged in age from eight to eighteen, though the majority were in their teens).[93] The wards clearly became children of God; they were now hailed as religious subjects. At the same time, the Sisters became the parental authority. Notably, the ideal child's body, particularly in the Bible, was represented as free from sin.[94] By setting up a new system of identification, the girls were radically introduced to their new environment. Nearly everything in the atmosphere worked to set up an entirely new "system of meaning, hence a wholly different speaking subject."[95]

Despite this new Catholic subject, one element of the girls' former selves was preserved within the walls of the convent: race. An article in the *Catholic Louisiana* noted, "For wise reasons the Convent is divided into sections according to the different classes of those who live therein."[96] Though the Sisters had little extra space, the convent was divided strictly—not by class, as the *Catholic Louisiana* neatly phrased it, but by race on the one hand and by level of sin on the other.[97] White girls did not live, play, work, or worship beside black girls.

Sociologist and Protestant reverend Edward Coogan's 1954 study of Houses of the Good Shepherd located across the country underscored the importance of religious pedagogy in remaking sinful girls anew. In preparing his study, he wrote to juvenile courts that dealt specifically with the Sisters of the Good Shepherd. He asked if the homes' efforts were "helpful at all." Judge John Wingrave from the New Orleans juvenile court replied, "In ninety-five percent of these cases the Sisters [in New Orleans] are able to work wonders with these girls, because of religious training and the general spiritual atmosphere."[98] The moral pedagogy of the convent created the "spiritual atmosphere" and relied on several factors: a notion of the body that placed sin in the flesh, spatial isolation that would help keep the girls from returning to sin, confession, and feminine notions of hard work. These aspects of the "spiritual atmosphere" attempted to refashion girls into Catholic subjects.

Because the Sisters knew, upon entrance, if girls were "sexually delinquent"—or more precisely, "sexually active," since the two were conflated according to Catholic doctrine—they worked to rid the wards of the sins of the flesh.[99] Sisters of the Good Shepherd tried to help the girls repress sinful actions and desires and become bodies without sin. To do this, the Sisters created a safe and sacred space: the imposing walls of the convent separated the corrupt from the pious. But it was not just a matter of keeping sin outside—the nuns need to keep temptation at bay.

For that reason, the "spiritual atmosphere" of the House of the Good Shepherd began with the physical space of the convent. The spatial seclusion protected girls' moral safety from the sexualized public space of the vicious city and violent world. By barricading girls off from the world, the Sisters hoped to keep temptation out. The interior was simply adorned, as were the girls themselves. The space of the inside was purified from the excess of the world: there were no extra books, magazines, newspapers, or movies that might distract a ward's attention from purity. Sister Mary Bernard explained: "We do not allow [the wards] to read anything of loose moral or crime, but all current news and any other article of interest is always cut out and put on their bulletin board. With regard to magazines, besides many fine Catholic magazines they have *American Girl, Southern Agriculture, Current Science, Modern*

Mechanix, Popular Science, and others, but *Life* and other sensational books are forbidden."[100] The Sisters controlled the discourses that entered the walls of the convent. The bulletin board told the girls what they needed to know of the world—presumably this excluded stories of racial violence (as it excluded crime as a rule), war, poverty, and probably anything from the world with which girls like Ramona Cruz or Dorothy Jackson were familiar.

Before girls could refashion a new self, they had to account for their sinful self. Despite being told to hide their past from their peers, the convent provided girls with the opportunity to confess their sins either to the Sister in charge of them, to a counselor, or to a priest.[101] Some girls may have taken this act of confession seriously, while others may have refused to speak or fabricated narratives of their past "misdeeds." Honest, silent, or fictionalized confessions will never be found in the archive. Nonetheless, the Sisters treated the act of confession seriously, as an important moment in the ward's refashioning. In preparation for confessing their "misdeeds" of the past, girls of the Good Shepherd were told, " 'Look into your hearts, but with cheerful eyes.' Even a misspent past has its uses."[102] The Sisters compelled the girls to speak—to say something. Especially when confessing to a priest, such a speech act brought the most intimate matters of a girl's past into the hands and judgment of another. Such an act (even when falsified or refused) laid bare something of a ward's interior self.[103]

Confessing sins of the flesh was especially important for affecting a Catholic subjectivity.[104] Black Creole Aline St. Julien grew up in a New Orleans household steeped in Catholic culture. Thinking back to the ritual of confession, she recalled the emphasis on impurity in the confessional as a girl:

> I was so scrupulous, so not only was I going to confession telling my
> sins, which I thought were sins, they weren't even sins. Everything
> was a sin in those days, girl. I was confessing things like stealing a
> piece of meat out of my mama's red beans. . . . And, oh Lord, if you
> did a little sin of impurity! If I'd say, "We'd be looking at each other's
> breasts" or . . . "I was in the bathroom pasting a lemon peel on my
> little nipples," I'd have to go tell [the priest] everything. It had gotten
> to a point where I think I was a little too scrupulous.[105]

The practice of confession, even for a "nice girl" like St. Julien, depended on speaking of sin. And the very act of confession created a "scrupulous" way of interpreting one's actions and one's self. Eileen M. Julien told a similar story about "sins of impurity" in her memoir, *Travels with Mae*. One evening she saw her cousin Connie, two years her elder, nude. Eileen Julien remembered,

"I noticed these little buds on her chest. My eyes got big and I said, 'Connie, can I touch them?' She said, 'Sure, Leanie.' So I felt the bumps—soft and contoured."[106] Realizing that she was guilty of "the sin of touching," young Eileen "prayed that I would not die before getting to confession." Eileen Julien interpreted her actions in the same "scrupulous" manner as Aline St. Julien. She was "panicked" and understood immorality and morality through a Catholic lens. This scrupulous way of interpreting her own actions sexualized play between herself and her cousin. Eileen Julien remembered that at confession, the priest "asked who did the touching. When I said I had, he asked how long it had lasted. I replayed the episode in my mind and estimated perhaps five seconds. With three Our Fathers and three Hail Marys, I was free to go and sin no more!"[107]

Confession controlled not only Eileen Julien and Aline St. Julien's actions but also the way they came to understand themselves in relation to sin and sexuality as girls. Catholic subjects (like Julien and St. Julien) confessed "freely"; they felt compelled to speak of their sexuality to a priest. So, for a black girl coming into the House of the Good Shepherd, the act of confession asked her to speak of herself as a sinner, reinterpreting her life as a religious subject even while segregation had taught her to see herself as a "colored" New Orleanian. No matter what their past had been, girls of the Good Shepherd were advised by the Sisters and priests to continue to do their "best." Once they had confessed the ways of their sin, they were to "treat the past as dead."[108] In this way, the Sisters, the priest, and God were to be directors of a girl's changed self, reinforcing the hierarchal authority of the delinquency home.

Because so many girls sent to the House of the Good Shepherd by the courts grew up around "immorality," the sisters believed they needed to teach and reform the girls' internal sense of decency and propriety. They concluded that girls needed to be "re-educated" in family life because they did not fully understand the value and virtue of domestic industry.[109] Thus, the Sisters of the Good Shepherd turned to lessons in proper feminine industry as a cure for the sins of the flesh. In this atmosphere, black girls who became "reformed" had to sublimate bodily desires through hard work and simplicity. A clean and proper domestic space renewed and cleansed the spirit, and the Sisters used their authority over the girls to exhibit a work ethic that relied on focus, hard work, and feminine duty.

Therefore, wards of the Good Shepherd of all colors were expected to work hard. Wards of compulsory schooling age received educational instruction for four hours a day.[110] Additionally, the girls were taught how to properly be a woman. They learned how to cook, sew, and nurse as part of their "vocational" training. The Sisters of the Good Shepherd believed that a reformed girl would go on to be a mother and nurturer, passing on what she learned at the convent to her own children, or in black girls' cases, to the white children they cared for. In 1937 the convent allowed an "intimate view" of life inside the convent to a writer for the *New Orleans Times-Picayune*. The ACC let the female author interview one (presumably white) ward. The sentimental article extolled the "kindness and devotion of the sisters who take such a bruised reed, mend its soul and body and prepare it as best they can to meet the new stresses of life when again the girl issues forth and takes her place in society."[111]

To be in their proper "place" in society, young women had to be "useful." Ideally, girls' stay at the convent would turn them into valuable women— women who could cook, clean, and take care of a home. If the Sisters could mold wayward girls' bodies into useful bodies, then they could claim the successes of their reformation project. For example, in the 1920s an author for the *Catholic Louisiana* made such a claim about the convent's value:

> Since the opening in 1859, over 20,000 have been received and
> sheltered in the Fold. Of those who have returned to their homes,
> thousands have become *useful*, honored members of society. There
> are homes in every section of the country where mothers are teaching
> their little ones lessons they learned while under the care of the Good
> Shepherd. Everything possible is done to improve this condition so
> that they will be better equipped to make their living after leaving
> the Convent. Plain and fancy sewing, shirt and umbrella making
> and laundry work: each girl spends a part of the day in one of these
> departments besides the household duties which are assigned for
> their instruction.[112]

The Sisters, then, had a deep commitment to teaching proper femininity.

Of course, there were different standards of "use" for black and white girls in the Jim Crow South. Most jobs were not open to black women in New Orleans. Black women could work as domestics in homes or companies; as laundresses or seamstresses; or in restaurants. The black girls at the convent, then, worked in only one capacity: as domestics for the convent.[113] They were expected to clean the "colored" wing, the visiting and common areas, and the nuns' buildings. The designation of "useful" also worked against what both white and black girls were before they came to the convent: wayward and, thus, worthless. At their entrance to the House of the Good Shepherd, they were the antithesis of "nice girls."

Capturing Good Shepherd Girls: An Intimate Archive

A series of photographs taken in the 1950s demonstrates the ways in which the Sisters of the Good Shepherd worked to present "useful," pious girls to the New Orleans community. In 1955 the Sisters decided they needed a new building to better care for the girls, to update their methods, and to respond to the concerns addressed by local juvenile court judges. To help raise donations, articles were published about the Sisters of the Good Shepherd in local newspapers, and they printed their own materials explaining their work. As part of this broad advertising campaign, the House of the Good Shepherd allowed a photographer inside the convent to capture the images of a handful of girls, both black and white, to prove the civic good done by the house. This small collection of photographs, then, shows the girls in their supposed daily life and claims to offer a glimpse into the inner world of the convent (see Figures 5.2, 5.3, and 5.4). Most of the photographs were never published, and as we will see, the Sisters chose carefully how to present their work to the public.

As narratives, the photographs work to demonstrate the "truth" of the interior of the House of the Good Shepherd. But the images also obscure as much as they reveal because photographs are coercive. Images perform effective ideological work: social categories such as race, class, gender, and sexuality appear natural, and the photograph becomes evidence for the stability of these categories.[114] As the image is put forth as evidence, "the institutions of production, circulation, and reception of photographs effectively discourage inquiry into how things got to be the way they appear."[115] With very little background information on the scenes shown in the photographs or the girls who sat for them, how, then, should we approach the photographs of the House of the Good Shepherd?

This grouping of photographs constitutes an archive. As Shawn Michelle Smith explains of photographic archives, "An archive circumscribes and delimits the meaning of the photographs that comprise it, investing images with import calculated to confirm a particular discourse. Even as it purports simply to supply evidence, or to document historical occurrences, the archive maps the cultural terrain it claims to describe. In other words, the archive constructs the knowledge it would seem only to register or make evident."[116] The House of the Good Shepherd images worked to construct local knowledge about the inside of the convent, presenting the work the Sisters performed for the New Orleans community. The photographs were not natural; they were staged. By examining the ways in which they were staged,

FIGURE 5.2. Convent of the Good Shepherd dance class (The Charles L. Franck Studio Collection at The Historic New Orleans Collection, accession no. 1979.325.2280)

we can more clearly articulate the type of "good" the House of the Good Shepherd wished to perform and present to New Orleans society.

Some of the photographs appeared in a pamphlet produced by the ACC to raise funds for the new building. Next to a series of four photographs, the pamphlet included large letters floating on the page:

Awaits new Hope . . .
for those in need of guidance, re-education and training
for self-supporting
self-respecting
family and community living[117]

The four images on the page included white girls in a chemistry class (with a Sister in a habit instructing them), white girls sewing or ironing a garment (with what looks to be an instructor overseeing their progress), three white girls cooking, and three black girls in the sickroom (with a white nurse). Save for the chemistry class, the photos are all domestic images: they emphasize both the "family" atmosphere and the "community living" within the convent. And just like the quotation that accompanies them, the images stress that the convent is a space of instruction—a learning environment where girls are "re-educated." Therefore, the images neatly pair domesticity with education. By drawing on viewers' notions of proper gender roles, all

FIGURE 5.3. Sewing room at the Convent of the Good Shepherd (The Charles L. Franck Studio Collection at The Historic New Orleans Collection, accession no. 1979.325.2277)

of the photographs depict the girls performing legible feminine tasks that were deemed appropriate for teenage girls, such as comforting and cleaning, but not, for example, anything overtly sexual. Just as they rely on these dominant systems of meaning, the photographs simultaneously create their own meaning.

The girls in Figure 5.4, for example, appear to be learning how to care for a sick loved one. With the dark background and light on the starkly white sickbed, the girl being cared for appears to be undergoing some sort of religious transformation. The girls photographed play the role of nurturer (rather than being nurtured or punished, which is why they ended up in the convent in the first place). It is clear, however, that this is only a learning environment. Each person in the photograph has a pleasant look on her face. The instructor is smiling broadly, and the "infirm" agreeably allowed a photograph to be taken of her. This type of training would be useful in a family setting or in working as a caregiver for a white family. Although they are playing at nurse, it is unclear if this photograph was actually taken in the infirmary. The large number of beds suggests instead that it is the black girls' dormitory. A series of dresses is barely visible in the periphery of the photograph—perhaps the wardrobe for the black wards.

In contrast to the room that is the setting for the nursing photograph is the pamphlet including another image that clearly shows a dormitory room.

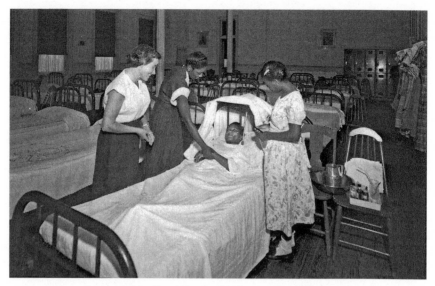

FIGURE 5.4. Convent of the Good Shepherd infirmary (The Charles L. Franck Studio Collection at The Historic New Orleans Collection, accession no. 1979.325.2279)

This photograph is meant to give an inside peek at the living quarters for the white wards of the Good Shepherd. Smiling white girls line up to have their image shot. They all wear matching white dresses and have simple curled hairstyles; all look at the camera. The beds are neatly made and the room is plain, although it has drapes with flowers. In comparison to the infirmary, the scene comes across as much more intimate and warm. Although the beds and the bedframes are identical to the infirmary beds, the comforters in the dormitory are decorated with patterns and flowers. The intimacy of the photo charms the viewer into believing that this feminine, indeed girl-ish, space is where delinquent children are sent to live. The room is not presented as a space in which young women were unwillingly confined or imprisoned.

The photograph tells the viewers that the girls of the House of the Good Shepherd are happily domesticated. They sit, feminine and proper, with legs crossed and folded in their conservative and unadorned dresses. Although the girls recline across beds, the scene is not sexual. The simple mode of dress and hair inside the bare room purifies the space. These girls are not a sexual threat to the social order; they are happily plain and properly feminine. Yet this is also the only photograph in which the girls are not doing anything, are not in the act of learning, exercising or working. There is no parallel photograph of black girls sitting happily, presenting their femininity or at leisure in their beds, perhaps because a "useful" black woman would not be at leisure in this way. However, in the larger collection taken by the photographer, but not included in the ACC pamphlet, there is a photograph of black girls in "dance class"—according to the archival record. The girls seem to be learning how to perform a respectable feminine posture, with arms daintily raised and necks long and elegant (Figure 5.2).

The plain adornment and identical hairstyles are common elements throughout the Good Shepherd photographic archive. Both suggest that once inside the convent, the girls' individuality was forsaken for a communal identity. The girls' new clothing redefined who they were, replacing the old self and wardrobe. But instead of wearing white dresses, as the white wards are, the black girls appear in the photographs in dark-colored dresses. The color difference clearly marks the girls' racial difference for the viewer. The difference in dresses suggests that black wards were, at least symbolically if not actually, treated differently from the white wards. And, in a photograph showing the black wards in class, the girls sit with their hair pulled back in indistinguishable braids.

The building fund pamphlet explained that girls received the benefits of a "thorough educational program."[118] In an earlier set of promotional materials, the convent explained that "the Girls of school age attend school four hours daily. This is compulsory. Classes also are held for girls over school age who are defective or whose early education was neglected, and who may wish to avail themselves of this opportunity."[119] The photograph of black girls in class is meant to demonstrate the education they receive. Yet again, the photograph was staged. A close-up of the photograph reveals that the girls' books are open to different pages, and the student writing on the board wrote nothing at all.

"The secret of the success of the Sisters in their efforts to reform those under their care," argued a 1909 description of the House of the Good Shepherd, "is industry. From the superior to the smallest child there is no one idle; the sisters set the example and in the kitchen, laundry, sewing and class rooms are always in attendance watching over and directing every employment."[120] The photographs from the 1955 archive reinforced the notion that industry, particularly feminine industry, was the cornerstone of the Sisters' rehabilitative work. The tasks performed in the photographs seemed not to matter much in and of themselves; instead, it was working that was important. In all the photographs (except the white girls' dormitory), the girls are at work, in action, are doing something. A photograph of black girls in sewing class demonstrates the notion of industry the archive attempts to propagate (Figure 5.3). Every single girl in the frame is busy; none look up at the camera. By setting the photograph in a seeming "learning" environment (just as a similar photograph with white girls does), the archive obscures the white girls' daily work in the convent's laundry that helped to raise money and paid for upkeep of the facilities; the archive also hides the work of the black girls as domestics for the convent. The "industry," described in 1909, remained literal—girls continued to work hard as laborers for the convent at the start of the 1950s as well. Their work helped provide their food and shelter. This type of work was not for the sake of education but for the sake of diligence and penance.

Throughout this photographic archive, the convent is a place of performance. Indeed, performance for the Sisters was a thing of healing power. If we think of the work the girls did not only as education, as the Sisters attempted to present it in the 1955 pamphlet, but also as penance, as they suggested in earlier material, then the compulsive need for "industry" and "work" was a religious necessity. For penance, it did not matter what type of work the girls learned or did; the emphasis was on the doing, the performing of physical labor, not on the final product of that labor.

The complex relationship between work as penance and work as education is highlighted in a photograph titled "Convent of the Good Shepherd Kitchen." The girls appear to be practicing proper kitchen techniques for baking and setting the perfect table for a family meal. Such a session represented an educational lesson in femininity and simultaneously a lesson in the proper role for black women in a Jim Crow economy—a lesson the girls appear happy to learn, with their large smiles. However, a close-up of the photograph reveals that there is nothing inside any of the bowls, in the oven, or on the table. In fact, there is not any food or edible product (such as flour) out at all. Just like the shot of the girls in the classroom, the photograph was staged. If the girls were working merely for penance, the emphasis would not be on aesthetics, such as on the proper look of the table; instead, it would be on the labor put into cooking the meal.

In creating an intimate knowledge of life behind the convent walls, the images worked to give the citizens of New Orleans—possible donors to the convent's cause—an ideal world of the life of a ward of the Good Shepherd. The images of reformation were not violent, coercive, or even policed, beyond the presence of a benevolent (usually lay) instructor. The photos displayed no resistance from the wards. Girls were not shown as imprisoned inside or kept against their own will nor do they show parents or family members. According to the photographs, everything came easy and neat for the Sisters of the Good Shepherd.

GIRLS WHO GREW UP in New Orleans knew about the House of the Good Shepherd. Many were afraid that if they acted badly enough or were caught in inappropriate relationships, they would be sent there and become stuck behind the walls. Although the records of the House of the Good Shepherd are limited in what they reveal, they do help us reconstruct the intersection of race, stigma, and sexuality in Jim Crow New Orleans. "Sexually delinquent" girls at the convent were accused not only of having acted immorally but also of having both diseased and criminal bodies. By linking girls' sexuality to criminality, the convent and city turned "guilty" girls into stigmatized bodies that wore their sin.

Many of the girls sent to the House of the Good Shepherd were victims of sexual and domestic abuse. And many of these "bad" girls were really just girls who had faced the difficulties of growing up in poverty in New Orleans. Some of the black girls sent to the House of the Good Shepherd had simply been in search of pleasure—attempting to find some balm to protect them from the harshness of life. But they found their bodies regulated by the state or by their families because this pleasure was stigmatized and considered illicit. The next chapter explores in more detail where girls might go to find pleasure within the boundaries of respectability.

CHAPTER SIX

Make-Believe Land

Pleasure in Black Girls' Lives

Figure 6.1 is a photograph taken at Claiborne Avenue branch of the New Orleans Young Women's Christian Association on Canal Street sometime in the 1950s. If we can assign emotions to the bodily characteristics of the girls in the photo, we might say that they look not only happy but also excited and proud. As discussed in chapter 1, the YWCA's location on Claiborne and Canal Street was controversial. As young women and girls walked to the facility in an area surrounded by white homes, they faced possible physical violence or insults from local whites. The *Louisiana Weekly* recorded the violence: white boys who resented the YWCA's presence threw rocks at passing girls.[1] Despite the hostility and segregation outside the doors, the interior of the YWCA presents us with an entirely different picture; it provides a glimpse into the inner world of the girls who entered.

In 1931 the New Orleans branch of the YWCA began discussing the possibility of opening a "colored" branch for black girls in the city. Directors of YWCA programs, who placed a "special emphasis . . . on helping people have a good time during their leisure hours,"[2] were concerned that black girls had insufficient space to safely develop into young women.[3] The need for "a good time," particularly a safe and respectable good time, seemed especially important for the black teenagers of New Orleans. Fun and relaxation could not easily be found outside the doors of the YWCA or down the road in the segregated shopping and entertainment district of Canal Street. How, then, did girls find pleasure despite the confines of segregation?

The girls in the "Make-Believe Land" photograph give us clues to the function of the "colored" YWCA. The teenagers did not just pose for the camera; they also created a whole world, a new landscape. Although there is a prearranged symmetry to their positioning, they do not appear stiff, because they stand "in character." Their costumes, inspired by fairy tales, were only one piece of a larger performance. The princess in the front sits regally with her legs carefully folded so that she can present the ruffles

FIGURE 6.1. "Make-Believe Land" at the Claiborne Avenue Branch YWCA (Courtesy
of The Amistad Research Center at Tulane University, New Orleans, Louisiana)

on her dress to the camera. The cross-dressed prince in the back (with
mustache and all) stands straight up, arms down at the sides, perhaps
trying to enact a masculine stance. Fittingly, the prince is also the only
person in the photograph not displaying an open smile: is it the smirk of
power that she wears? The camera, it seems, caught the girls *in the act* of
make-believing. Such make-believing supplied pleasure. And the YWCA
provided the materials, stage, and backdrop for make-believe—it was a
land of fantasies.

"Make-Believe Land" stands apart from the other chapters of this book.
What follows is a methodological discussion that highlights a history of
pleasure in black girls' lives. Finding pleasure in traditional archives is a
difficult, sometimes seemingly impossible project; but by rethinking the
archives and historical methods, pleasure and worlds of romance appear.
This is an important project. Without making an effort to recover pleasure,
black girls' lives are narrated only by the trauma of Jim Crow. To consider
black girls as full human beings, we need to understand their pleasures just

as much as their pains—even if, for some, pleasure was fleeting.[4] Black girls' make-believe land offered a critical black respatialization, a place to develop a black pleasure culture.

A Problem of Silence, a Problem of Sources

"Black women are the beached whales of the sexual universe, unvoiced, mis-seen, not doing, awaiting their verb," declared feminist theorist Hortense Spillers. In 1984, when Spillers attempted to locate nonfictional texts about black women's sexuality (written "by themselves and for themselves"), she failed to uncover the texts she was hoping to find. Instead of a record of black women's pleasure, she found an overdetermined silence.[5]

The ideological systems that defined black women's sexuality, silencing expressions of pleasure, had two principal components.[6] First, the silence stemmed from the overarticulation of black women's sexuality by racist ide-ologies. Black women and girls were defined as promiscuous, as Other, and as always an object of someone else's pleasure.[7] If not promiscuous jezebels, then adult black women, and sometimes even working teenagers, were defined as asexual mammies by racist ideologies; the mammy figure was always at someone else's command, with no desire of her own. Second, the silence surrounding black women's sexuality was caused by a self-imposed culture of dissemblance.[8] The silence was a reaction to the racist discourses that made black women objects of others' pleasure. Dissemblance afforded black women privacy; it was a way to shield their hurt and trauma. The culture of dissemblance was an affective culture because it provided a way to order one's emotional life in public. For black women, hiding pleasurable sexuality might have been just as important as concealing traumatic sexual experiences. Sexual pleasure or sexual experimentation might cause one to lose the status of a respectable "nice" girl or woman.[9]

In "Black (W)holes and the Geometry of Black Female Sexuality," Evelynn Hammonds argues that black feminist theorists have consistently described black women's sexuality only by this very silence. She contends that black women's sexuality "has been shaped by silence, erasure, and invisibility in dominant discourses."[10] In *Crescent City Girls* I have attempted to point to places where black girls' voices and concerns are articulated. Through a reading of space in chapter 1, I made girls' bodies visible—not simply as objects of desire but as intentionally moving subjects navigating the city space of New Orleans. In chapter 4, I looked at fears articulated by girls themselves. But still, none of the previous chapters made girls' pleasure the central analytic. Indeed, girls' own pleasures have been hidden behind the regimented and disciplining features of the Jim Crow order.

The various silences that seem to constitute and consume black women's sexuality are reflected in the archive. Newspaper articles, "expert" discourses on black sexuality, court documents, reform home records, and even oral histories are filled with silence. Part of the problem of sources relates to the problem of authorship. Hortense Spillers argues that black women's sexuality was rarely depicted by the "subject herself."[11] By interrogating authorship, we ask the question, "Who can speak about sexuality and who cannot?" Spillers reflects: "The discourse of sexuality seems another way, in its present practices, that the world divides decisively between the haves/have-nots, those who may speak and those who may not, those who, by choice or accident of birth, benefit from a dominant mode and those who do not."[12] The ability to speak, to imagine, to desire freely without fear of punishment or censure marks both privilege and autonomy. The white heterosexual men who left accounts of the racialized sexuality of the segregated South (in the form of political debates about black and white women's sexuality, political campaigns that terrorized the black community with lynching, newspaper reports) speak to the authority of white men in the Jim Crow order. Often, traditional archives reconstruct the vision of those in power.[13]

My work departs from other black feminist theorists and foundational work by Spillers, Darlene Clark Hine, E. Frances White, Evelyn Brooks Higginbotham, Paula Giddings, and Elsa Barkley Brown by suggesting that silence is not the only articulation of black women's pleasurable sexuality. By bringing together the analytic strands of geography, the body, and affect, we see black women's sexuality more fully. Thus, the methods used throughout this book become the methods used to explore sexuality and pleasure in black girls' lives. We must, therefore, turn to unconventional archives and fresh ways of viewing traditional archives in order to look beyond the silences. Rethinking what constitutes archives in New Orleans is made difficult due to Hurricane Katrina's devastation of buildings, homes, material culture, and personal archives.[14] Still, a reconsideration of source material is necessary. This chapter, then, answers Evelynn Hammonds's call to invent a method that pushes past silence, to "contest rather than reproduce the ideological system that has up to now defined the terrain of black women's sexuality."[15]

In *An Archive of Feelings: Trauma, Sexuality, and Lesbian Public Cultures*, Ann Cvetkovich argues that "lesbian and gay history demands a radical archive of emotion in order to document intimacy, sexuality, love and activism—all areas of experience that are difficult to chronicle through the materials of a traditional archive."[16] Such a statement is true for other minority histories as well—and, as we have seen, particularly for black women whose intimacy, sexuality, and love have long been silenced. To construct a "radical archive of emotion," Cvetkovich uses a wide range of sources, including film, oral history, essays, and poetry; but her sources also include performances and cultural space, such as women's music festivals. Her work asks us to reconsider the meaning of space and fellowship. She turns to these sources by looking specifically at communities and their public emotions. As I have demonstrated, space in Jim Crow New Orleans was particularly important in the maintenance of the racial order. During segregation, black girls had to carefully figure out places in the city where they were allowed and welcome. But, if space was an important regulatory feature of Jim Crow New Orleans, then finding spaces of freedom (even if they were small spaces) and creating respatializations were equally important for black girls.[17] Black girls found self-satisfaction in places where they did not need to consider others' views of them, worry about their safety, or worry if they belonged.

Exploring places of fun and fellowship through the lens of Cvetkovich's work can help us address the problem of sources. *An Archive of Feelings* explores "cultural texts as repositories of feelings and emotions," suggesting that emotions do indeed exist in the public world.[18] By disrupting the dichotomy between one's inner (emotional) world and the public world, Cvetkovich insightfully argues that emotional lives saturate public lives. Therefore, she goes looking for "trauma cultures."[19] Following this method, I have decided to look specifically for "pleasure cultures" that intersected with black girls' lives. Pleasure cultures formed in and around joy. They were found in public spaces where a community of black girls could enjoy them. Black girls' pleasure cultures were imaginative "make-believe" worlds; girls delighted in sharing these worlds with their friends.

Pleasure cultures existed in black girls' worlds to varying degrees depending on class, ethnicity, and location in the city. Certainly, black girls who went to school had more time and resources to devote to public culture and leisure. And school itself functioned as a particularly important site for developing pleasure cultures. Many black women who came of age during the 1930s, 1940s, and early 1950s—particularly those who graduated from high school—looked fondly on their schoolteachers, friends, and extracurricular activities. On the other hand, black girls who worked and/or raised children had little time to and for themselves. Still, these girls earned money, which could be used to purchase clothing or to go out and party. It is a radical suggestion that pleasure cultures could (and did) exist in Jim Crow New Orleans—or in the larger segregated South that millions of African American citizens wanted to (and did) escape from.[20]

There are many different avenues for exploring pleasure cultures. In segregated New Orleans, churches provided for the development of pleasure cultures. In 1936, Dillard student Thelma Bryant interviewed seventeen-year-old Georgetta Green and nineteen-year-old Doris Daniels.[21] Daniels was the daughter of the minister of Williams Chapel Methodist Church. The teens discussed some of the pleasurable activities for youth at Williams Chapel. Girls dominated most of these youth organizations, as male participation was low. Georgetta Green emphasized the fun they had during the summer: "Oh don't we have good times in the summer time? Child, we hire a truck and go on hayrides. You just ought to be there. It's plenty of kicks!" Doris Daniels added that in the summer, girls wore white dresses on Sunday. She then told Thelma Bryant, "You ought to be here in the summer. Everything is lively then!"[22] The space of the church, of course, was regulated by adults who made sure the girls' pleasure was respectably controlled.

While some black girls found pleasure in respectable church activities, others found fun in more forbidden pleasures. Eighteen-year-old Beverly Carter described a group of young women that partied at clubs like the Tick Tock Tavern on South Rampart Street. After a night of partying, the girls would pool their money and stay together in a rooming house rather than go home and listen to their parents or guardians complain about their lateness and behavior. Beverly and her friends found pleasure in spaces away from home. Using money they earned from work (Beverly Carter worked as a domestic in a "poor" white home), they continued their fun at the rooming house: "We play cards or anything—have cocktails—without being battered." "At my house we couldn't drink cocktails," explained Carter. The girls also engaged in girl talk, discussing "how bad we did some man or something like that. We have lots of fun telling each other how we carried somebody out."[23] Carter's behavior hurt her reputation among her family, but she found freedom in some of the unrespectable pleasure spaces of Jim Crow.

In grappling with pleasure cultures in black girls' lives, I have chosen to focus this chapter on elements of fantasy and make-believe—the same make-believe that seemed to delight the girls of the YWCA. These make-believe lands represent black girls' imaginings of pleasure and romance that allow for a radical redefinition of black girlhood/womanhood. The first pleasure culture I focus on is that of a widely popular writing culture among black teenage girls.

Fantasy, Romance, and Black Girls' Writing Culture

In the 1930s and 1940s, black schoolgirls spent time writing and reading. This writing culture emphasized pleasure and fantasy. Romance stories read by girls during their free time and poetry by black writers (such as Paul Laurence Dunbar) that girls recited in school all functioned to create a literary counterpublic.[24] By sharing and discussing these narratives with one another and even by writing their own stories, black girls constructed and imagined romantic subjectivities in opposition to their daily encounters with Jim Crow and to restrictive notions of black womanhood. These writings also disrupted the silence on black female pleasure. Although black girls' writings share some common features with black women's writings, youths' works diverge from themes of coupling in adults' works because girls' views of romance were built from make-believe and the hope of youth rather than on the disappointments and difficulties that often come with adult relationships.[25] The writing culture that emphasized romance, love, and sexual pleasure extended to autograph books, where girls wrote down witty sayings and poems (some original, others reproduced) and participated in a public culture of romance.

The romance/pulp fiction magazine *True Confessions* circulated as one of the most important pleasure texts in black (and white) girls' leisure worlds of the 1930s and 1940s. *True Confessions* was first published in 1922 in order to compete with the most popular pulp magazine, *True Stories*. By the 1930s, *True Confessions* was the second-most popular of the "confession"-styled magazines, selling over a million copies each month. Ostensibly, these magazines printed "true" stories written by "real" readers. The contests to submit writing into the magazines invited black girls to think about the construction of romantic stories, lives, and literature—even if they never sent in a story of their own.[26]

Marie Boyer Brown, a graduate from McDonogh #35 High School in the early 1930s, explained the importance of *True Confessions* in an oral history. Her tone, voice, and narrative interruptions during the interview help unveil multiple layers of meaning associated with *True Confessions* for black girls growing up during Jim Crow.[27] Brown first introduced the pulp magazine when trying to describe the contours of "girl talk" between her and her best friend Ida. The circular conversation that ensued illustrates how sexuality, intimate friendships, and girls' reading and writing cultures intermingled to create a pleasure culture. "Oh, we would talk about everything," she explained. "I used to read *True Stories* [and] *True Confessions*. My mama didn't like me to read that."[28]

As if further clarifying what girl talk was and was not, and in relation to what *True Confessions* represented and did not represent, Brown introduced a new thread to the story: "I didn't like nude pictures. Those girls would sometimes get hold of these pictures; I think the boys had them. But I never did like to look at nothing like that."[29] As Marie Boyer Brown attempted to explain "girl talk," she moved back and forth between the fun things girls talked about—including *True Confessions*—and romantic, erotic, and sexual relationships between boys and girls. In one sense, *True Confessions* functioned for Brown as a metaphor for the types of things best girlfriends might discuss. "Girl talk" included intimate discussions about sexuality, romance, and love. That Marie Boyer Brown associated *True Confessions* (and girl talk) with "nude pictures" (which she did not look at) speaks directly to the link between such magazines and the sexual content of the stories. Although the stories of premarital pregnancy, romance, mistaken identities, and dangerous relationships might seem passé to a modern reader, the magazine's stories were much more risqué by the standards of readers in the first half of the twentieth century.

To further clarify *True Confessions* to her interviewers, Brown compared the stories in them to soap operas: "And I was thinking, too, about how foolish they were. That story [that I had on the TV] when you came [to interview me] and I turned it off? . . . I look at that too. Some of those girls make the wrong decision. . . . [*True Confessions*] was like that. And I used to buy them. Mama would fuss. They were fifteen cents. And I would buy them; Papa would give me money."[30] In Brown's rendition of *True Confessions*, the stories were just as silly and over-the-top as modern-day soap operas. But just as she liked *True Confessions* back then, Brown enjoys her soap operas today. From a twenty-first-century perspective, perhaps, she realizes that "some of those girls make the wrong decision," all in the service of an entertaining story line.[31]

Yet, while *True Confessions* was an entertaining read, the magazine also performed important cultural work. The "wrong decisions" made by the main characters were not so clear to the teenage girls who anxiously read the stories for information on love and sex. Brown said that the magazine helped her learn about relationships between boys and girls and provided information on sex and love that her mother did not give her. To explain why she enjoyed *True Confessions*, for example, Brown responded, "Well, my mama didn't talk with me. See, that's another thing. No, my mama wouldn't talk with me. She didn't want to talk about things like that. I had other ladies that used to talk with me."[32] According to Brown, her mother "didn't want to talk about things like that" and, at the same time, did not appreciate her reading the lurid stories found in *True Confessions*. But for only fifteen cents, Marie Boyer Brown found a whole world of information on romance, love, and sexuality—information she later shared and discussed with her friend Ida.

Indeed, *True Confessions* served that same role in many black girls' lives. Nearly every girl—even those in the striving class—heard of or saw an issue of the magazine. In 1938 Beverly Carter brought the most recent issue of *True Confessions* to her interview with Thelma Shelby, a Dillard University researcher for the Allison Davis and John Dollard personality development project on youth in New Orleans. When Shelby asked Carter about *True Confessions* and *True Stories*, Carter replied, "So many [magazines] just lay around the house over there where I'm working, that once in a while I just decide to read some of them. I like to be reading something all the time, especially if I'm on the street car."[33] In an ethnographic and sociological study of black beauticians and their customers, a 1950 sociology student noted the most popular reading materials in the black beauty shops she visited for her study. The most popular of all was *True Confessions* and *Love Story* followed by *Ebony*.[34] And Marian Wright Edelman, a daughter of a South Carolina Baptist minister, remembered that when she was about thirteen (in 1952), she tried to "trick" her father "by slipping a forbidden *True Confessions* magazine into the *Life* magazine [she] pretended to read." When her father found out what she was actually looking at, he "asked [her] to read it aloud and comment on its value!"[35] By confessing this true story, Edelman wished to teach children a life lesson on the value of reading proper materials. Significantly, her memory also points to the ubiquity of *True Confessions*. Even in Edelman's religious household, she managed to sneak in a copy of the magazine and found it compelling enough to try to read where she might very likely get caught.

Not only did girls read these passionate love stories, but they also participated in a writing culture that emphasized romance. Marie Boyer Brown, who nourished a love of writing just as she loved reading, saved some of her love poems (written in the 1930s) in a scrapbook.[36] In one of these poems she declared:

Why I love and love to be in return
To have love, to hold
and keep and to yearn.

Love and romance seemed central in many teen girls' writings. Marie Boyer Brown did not date many boys as a teenager; nonetheless, she wrote love stories that emphasized the fantasy of love rather than its reality. In one poem she spoke directly to the boy "of my dreams":

My heart speaks out to one alone
It will not be cast aside
Like a rolling stone.
Though ages will pass with the coming years
My heart should never
Cause my eyes to dimmer with tears.
Why waste love on lovesick fools
When love itself has many tools.
To the serious boy my heart sends love beams
The one and only one of my dreams.
Caution, oh heart, to the romantic call
Of thee strings that are tugging at thy wall.
Open your heart let love in
Begging and pleading again and again
Oh heart will thou let love plead in vain?
Answer, oh answer, without causing thee pain.[37]

For Marie Boyer Brown, pleasure was not just found in imagining a "serious boy" with whom she could share her heart; it was also found in the construction of the poem itself: she loved to write. Therefore, writing and sharing the love poem was pleasure in and of itself. Decades later, when discussing her writing, Brown boasted, "I used to come up with them fast!"[38] Black feminist Audre Lorde describes this type of pleasure as the power of "the erotic." For Lorde, the erotic is expressed in the delight of sharing passions with others and in the fearless "capacity for joy" in one's life despite, or rather in the face of, oppression.[39] The erotic contains significant power, challenging that which causes "resignation, despair, self-effacement, depression, self-denial." Lorde envisions this type of erotic power in all women's lives, regardless of their sexual orientation. To explain the erotic in everyday life, Lorde writes, "There is, for me, no difference between writing a good poem and moving into sunlight against the body of a woman I love."[40] Audre Lorde's linking of different types of pleasure (sexual pleasure with the pleasure of writing) allows us to think about the ways in which pleasure may have been expressed in black girls' lives. Just as Lorde explains the self-affirming and erotic act of "writing a good poem," Marie Boyer Brown's oral history emphasizes the pleasure she found, and continued to find, in her writing. Saving poems from the 1930s in a scrapbook and looking back on these poems while in her nineties illustrated just how important this writing was to Brown's sense of self.

Writings saved from the 1930s reveal the centrality of the romantic ideal to black teenage girls' notions of pleasure. The Normal School of Valena C. Jones in New Orleans published its own magazine full of student writings.[41] One 1938 short story in the collection echoed the tone of a "confessions" piece while also demonstrating what the "ideal" romance might look like. "When Fate Takes a Turn," by Inez Jolivette, tells the story of a young man, Rhoderic, and a young lady, Joycelyn, who feel a romantic spark the instant they meet at a high school senior prom. The idealization of love expressed by the short story is distinct from the experience of love. As Eleanor Alexander explores in her study of Paul Laurence Dunbar and Alice Dunbar, "Paul fell in love with his idealized mate, not Alice; for to fall in love at first sight—as did Paul with a photograph of Alice—is to love a concept of perfection."[42] "When Fate Takes a Turn" is structured around the idea of romantic love as a concept of perfection.

The short story clearly describes an ideal young man—perhaps the fantasy that Inez Jolivette had cultivated over months of imagining what the perfect boyfriend would be like. Rhoderic is manly but polite, strong yet respectable. Jolivette describes Rhoderic's high school years in terms of his athleticism and determination: "Rhoderic loved football and all his spare time was spent in practicing with the 'fellers.' . . . [His mother] would become angry when he would rush home from school, eat his dinner, and then be off again to come back begrimed with dirt. She tried scolding him many times, but would stop when he would tell her that a 'feller' had to practice if he wanted to amount to anything on the football team. A few months later, however, he was made captain of the high school football team."[43] He is clearly a leader at his high school and therefore sure to be a success in life despite the constraints of Jim Crow (which never fully enters the narrative). Rhoderic, above all else, is intelligent. He goes north to an integrated school—U Pitt—and after a possibly derailing encounter with a wild roommate becomes a successful doctor who performs the types of surgeries no one in the medical community thought possible. This was, possibly, the type of man Inez Jolivette wished to meet herself. She had chosen to become a schoolteacher and may have wanted to date an educated man who had made a career and name for himself.

As for the portrait of an ideal lady, Inez depicts Joycelyn as modest and willing to be Rhoderic's helpmate but with goals of her own. "When Fate Takes a Turn" introduces Joycelyn to the reader in comparison with another girl—the one Rhoderic had chosen as his prom date: "Rhoderic felt towards Joycelyn as he had never felt before towards any girl. Moreover, between her and Lorraine there was quite a contrast. Lorraine was selfish, flirtatious, haughty and spoiled; while Joycelyn was well-bred, ambitious, demure and above all had a pleasing personality. . . . [W]hen the dance was over they seemed to have known each other for a long time."[44] Right away, the scene is set with competition between two young women for Rhoderic's attention. Joycelyn wins this competition by being the "nice girl" who is ladylike. Yet part of this "nice" description includes a surprise: ambition. When writing the character of Joycelyn, Inez Jolivette created a young woman whom she, too, could become. On a path to her own respectable career, Jolivette created a character who was not simply a respectable woman but also an intellectual with concrete goals for her future. The intimacy and romance in the story is clear from this early scene featuring Joycelyn's ladylike behavior. On the space of the dance floor, the characters touch and look at each other in the eyes, feeling as though they had "known each other for a long time."

Jolivette's story is full of the failures and half-starts of any confession story. The two lovebirds part ways almost as soon as they meet and only accidentally become reacquainted years later when Joycelyn applies for a job as a nurse in Rhoderic's medical practice. After working together as nurse and doctor, they "grew more and more fond of each other, and likewise grew to become lovers. They made a perfect pair, for it seemed as if they were made to be together having so much in common."[45] Inez Jolivette's work expresses what it meant to have the intimacy of lovers. The main characters work together as intellectual partners, grow together, and finally become emotional and physical partners.

Black and white adolescent girls of the generation in this study lived in a world where romance was deemed particularly important.[46] The emphasis on romance was true for a wide range of young women—including working-class girls. As Kathy Peiss has discovered for working women in New York during the early twentieth century, "the work culture of women encouraged an ideology of romance that resonated with explicit heterosexual pleasures and perils at the same time that it affirmed the value of leisure."[47] Romance for many black and working-class girls like Inez Jolivette was often idealized rather than realized—the romanticized idea of the "perfect" mate, influenced by popular culture, held tremendous sway, even though men like Rhoderic rarely existed. Yet the very notion of romance was a pleasurable fantasy for many adolescent girls and young women.

In her poetry, Lois Williams, a Dillard University student, implored her fellow students to experience sexual pleasure for themselves. Williams wrote:

Sweet is a kiss,
   That you should not miss!
Once you get the feeling,
Sweet is a kiss.
It may leave you reeling,
   In a heavenly bliss;
Sweet is a kiss;
   That you *should not* miss![48]

But black girls' love poems and intimacy narratives also often featured heartbreak poems. These poems displayed the flip side of romantic love: rejection, breaking up, or, commonly, moving away. Heartbreak poems are one way to assess the pleasure culture of black girls' writing because although they focus on the distress of losing love, they nonetheless delight in the intimate relationship the couple once had. Some of these poems, just like the love poems, were likely based on fantasy rather than on experience with the dramatic breakups or rejections the writings depict. Yet black girls in the South often did deal with losing loved ones to migration—best friends, family members, and lovers moved north and west, leaving behind intimacies and memories.

Lillian Voorhees, a teacher from Talladega College, a historically black college located in Alabama, collected the writings of her students. Many of these poems and short stories displayed extreme skill and nuance. A large number of them represented a genre of romantic writing similar to what I found in New Orleans. As such, this larger collection enables a more inclusive examination of the pleasure culture of writing in black girls' lives. One 1930s heartbreak poem from this collection depicts the longing for intimacy expressed in girls' writing. Helen Hagin unveils a lost love to her reader in the poem "Explanation":

I asked her for a kiss
Her lips were sealed,
Her touch was cold,
She saw me not, nor heard my plea.
No, friend, she was not dead—
She was in love,—
But not with me.[49]

As the tale begins, Helen expertly allows her reader to guess at her meaning by writing as if the narrator's lover has died. But soon the reader finds that the narrator has simply been rejected and ignored. "Explanation" is intriguing precisely because of its mystery—it is open to multiple interpretations. The gender of the narrator is never clear, but the object of the narrator's love is a "her." It is possible that the two characters in the poem are both girls, maybe even best friends. The kiss and intimacy between one of them is romantic, while the other feels only a friendship because she is in romantic love with someone else. The suggestion is that the "her" is now emotionally dead, although presumably she was alive at one time—always at her friend's side. If this is the case, then the title of the poem becomes at once an allusion toward the ending of the poem and an "explanation" for the soured relationship between the two girls. Alternately, maybe Helen decided to write from a male perspective, imagining a female character being chased by multiple lovers.

Whichever was the case, the intimacy and longing in this poem is tangible. The narrative's complexity is built through an "erotic imagination" of what the relationship could have been.[50] Helen Hagin works with intimacy by figuring the romantic yearning through a tactile description, using words that emphasize physical contact such as "touch," "kiss," and "sealed." Although the narrator is rebuffed, physical intimacy never seems far away. And the narrator does indeed feel her loved one, only to find that she is "cold." Because Helen Hagin addresses her reader directly as "friend," the longing for intimacy feels near and is almost transferred to the reader herself (or himself). The heartbreak described is indeed chilling. Helen Hagin's work speaks directly to the erotic in girls' writing culture. Even though the love expressed is not reciprocal, her poetry reveals the ways in which black youth wrote and fantasized about pleasure.

Another heartbreak poem in the collection portrays the type of sadness caused by migration and movement. Beulah Jones writes about missing a lover in the poem "Absence":

I thought if long miles were between the towns where you and I
Performed our tasks and kept our dreams,
    Perhaps as days went by,
I would forget the little things
That made you dear—too dear,
And I should find happiness
Again, if you weren't near.

But I have come to love you more
Of that I am sure.
They are so wrong who would have me think
    Absence is a cure.[51]

"Absence" displays how youths' writing often simultaneously emphasized both the pleasure and pain of losing one's lover. The term "too dear" is the most intimate phrase of the poem. It may allude to a relationship that had overstepped the boundaries of niceness and subtly expresses the physical pleasures that made her lover so special. The pleasure and intimacy in this poem is conveyed in "little things" that go unnamed.

Dillard University undergraduate Countess W. Twitty wrote a heartbreak poem as a student of Professor Oakley Johnson, a white radical activist and English teacher in New Orleans. Johnson's students often submitted their work to *"America Sings": Anthology of College Poetry*. Twitty's heartbreak poem "Loneliness" appeared in 1947. The intimacy in the poem begins with an intense need:

I wanted you today.
In the rain I stood alone
And looked at the grey clouds,
Felt the raindrops on my face
And hardly knew whether they were raindrops
Or tears.
Where were you? Gone home?
I know I did not tell you,
But I needed you so terribly
I wonder that you did not
Sense my need
Or hear me call your name.[52]

"Loneliness" could have been written for a loved one passed away or moved home at the end of the semester, just as it could have been written after a breakup. The narrator is alone throughout the poem while the lover's absence haunts. The narrator's "need" drives the poem and is a longing for the company of her loved one, a physical closeness. The need can also be read as a sexual desire, as the narrator says, "I wonder that you did not / Sense my need." The poem is both solemn and heated. Romantic love and passion are expressed just as the subject of desire has "gone home."

Romantic love and fantasy are echoed in a wide variety of black girls' writing. These writings together constitute a pleasure culture. Part of the pleasure in this writing culture was the joy of writing itself, but the joy also came from the creation of a black counterpublic. Countess Twitty spoke of her work in this way, explaining that the collection of poems that Dillard students self-published were "the outcomes of many sessions of work, criticism, revision and good fellowship."[53] In this setting, girls wrote for fun, for friends, and to express the love (and fantasies) in their life.

Not only did black girls write such poems, so too did boys write to them. Although much less numerous in the archive, boys' romantic writing often took the same form as girls'. Not surprisingly, perhaps, much of boys' romantic writings were written directly to a specific (real rather than imagined) girl. In an autograph book once owned by Onelia Sayas Cherrie (a classmate of Marie Boyer Brown's at McDonogh #35 in New Orleans), numerous little poems and sayings hint at the pleasures of imagined romance, love, or intimacy. These "autographs" reveal the ways in which writing became a pleasure culture.[54] First, the signer had to think of something clever or cute to say, and then others delighted in what he or she had written as the autograph book was passed from classmate to classmate. One young boy wrote to Onelia Sayas:

I had a heart which
Once was mine
And now it's gone from me to you
So treat it well, as I have done,
For I have none and
You have two
(The author)
—Wilbur[55]

Sharing, discussing, writing, and circulating love stories were sources of pleasure in black schoolgirls' lives. This writing culture was one of a particular class: school was a space in which black girls had the opportunity and time to write and share with friends.[56] Additionally, schoolgirls were aware of and learned about important black writers and intellectuals. Black girls created a discursive culture around romance and pleasure. Their entrance into this writing culture was influenced by popular culture, such as their reading of *True Confessions*, as well as by their teachers' insistence that they, too, could be writers like Paul Laurence Dunbar, James Weldon Johnson, or Langston Hughes.

Make-Believe at the "Colored" YWCA

I want to return to the photograph (Figure 6.1) taken at the YWCA's "Make-Believe Land" in order to suggest that make-believe and fantasy are productive ways to envision black girls' performances of pleasure. The YWCA revealed a world where black girls performed their ideas of pleasure and fantasy—often on a dance floor. The "Make-Believe Land" photograph is a compelling symbol because of its location on Canal Street in the midst of segregation. At the same time, Make-Believe Land appears to be a place of pure pleasure and fantasy. When I stare at the photograph, analyzing it, looking for the "little things," I find myself smiling at the faces who stare back at me.

The Claiborne Branch YWCA on Canal Street functioned as a central gathering place for black girls and young women in New Orleans—particularly Protestant girls. Ellen Hill, who was so concerned with niceness (see chapter 4), was one of many girls who enjoyed the world created by the YWCA.[57] In 1938 she joined the Girl Reserves Club that met at the Y. The interviewer who talked with teenage Ellen Hill reported that she "seemed very happy" to be part of the club and spoke excitedly of the club's plan for fixing up a special room where they would hold a Halloween party.[58] The YWCA functioned as a cultural space where girls like Ellen Hill were free to construct their own make-believe lands. By joining the YWCA, Ellen found herself connected to a group of black girls and young women who worked together to build and maintain the shared spaces of the YWCA. The official purpose of all YWCAs was to "build a fellowship of women and girls devoted to the task of realizing in our common life those ideals of personal and social living to which we are committed by our faith as Christians."[59] Yet the notions of "social living" and "fellowship" were extremely important in the southern, segregated "colored" branches of the organization. As historians of African American life have observed, black institutions such as the YWCA provided a space for political discussion and a rich civic life for African Americans, despite the confines of segregation.[60] Yet the YWCA provided much more than just a space for political discourse—it also offered a space for pleasure and leisure. This pleasure geography provided girls the room necessary to construct alternate subjectivities around enjoyment, intimacy, and fantasy.

Girls' experiences inside the Claiborne Branch of the YWCA and at the Girl Reserves Club are difficult to trace. The space of the YWCA, though public, was also insular. It included only African American citizens of New Orleans, and unless there were special parties or club meetings, the YWCA included only girls and women. The images produced at the YWCA and the dances, games, clubs, and news stories about the Y reported in the *Louisiana Weekly* made imagined worlds real for just a moment.

Understanding the pleasure culture of the Colored YWCA is much easier when we work with juxtaposition. Fully appreciating the happiness a girl like Ellen felt when entering the world of the YWCA makes more sense after sketching out the realities of Jim Crow New Orleans. Much of the public space and culture of New Orleans was organized around a geography that reinforced and recreated dominant ideologies of race, gender, and sexuality.[61] When girls opened social studies textbooks, those books told the story of "The White Man's Burden." The images inside local newspapers and at the movies privileged whiteness, offering raced definitions of beauty. And as black girls walked down the street, they saw the racist memorabilia (of mammies, for example) displayed in the windows of New Orleans' tourist shops.[62] But the worlds created by the YWCA, and in similar spaces inside of the black community, created a different, often positive and hopeful, conversation. This space was organized around pleasure rather than trauma.

The building became a space for dancing and for parties sponsored and organized by the various clubs. There was pleasure (as Ellen Hill expressed) in the planning process of the parties: making the costumes, hanging the decorations, inviting girlfriends and boyfriends. Group work—coming together and creating together—provided the bases for the YWCA's approach to working with girls and young women. The YWCA's leaders believed that by working together in clubs or planning social events, young women learned that "social adjustment and growth of the individual are all closely related."[63] Further, at the parties, girls learned the value of "good taste" and "general refinement."[64] When the girls chose whom to invite to their parties, they were drawing ties of intimacy to boys and girls their age while marking difference between those invited and those left out. For the girls involved, the YWCA created a sense of belonging.

Les Jeunes Filles Club (The Young Ladies Club) participated in and helped create the make-believe world of the YWCA. In the archive at the Amistad Research Center (an archive devoted to black history), a series of photographs is dedicated to the activities of Les Jeunes Filles. Some of these are photographs of girls in various outfits and costumes. Alongside these posed costumed photographs are pictures of the young women at the YWCA being taught to sew. It is possible, therefore, that the outfits they displayed in the posed photographs were made by the club members themselves.

FIGURE 6.2. King and queen at the Claiborne Avenue Branch YWCA (Courtesy of
The Amistad Research Center at Tulane University, New Orleans, Louisiana)

The shards of evidence left behind by Les Filles Jeunes Club show traces of
a fantasy world. The outfits they wore (and possibly made) were role-playing
costumes. Members of Les Filles Jeunes Club turned themselves into genies
and cowboys. What made the clothes fantastical was the fact that they were,
in a sense, useless. Because the clothing was most often made for themed
parties with a focus on make-believe, the costumes had little use outside of
this fantasy world.[65] The girls' goal was not to learn how to sew or to mend
their own clothing (although they most likely acquired the skills to do so),
nor were they making work or school clothes. These were not clothes for
the "real world" outside the doors of the YWCA. They were purely pleasure
clothes—with no other purpose. In this, the YWCA created a place of pleasure where girls escaped their daily world and instead "made believe."

Figure 6.2, a photograph taken in 1959, characterizes a later period of the
YWCA. The fantasy in the picture is clear—a couple has been named queen
and king and will rule the night (likely during Carnival time). Depicted in
the photograph is the full-blown world of make-believe culture inside the
YWCA. The fantasy world was created by decorations: large, painted masks;
oversized fans; and ribbons flank the walls while perfectly spaced plants
border the dance floor. The image created is striking for its symmetry. The

couples who surround the king and queen are almost symmetrical (except for the fact that the boy-girl pattern is inverted on one side). The heterosexual couples on the sides descend in height; the ballerinas, en pointe, strike their pose in tandem.

Every single detail in the photograph is perfect—but in considering this coincidence of perfection, it is clear that the scene is posed. Inexplicably, nobody in the photo is looking at the photographer; not one boy or girl's gaze is misplaced. It is clear, then, that this is a make-believe world with every detail worked to perfect precision by the girls involved. The girls who created the party worked incredibly hard to create a "make-believe" world that would appear completely real in the photo. Did the girls hope that the photograph would be published in the society section of the *Louisiana Weekly*? The pleasure of the dance was meant to be seen, shared, and admired.

The dance (depicted by the posed precision of the photograph—which is not a substitute for the real dance) was saturated with safe, heterosexual coupling. Everyone—at least on the dance floor—is coupled boy-girl. The pleasure environment of the YWCA was molded specifically for respectable leisure. According to the New Orleans branch, the space was for "Negro girls and women . . . a community investment in healthy, happy, efficient womanhood."[66] This photograph reflects the YWCA's commitment to "the *right kind* of social relaxation," the type of relaxation that would teach girls to be pretty partners to the men in their lives.[67]

Also notable about this particular photograph, the dance, and more precisely the image created is its mode of Cold War intimacy.[68] A scene of this type could have been played out anywhere in America. The photograph endorsed Cold War consumption and was built on excess and extravagance; this image, decidedly middle class, was clearly not part of the 1930s YWCA. And lining the rafters are servicemen (in fact, here, there are more servicemen than girls, as if the scene was created not only for the photographer but also for the young men watching from above). In the photograph, pleasure is represented in coupling, in hand holding. There is also a pleasure in lavishness of the scene. The girls wear beautiful dresses—some even strapless. But what makes this scene particular rather than ubiquitous was the world that existed outside the walls of the YWCA. Just down the street from the dance, at the shopping/entertainment district of Canal Street, was a world of segregation. On Canal Street stood Loew's movie theater; Loew's extremely long series of steps leading to the colored entrance served as a physical reminder of Jim Crow. With each step, youth knew they were entering the colored-only section. This, along with the unfriendly world of Canal Street department stores, reminded black youth of their second-class citizenship.

The make-believe world offered by the YWCA images shows an alternate world to the segregated streets outside; it was a critical respatialization where black girls could resist the geography of Jim Crow. The performance culture that emphasized dancing, costumes, and sets created a make-believe land where fantasies could be realized. That this detailed, incredible world was made from construction paper, cloth, and the perfect photograph shows the care and time the club girls put into their lives at the YWCA. The creation of such a world was part of the pleasure itself. At the same time, girls sought to have a good time at dances where they could take part in the act of make-believing.

Performance, Respatialization, and Make-Believe at Mardi Gras

As is clear from the history of the YWCA, dancing, balls, dressing up, and parading were central aspects of the pleasures of make-believe. Nothing represents the performance of make-believe in black girls' lives better than the public pleasure cultures of the New Orleans Mardi Gras and Carnival season. The pleasure cultures of Mardi Gras were represented in fleeting moments of performance: in dancing, masking, attending parades, and catching/throwing. These pleasure cultures are not easily found in an archive, which privileges texts; meanwhile, scholars of performance studies have argued that instead of looking at the text, our method of analysis should turn to the repertoire. The repertoire is a counter-archive containing "traditions stored in the body" that decenter texts and challenge what historians might think of as evidence.[69] So, pleasure cultures can be traced through the repertoire, through "embodied memory: performances, gestures, orality, movement, dance, singing."[70]

In the 1930s and 1940s, many of the Mardi Gras balls and floats were arranged by various all-white krewes; this was the public Mardi Gras centered on a particular kind of whiteness. Margaret LeCorgne came from a wealthy white uptown family. Her parents were invited to balls, and as a girl she dreamed of attending. She remembered the Mardi Gras krewes, "only Momus, Comus and Proteus in those days."[71] Black New Orleanians might work *for* these krewes and at their balls and dinners but could never dream of participating in their festivities except as viewers at the parade. One black visitor to New Orleans remembered seeing the Proteus Krewe at the parade in the 1930s. "I saw Proteus parade and it was beautiful," she said. "I don't see how they could afford to spend so much money and hundreds of thousands of people are starving."[72] Jewish New Orleanians and working-class and poorer whites also did not have access to these worlds. One white New Orleanian recalled that as a young girl, "I was not aware of the balls and supper dances, of the social whirl that centers about the kings and queens, the maids and courts of Carnival."[73] Eva Augustin Rumpf, who grew up in uptown New Orleans, remembered that "the balls were run by these private organizations called krewes . . . and you had to have money to be a part of a Carnival krewe. Or, you had to know someone who was a member in order to get an invitation to a ball, so we never participated in the balls."[74] Thus, these official krewes and their balls marked the white social elite of New Orleans.

Travel writer Eleanor Early, a white woman from New England who had traveled the world, wrote about Mardi Gras and Carnival season in *New Orleans Holiday*, published in 1947. She described the pleasure culture of Mardi Gras as one of romance, elegance, and exclusivity:

> Mardi Gras in New Orleans is mad and wonderful and the greatest free show on earth, and it is strange that visitors know so little about it. People expecting to attend Carnival balls often arrive in town with beautiful costumes, especially people from Hollywood, and when they learn that tickets cannot be bought for love or money some of them get angry. Visitors may watch Carnival parades, wear dominoes, and dance in the streets. But they have about as much chance of going to one of the exclusive balls as the camel had of going through the eye of a needle.[75]

Eleanor Early captured the spectacle of the public pleasure culture of Mardi Gras, of masking and of "dancing in the street," open and "free" to all New Orleanians. But she also emphasized the elite and exclusive culture of the white krewes. Not even Hollywood stars could enjoy the pleasure of Carnival balls without a ticket or an invitation.

But Mardi Gras incorporated much more than just these white krewes; black New Orleanians created a Mardi Gras world all its own. The *Louisiana Weekly* noted this black counterpublic by welcoming black visitors to Mardi Gras on a special advertising page announcing, "This Year Greater Than Ever Before. Notice Our Beautification, Our Many Newly Paved Streets. All for Your Joy and Comfort. Visit These Places and Get Acquainted. Read the Zulu King's Schedule on This Page, Then Wait on the Best Corner to See Him. He is One of Our Carnival's Greatest Attractions."[76] The paper emphasized "our Carnival" and "our" city streets, claiming the urban land-scape for black New Orleanians and their visitors. The advertisers touted the city's 1929 beautification project, taking pride in the city's remaking. Black businesses advertised lunch specials and informed visitors where they would be welcomed, important for black travelers coming to a segregated city. And, of course, they advertised the Zulu King's schedule. The Zulu Social Aid and Pleasure Club represents one of the most famous aspects of black Mardi Gras, but there were also the Black Indians, Skull and Bones Gangs, and the Million Dollar Baby Dolls.[77] The black Mardi Gras counterpublic came into being not through texts but through these performances and parades.

Eleanor Early cleverly noted the ways in which black New Orleanians cre-ated a Mardi Gras counterpublic, playing with raced and gendered expecta-tions. Her description of black Mardi Gras is breathtaking for its complexity. She read the Zulu performance as invested with racial meaning, upending the racial-sexual domination of space. But central to her reading of the black Mardi Gras counterpublic was black women as "real" and "true" queens:

> Zulu's extravaganza is a witty travesty of the white folks' Mardi Gras. In his rattrap float, trailing clouds of tarnished glory, he mocks the white parades and in his mangy robe, he mocks their Kings. His hilarious floats burlesque all the gaudy show of the white Krewes, his horned men imitate their Dukes, and the Big Shot of Africa carica-tures their Captains.
>
> But there are two things in Zulu's Mardi Gras that are real. And one is his band, and one is his Queen. The band plays Dixie-land rhythm. And the Queen wears a true satin gown and a rhinestone crown. The gown has a beautiful sweeping train. The crown is as bright as the morning. And the Queen has a party in the undertaking parlor with champagne and sandwiches, and that is real too.[78]

Early enacts a diasporic reading of the Zulu King's performance that does not take his representation of "Africanness" as authentic. Instead, she recog-nizes a repertoire of parody that critiques white racism. Her writing is sub-tle; one gets the sense that wealthy white New Orleanians might have missed her critique, just as they had missed the Zulu King's critique. Eleanor Early's analysis of black Mardi Gras probably comes from her travels in Africa and the Caribbean. In *New Orleans Holiday* she makes reference to these other trips as a way to enhance her authority as an observer of race relations and to challenge the "knowledge" of southern whites who understood "their" blacks.[79]

Even as Early marks the Zulu King as a cunning performer, she notes that the black queen is "real." At stake in this reading was the respectability of black femininity. For Early, the black queen was not a parody; rather, her costume was terribly serious, her beauty authentic. Early seemed to recognize that in this moment of parading, masking, and playing, black women deserved respect, just as did black music, a true art form. Thus, for Early, the imaginative act of the black queen at the ball was not ironic nor mimetic. Early's interpretation of the black queen is notable; the queen's performance was one enacted by black teenagers throughout the city, as, too, was the scenario of the royal ball.

Scenarios are "portable framework[s]" that "bear the weight of accumulative repeats. The scenario makes visible, yet again, what is already there: the ghosts, the images, the stereotypes."[80] Noting the scenario of the royal ball during Carnival season makes visible the "construction of bodies in particular contexts."[81] The royal ball worked to reconstruct the black female body as royal, regal, and on display but *not* for sale. This bodily reconstruction was visible to Eleanor Early in her retelling of the Zulu parade. The queen's performance was a devastating reworking, haunted by the "ghosts" of enslavement and the "images" of Jim Crow subordination. At the same time, the scenario of the royal ball helped to hide the subordination of Jim Crow, directing the viewer to the regality of the queen. This framing was especially important for black girls performing pleasure in Jim Crow New Orleans. Through the familiar scenarios of balls, particularly of royal balls, black New Orleanians unsettled any referent to a servile black body. Instead, the Carnival ball invited dancing and coupling and evoked imagery of weddings with kings and queens and courts.

In 1939 the *Louisiana Weekly* published a picture from one of these Carnival balls, announcing "Beautiful Pageant Staged by Wicker [Junior] High."[82] The use of the word "staged" indicates the scenario of the royal ball: this was an embodied performance as elaborate as a theatrical play. The king, queen, and court line up for the photo; younger girls are dressed up like court jesters. The ornate scenario enacts royalty through the use of the stage, draped fabric, ball gowns, and tuxedoes. The elaborate dress was a key piece of the performance; dressing as royalty allowed for an imaginative embodiment of prominence. The students' gestures and posture are majestic—signifying magic and class privilege and erasing blackness as abjection. When black girls enacted such scenarios, their bodies appeared in a new context. The "new context" of embodied pleasure was particularly evident in one girl's posture in the pageant staged by Wicker Junior High School. The girl, Selina

Gray, is wearing a ball gown that flows just past her feet; the gown has puffy sleeves that reach down to her elbows. She holds a grandiose bouquet of flowers, so large that they cover nearly half of her body. Yet she holds the bouquet just so, so that the photographer may capture her full face. She is performing within the repertoire of the royal ball, her gestures and posture informed by monarchs. She is standing perfectly erect—her head held high; her chin slightly elevated, matching her gaze; her shoulders pushed back. Her stance emphasizes an elegant and long neck. The posture is purposeful. Here, Selina Gray uses the physical body to claim a space and a self worthy of pleasure.

The Girl Reserves Club and Hi-Y—a High School YMCA club— produced and sponsored the Wicker Junior High Carnival ball, highlighting the importance of girls' and boys' clubs and the YWCA as critical counterpublics that made space for pleasure cultures. Elementary, junior high, and high schools replayed the scenario of the royal ball every year during Carnival, always punctuated with royal courts. The photographs of these festivities routinely appeared in the pages of the *Louisiana Weekly*.[83] Such a replaying of Mardi Gras balls was singular to black New Orleans. White writer Eva Augustin Rumpf remembered that "there was no official connection with the [Carnival] organizations. . . . In school you do little things to acknowledge Mardi Gras just like you would for Christmas or Valentine's Day; I don't remember anything outstanding."[84] But in black schools, both public and private, Mardi Gras represented a spectacular event.

Balls and courts were not just for the youth of New Orleans. The parades and balls that young girls attended were replicas of the lavish Mardi Gras festivities celebrated by black New Orleanians throughout the city. For example, the Young Men's Illinois Club staged yearly Carnival balls for the fashionable set of black adult New Orleanians, presenting teenage girls as the queen and court. Such presentations introduced girls into society, marking them as privileged, popular, and stylish. The Young Men's Illinois Club's sixth annual ball in 1932 enacted the scenario of "In Old Japan" on the rooftop garden at the Pythian Temple, a center of black social, economic, and cultural activity in New Orleans. In addition to the "famous rooftop garden," the building housed social halls, auditoriums, and business offices. A race man from Tennessee visited the Pythian Temple when he cataloged the best of Afro-America. He proclaimed: "The Eighth Wonder of the world is not located in the Orient, in the Occident, nor at the North Pole, but right in the city of New Orleans."[85] When he visited this imposing building built by black New Orleanians with black capital, he was most impressed with its ability to promote respectable pleasure cultures: "On the top of the building there is a roof garden, where concerts, moving picture exhibitions and other creditable entertainments are given, and altogether the roof garden is as much of a necessity as it is a novelty for the proper kind of social pleasure."[86] His emphasis on "creditable" and "proper" pleasure made clear the respectability of the space. It was, therefore, the ideal geography on which to create the scenario for a ball that transported black New Orleanians from the Jim Crow South into the fashion and sophistication of "Old Japan." Indeed, the placement of the garden (on the roof) was as far away from the Jim Crow street as possible. One advertisement for the Pythian Temple's rooftop garden noted this geography, declaring it "200 feet in the air."[87]

For the Young Men's Illinois Club's sixth annual ball, the rooftop had been turned into a Japanese garden, with cherry blossoms and wisteria carefully placed to transform the space. The "lovely little queen," fifteen-year-old Clyde Angle, was dressed in white satin and adorned with a rhinestone crown. She gracefully held a large bouquet of white roses.[88] The rooftop garden at the Pythian Temple provided a different sense of place, undoing the racist geography of Jim Crow.[89] As the site for innumerable Carnival balls during the season of Carnival, black women transformed the rooftop night after night from one party's theme to the next. Thus, the rooftop garden as "Old Japan" revealed how geographies of domination like Jim Crow were flexible. Fifteen-year-old Clyde Angle's appearance at the ball, being "displayed" by the Young Men's Illinois Club and waving to the crowd of gowned and tuxedoed partygoers, undid the racial-sexual domination of space by renaming black female bodies and their capacity for freedom, pleasure, and regality.[90] The imaginative capacity of "In Old Japan" demonstrated "the ways in which black women think, write, and negotiate their surroundings," indeed, perform in their surroundings, as "place-based critiques, or, respatializations."[91] Respatialization was critical to Carnival-time imaginative acts. And so, it is crucial to note here that the repertoire itself had a geography its own. The respatializations provided spaces for rethinking the self and for constituting subjectivities momentarily free from the racism of Jim Crow.

Respatializations happened in a multitude of moments during Mardi Gras. Some of these respatializations took place in gestures and physical encounters at parades where black girls were often masked, dressed up in costumes ranging from Indians and dolls to characters from books. In Jim Crow New Orleans, black girls carefully navigated the city streets; their physical comportment was often deferential, hushed, and solemn. But the scenario of Mardi Gras masking made way for new gestures and a new relationship to space. During masking, black girls' everyday bodies were hidden, destabilizing the segregated body. Within their Mardi Gras performances, black girls might develop a new way of being next to whites on the parade route, and of moving in space. Sometimes costumes could transform a black girl or woman into something entirely new—a new race, a new look, a new body. Eleanor Early, too, noted this when she remarked that "most of the [black] women are Baby Dolls with blonde wigs and white faces."[92] The white face (to mimic porcelain dolls) and blonde wigs allowed black women and girls to play with the racialized body. They were neither white nor "colored" but something new entirely. As Kim Marie Vaz has explored, the Million Dollar Baby Dolls were a sorority of black women masked as baby dolls, enacting a sense of themselves that allowed them to escape from raced, gendered, and classed expectations of black womanhood and sexuality.[93] Black girls masked as Indians, pirates, dolls, or characters from books were doing much the same. Masking provided the opportunity to run the city streets, attending parades as a make-believe character rather than as a second-class citizen.

In 1936 a black college student at Dillard University interviewed Mary Johnson, a black visitor from Baton Rouge. Mary Johnson had just taken part in her first Mardi Gras and Carnival season. Johnson emphasized the repertoire of masquerade and parading and its potential for respatialization, a momentary rewriting of race and space. "In New Orleans, Mardi Gras seems to be the day one can do anything he or she wants to do and get off with it," Johnson said. She described Mardi Gras as a moment where blacks had more freedom: "It seems that on this day the white and colored are all together. You see white and colored standing side by side to see the parade, whereas on any other day the whites would move rather than stand by a Negro. I noticed people knocking into each other and passing by just smiling, nobody seemed to be insulted because somebody stepped on their foot or knocked their hat off. . . . They should have Mardi Gras every day so all the people would be more friendly both white and colored."[94] Eva Augustin Rumpf, too, remembered the way in which Mardi Gras culture created new integrated spaces in the city. "They couldn't segregate the parade route," she recalled wryly.[95]

It is important to note, however, that the respatialization allowed by the repertoires of masquerading and parading did not undo Jim Crow permanently; black girls were not completely "free" from racism. Instead, masking offered fleeting reprieves, allowing black girls to reimagine themselves, remake blackness, and survive the traumas of Jim Crow. Still within Mardi Gras also existed the racial violence of Jim Crow. Even Mary Johnson interrupted her account of white and black harmony to note, "But I noticed a group of people that must have been lower class people because a Negro knocked into them and they began cussing in a very loud voice [so] that everybody around them turned around to look at them and from their expressions they didn't seem to approve of it."[96]

Mardi Gras racial violence was often remarked upon in the *Louisiana Weekly*. In "Killings and Cuttings Are Sore Spots," the *Weekly* argued that Carnival was "marred" by white supremacy and racial tensions. Far from just the "lower class" whites of Mary Johnson's story, a group of white college students from Tulane were "insulting" and "throwing trash" on black passersby. The white college students' behavior is a potent reminder that black New Orleanians faced daily insults in the space of the Jim Crow city. The *Louisiana Weekly* argued that the college students' violence "caused several men of color to resent their actions." The students chased down the men and a fight broke out, ending with the death of a white student. This incident was reported alongside another conflict over Mardi Gras space: ten white boys wanted a black boy's spot on a parade route and "without even batting an eye . . . made the usual request, 'move on nigger.'" The paper's description of the request to move as "usual" underscored that white New Orleanians felt as if they owned the space of the city. When the lone black boy asked for protection from a police officer, the officer told him to "keep moving"; he was then chased to North Rampart, where he was beaten unconscious by the white boys.[97] These reports from the *Louisiana Weekly* function as reminders that the geography of Mardi Gras could be at once confining and liberatory. This is what Katherine McKittrick calls "paradoxical space" full of "painful contradictoriness" of both freedom and domination.

Black girls and teenagers negotiated this paradoxical space in multiple ways, attuned to both interracial and intraracial violence. In 1938 Beverly Carter recalled Mardi Gras of two years prior, when she had been sixteen years old. She had fun running around the city and masking. She and her friends went into "different beer parlors disguised[;] nobody knew me and I had some fun." Beverly Carter and her friends went for a ride with some black men "five miles outside of the city limits" to enjoy some "fresh air." But instead, they found themselves in a house where the men said, "We have planned something and you do what we say or get home the best you can." After a struggle, Beverly Carter made it out of the house and hitchhiked with her friends back to the city. The girls "could not tell" their story, so for two years Carter "just kept the matter to [herself] and went on" as if nothing had happened.[98] Later that night, she went back out to dance, drink, and enjoy Mardi Gras. Thus, Beverly Carter disguised herself, delighting in the anonymity of masking, but also experienced the ways in which men, white and black, could take advantage of space and geography to impose their will. Here, taken outside of the city, she was forced to find her way back home. Her day, as well as the space of Mardi Gras, included both pleasure and fear.

Respatialization within paradoxical space can also be captured through the scenario of throwing and catching, acted out again and again at Mardi Gras. In *Travels with Mae* Eileen Julien describes throwing and catching as a bodily and affective event embedded in the city of New Orleans:

> There is something sublime about throwing or catching a throw dur-
> ing a parade. If you're doing the throwing, there is such joy in making
> people happy, in seeing eyes light up. And such ecstasy in catching
> something, in being part of the emotion, the event, the communion,
> sharing an hour or two in a crowd with people you don't know and
> will probably never see again. Bart Giamatti thought it was baseball.
> But I *know* it's Mardi Gras. Children who grow up in this tradition,
> from infancy to 96, believe in color, community, disguise, metamor-
> phosis, fun, seasons, ritual, sensuality, luxury, plenty, the body![99]

Julien's description of throwing, of "making people happy," emphasizes the pleasure culture of Mardi Gras. Throwing and catching is a "repertoire of embodied knowledge."[100] For Julien, it is only "children who grow up in this tradition" who truly understand the transformative spirit of throwing and catching. The respatialization found in the performance of throwing and catching inscribed meaning onto the city streets, creating a moment of "metamorphosis": changing the cityscape from one of segregation to one of fun, pleasure, and sensuality. It was in this performance of throwing and catching that black girls' bodies became embedded in the space of the city, embedded in the city's luxury. What made this moment "sensual" was the ways in which black girls were able to use their bodies to claim space and self. Eileen Julien's remembrance makes clear the nexus between "landscape, body, and imagination" as a place of possibility for black girls and women.[101] Throwing and catching lasted for only moments and represents a fleeting pleasure culture.

But even in the metamorphosis represented by throwing and catching, racial meanings haunted interactions between Carnival-goers. White New Orleanian Eva Augustin Rumpf remembered that "the one setting in which we sometimes stood side by side with black folks was while watching parades during the Carnival season. . . . My sisters and I would be cautioned to stay close to our parents and to never challenge a colored person over owner-ship of the beads and trinkets thrown from the floats."[102] In these moments, Rumpf's parents taught her lessons in white supremacy. They told her that challenging black New Orleanians threatened her safety as a white girl. This same lesson, however, simultaneously taught her that black New Orleani-ans had the right to possess Carnival beads and trinkets. Blacks, too, could catch. But racial hierarchies reemerged intact as soon as the throwing and catching ended. As a young girl, Rumpf noticed that "it was not unusual for the black child or adult who'd captured the prize to willingly hand it over to one of us."[103] The word "willingly" haunts Rumpf's sentence. Rumpf high-lights the ways in which the integrated scene of Carnival parades collapsed the rules of segregation and yet reinforced them all the same. "Willingly" giving up a prize to a white girl represented the reinscribing of the racial-sexual domination of space. For black girls, throwing and catching might be a sublime instant of pleasure, but taking home their prizes presented a more difficult problem. If challenged later for some fancy glass beads, black girls might be forced by the racial etiquette of white supremacy to give up what they had caught.

Carnival beads, especially, represent a significant piece of the material culture of Mardi Gras. Beads can be understood as "a scriptive thing." A scriptive thing, as Robin Bernstein describes it, is "an item of material culture that prompts meaningful bodily behaviors."[104] Scriptive things invite certain performances. Beads, when thrown as they were during Mardi Gras, invited black girls to catch, take, and possess. If black girls were lucky enough to take the beads home, the beads turned into ornaments inviting other sorts of behaviors. Beads, for example, could be hung around one's neck, worn as jewelry for play. Beads could also be hung in one's house, displayed for dec-oration and adding color and flourish to everyday spaces. One white New Orleanian recalled the performance invited by Mardi Gras beads. At Mardi Gras parades she always sought the fanciest glass beads, which reminded her of "costume jewelry" that she could wear to high school.[105] Beads, of course, were not the only things thrown at Mardi Gras parades and parties. In 1932 the Original Illinois Club organized a debutantes ball during the Carnival season. Throwing (and catching) became a highlight of the ball, making it into the society pages of the *Louisiana Weekly*: "About the hour of 12 mid-night the hostesses, to the surprise of their guests, threw kisses and peanuts to the tunes of 'The Kiss Waltz' and 'The Peanut Vendor,' respectively."[106] A black counterpublic—a public pleasure culture—came into being at the debutantes ball and in the retelling of the ball and the throwing/catching.

The public pleasures of Carnival season did not pass without its detractors. One editorial in the *Louisiana Weekly* noted that although visitors may fixate on the pomp and circumstance, those who lived in New Orleans can "see deeper than the veneer of good times." "Carnival with its thin veneer of pleasure soon passes," the author argued, "and with it goes the hard-earned cash of the weak-minded members of our group."[107] The history of Mardi Gras pleasure as I have told it is also a history of black class privilege. The rival geography of the rooftop garden at the Pythian Temple was not an open space, available to all black New Orleanians. It represented a space of exclusivity. Just as it allowed some black girls and women a place to enact a performance of regality, it also purposely excluded others. The story of exclusivity points to the contradictions within make-believe lands. Some of these respatializations—free from the racial-sexual domination of space—inscribed other types of domination and highlighted intraracial tensions of class, color, and ethnicity.

THE HISTORIES OF PLEASURE that I have told are only bits and pieces of a larger history of intimacy, love, and joy in black girls' lives—a small piece of the puzzle in reconstructing girls' inner lives.[108] In some crucial ways, my discussions of black girls' pleasure culture builds on Robin Kelley's *Race Rebels*, a "history from way, way below" that seeks to explore the politics of the everyday.[109] In the chapter "We Are Not What We Seem: The Politics and Pleasures of Community," Kelley argues that historians of African American life need to "strip away the various masks African Americans wear in their daily struggles to negotiate relationships or contest power in public spaces, and search for ways to gain entry into the private world hidden beyond the public gaze."[110] His assertion suggests that behind the cultures of dissemblance, silence, and feigned smiles, African Americans cultivated cultures of pleasure with one another. Analyzing all-black spaces such as the YWCA and the Pythian Temple partially answers Kelley's call. In fact, Kelley, like historians Tera Hunter, Stephanie Camp, and Earl Lewis, attempts to explore life behind the masks by looking for spaces of black cultural life— at dances, at parks, even at church.[111] These scholars of African American life discuss the political ramifications of pleasure in black lives by invoking the analytical terms "resistance" or "infrapolitics." From their work we learn that pleasure cultures can be found in a myriad of public spaces. This discussion pushes the conversation to seriously consider the ways in which performance has a geography. This chapter also adds to the discussion of pleasure and politics by grappling with the ways in which pleasure cultures helped individuals forge intimacies with one another.[112] There is much to learn from friendships between girls and among groups of women. These relationships helped women survive the traumas of Jim Crow and provided an alternate space to construct subjectivities. Further, through a detailed account of pleasure cultures in African American lives, we may also be able to reconstruct a history of love and relationships in black communities. The intimate and romantic relationships cultivated by girls give us a sense of their hopes and dreams. At the same time, these pleasure cultures provided an alternative identity for girls who participated. In "Make-Believe Land" at the YWCA or at Carnival balls or as the heroine of a love story, girls were no longer "colored," second-class citizens being insulted on the streets. Instead, they were the heroes of their own lives, able to fantasize and play.

Epilogue
Jim Crow Girls,
Hurricane Katrina Women

Nina Simone, who came of age in Jim Crow North Carolina, sang of segrega-tion in "Old Jim Crow," a protest song from 1964. The song referenced the wea-riness felt by so many African Americans frustrated with the pace of change in the fight for racial justice. Simone lamented, "Old Jim Crow / I thought I had you beat / Now I see you walkin' up and down the street." In the song, Jim Crow haunts the geography of the American South. She asks, "Don't you know? It's all over now."[1] The reinscribing and returns of racial injustice on the city streets mark a continuing struggle in New Orleans and in the Amer-ican South. On August 29, 2005, Hurricane Katrina slammed onto the coast of southeast Louisiana. The levees, constructed to protect low-lying New Orleans from floodwaters and storm surges, failed. Their failure caused flood-ing, mass destruction, and death in New Orleans, even though the hurricane just missed a direct hit of the city. After a slow and stumbling response from George W. Bush's federal government, New Orleanians who had stayed in the city to wait out the storm were stranded, many without food or water. New Orleans remained underwater for days; citizens were displaced for months, even years; and the city continues its slow rebuilding process ten years later.

Onelia Sayas Cherrie was a fourteen-year-old high school student at McDonogh #35 in 1931 and appears in the front row of the class photo on the cover of this book. She was born during segregation and died as a result of Hurricane Katrina in 2005. Cherrie's home withstood the storm, but the dam-age to the city left her and her son, Eddie Cherrie, without electricity or run-ning water. Mayor Ray Nagin had advised all remaining New Orleanians to try to make their way to the Superdome or Ernest Morial Convention Center for further support and transportation. Onelia Cherrie was one of many elderly black New Orleanians at the convention center. "Once there, we were forgot-ten," wrote Eddie Cherrie a month later.[2] After three days of dehydration, she fell and hit her head; only then was she evacuated by helicopter to Armstrong

International Airport, where medical help and a flight outside the city waited. At the airport, she was separated from her son by medical personnel promising to care for her. She was conscious and they had her information. What happened next, no one knows for sure. Her son waited for her to come out of the triage area, but workers told him they could not locate her and that she might have been evacuated by FEMA to a shelter or hospital. But Onelia Cherrie never made it out of the airport alive. Her family learned of her death just before Thanksgiving, nearly two months after the breach of the levees. What did she see and think as she looked around at the horrific scene at the convention center? What framework did she have to comprehend her experience, herself, and the geography of the city she had known all her life? Did she see "Old Jim Crow" walking down the street again? In 1931, when Onelia Sayas Cherrie transferred from the public high school for black students, McDonogh #35, to the local black Catholic high school, Xavier University Preparatory, a classmate wrote good-bye to her in an autograph book:

Dear Nellie:
Tis the sad, sad fate of a
Schoolgirl's heart
To meet, be friends
and then to part.
Always remember me as a friend.[3]

Hurricane Katrina presents only one ending to the story of the generation I have followed; there are other conclusions that could be written. But Hurricane Katrina hit just as I began research for this book. In oral history interviews, then, women talked about their relationship to the city through the lenses of segregation and of the storm. Elderly women who lived through or died in Hurricane Katrina due to the storm's attendant governmental neglect and racism came of age during legalized Jim Crow in New Orleans and a white supremacy supported by the state. Therefore, these women's notions of citizenship, their sense of belonging to New Orleans, and their subjectivities are irrevocably tied to these two epochs in New Orleans' history. As George Lipsitz reminds us, there has been a "perpetual struggle for dignity and self-identity waged by working class blacks in New Orleans."[4] The stories collected throughout *Crescent City Girls* reveal that, for women, this "struggle for dignity" was a struggle against gendered forms of violence as well. Although some believed that America had "gone far to disinherit the Negro boy" while girls "fare better," the truth was that black girls faced struggles of their own.[5]

At the ten-year anniversary of Hurricane Katrina, as scholars begin to grapple with the hurricane as a historical moment, we must also remember that the people who lived through and died in the storm have individual life histories.[6] Women in New Orleans were tied not only to the trauma of Hurricane Katrina but also to the trauma of segregation. These histories, seemingly far apart in time, are intimately interwoven by the people who lived through them. By considering Katrina in the epilogue of a book focused on segregation, I answer Nell Painter's call for us to consider our "interrelatedness," not only across the color line but also across time.[7] An analysis of such interconnection reveals two crucial moments in generational memory. Even as civil rights and black power movements transformed the racial structure of New Orleans, a generation of black citizens experienced the state's denial of their subjectivity and material and psychic pain during different stages of their lives. The women most vulnerable to the hurricane and its aftermath came of age during Jim Crow. Furthermore, the contemporary struggle for state accountability in post-Katrina New Orleans is informed by a much longer struggle for citizenship rights in New Orleans.

The preceding chapters lay out the ways in which young black women and girls struggled against geographic dislocation and dispossession during Jim Crow. Black girls coming of age during Jim Crow knew they were often unwanted or out of place in the urban landscape. And young black women learned that the space of the city could be dangerous—they might be insulted, sexually harassed, or subject to physical and sexual abuse. Hurricane Katrina, then, represented yet another moment of geographic dislocation and dispossession for women who had grown up during segregation.

In an oral history interview, New Orleanian Joycelyn Hyman pointed to the interconnections between the historical trauma of segregation and the trauma of Hurricane Katrina. Her intertwined stories of the past and present city noted the ways in which "the category of black woman is intimately connected with past and present spatial organization and that black femininity and black women's humanness are bound up in an ongoing geographic struggle."[8] This geographic struggle works against dislocation and the forgetting of black women's place in the fabric of the city, both in the present and in the past. Hyman began by trying to explain that segregation had affected her "in every, every way." She then moved from the memory of segregation to the memory of Katrina as she attempted to express how historical trauma rested inside of her, causing psychic pain:

> But it's just the things you remember, that you don't forget. I remember after Katrina, the Sisters (not the Sisters of the Holy Family,

but the Sisters of the Sacred Heart; they are a white community of nuns) . . . they were housing a lot of people that were coming down here to help with the rebuilding, and they would ask me to come and tell my story about Katrina. And I did that for a while, and then all of a sudden I said to Sister, "I'm sorry, but I just can't keep reliving this." They didn't realize what this was doing to me. And at first, I didn't realize what I was doing to myself.[9]

For Hyman, this story of reliving and retelling her experience of Hurricane Katrina, a site of trauma and loss, paralleled a similar story, this time about race and segregation:

Now I'm on the Racial Harmony Committee for the archdiocese, and when we have retreat, we relive [segregation]. And I find, last year, when I did this, and I was reliving my life, I started crying; I was in tears. And the archbishop came over to kind of comfort me. And I said, "I'm really sorry, but I find that this is too painful for me to keep doing this all of the time. I don't want to keep reliving that." . . . Because it is with you. But you just don't want to keep talking about it all of the time.[10]

Hyman moved between the two experiences, creating a "present-past time-space"[11] in the urban landscape. In doing so, she explained "sites of memory," the process of remembrance, and the emotional cost of retelling. In her narrative of her life, she continued to move back and forth between the segregated city and the flooded city. These places—the segregated city and her lost city, home, and possessions during the flood—both remained within her. As she stated when talking about coming-of-age in Jim Crow, "When you've grown up in a segregated environment, things that have affected your life are always going to remain with you."[12]

Past geographies of Jim Crow that were undergirded by violence, dislocation, and emotional trauma constructed New Orleans' urban and suburban spaces and haunt the city's landscape of today. Spaces that flooded after the storm and black neighborhoods that remain unbuilt are influenced by histories of residential segregation.[13] And so the flooded city of Hurricane Katrina, as well as specific material places within the city during that time, acted as a "site of memory,"[14] a place where black women would remember and grapple with forms of racism, historical trauma, and memories of dislocation. Sites of memory are places "where black people were and are denied humanity, belonging and formal citizenship."[15] Although a devoted servant to the Catholic Church and a volunteer for numerous Catholic organizations, Hyman noted the continued racism within her home parish while thinking through meanings of racial "harmony" in a post–Jim Crow, post–civil rights, post-Katrina New Orleans. Her friend Ann Stuart noted, "Segregation is alive and well. In every way."[16]

Thus, recognizing these sites within New Orleans, as well as the past/present interconnectedness in these places, brings into view black women and girls' lives in New Orleans. Oral history interviewees Hyman and Stuart both emphasized the uneven rebuilding after Hurricane Katrina. Some neighborhoods were reconstructed quickly, while others are still overlooked. Hyman explained the difference: "Some neighborhoods are black and some neighborhoods are white. Some people won't say it, but that is the way it is. Because as far as having a hospital, in a community that is predominantly black [New Orleans East], that should have been a priority." Hyman argued that every neighborhood deserved a grocery store, drug store, and hospital; but black spaces, such as New Orleans East, remained without them.[17] As Katherine McKittrick explains, sites of memory are also "the *sight* of memory," the ability to remember and make visible black female struggles and subjectivities when dominant geographic stories would erase those experiences.[18] The *sight* of memory for Hyman and Stuart, then, is also the ability to see the interconnections between past and present geographies, to see the connections between past and present traumas, and to make the connection between past and present modes of segregation.

The impulse to reflect on coming-of-age stories in the face of Hurricane Katrina is seen in writings published in the wake of the storm. Since Katrina, both black and white women who grew up during Jim Crow have written a number of memoirs about New Orleans girlhood.[19] Some of these are self-published. The storm has brought the space of segregated New Orleans and of these women's pasts into relief. For these writers, Katrina's devastation caused flashbacks, connected past and present geographies, and asked them to remember the city's influence and its geography on the construction of their subjectivities. Beverly Anderson, a black Creole writer and educator, had always thought of writing a book about her childhood in the 1950s, but, she reflects in her introduction, "I didn't really get started on it in a serious manner until after Hurricane Katrina hit New Orleans on August 29, 2005, three months after I attended activities in New Orleans celebrating the fortieth anniversary of my graduation from Dillard University."[20] Anderson thought fondly of some of the spaces of her past that are now gone—destroyed and displaced first by suburbanization and then by the storm.

For some, this looking back to the past provided a space of mourning for a city lost, for family members passed away, for homes destroyed, and for photographs and keepsakes moldy or completely washed away. In *Cherished Memories* Anderson catalogs her family's losses, from the simple to the cataclysmic, in a paragraph. She writes, "[T]hese siblings, seven sisters and one brother, lost their homes, at least one car, their jobs, their mementos, and their way of life. They lost material wealth and much of the mementoes that were even more precious to them. They lost contact with family and friends scattered all over the country." It is only after this cataloging, which includes the mundane and replaceable (a car) as well as the symbolic and irreplaceable (a way of life), that Anderson reveals another, more profound loss: "We lost our mother, Dorothy Angelety Jacques, who was on life support at Lafon nursing home at the time of the hurricane. My mother was one of seventeen senior citizens, along with her first cousin Renette Mercadel Peters, who were on life support at the time. . . . They all perished as a result of this horrific storm."[21] For Anderson, the flooded city becomes a site of memory, a way of reconstructing things lost and a girlhood long gone.

Poet Natasha Trethewey writes about the site of memory and loss in *Beyond Katrina*, a look at the geography, memory, and devastation of Katrina not in New Orleans but in the Mississippi Gulf Coast of her home. She too argues for connections between geographies of past and present and of *sights* of memory. She meditates on other storms from her personal history and the possibilities of returning home. The book begins just as her Pulitzer Prize–winning *Native Guard* began, "with a journey home— my *nostos*. 'Theories of Time and Space.' . . . Writing it nearly ten years ago, I was thinking figuratively, *You can get there from here, though / there's no going home.* Although I had intended to consider the impossibility of returning to those places we've come from—not because the places are gone or substantially different but because *we* are—by August 2005, the poem had become quite literal: so much of what I'd known of my home was either gone or forever changed."[22]

Eileen Julien, in *Travels with Mae: Scenes from a New Orleans Girlhood*, remembers returning to New Orleans after the storm and finding "mold. Mildew. Climbing the walls, filling the air. Ashen, curled floorboards. The contents of the cupboards low to the floor, filled with the waters of the sea. Furniture overturned, swollen. Mae's piano, a bloated prehistoric monster lying on its side."[23] The material geography of her home, the home that had been her parents', connected Julien with the past of her mother (Mae) and her father. The sight of the mold and the destruction of pieces of the house (such as a beloved porch) brought back memories of her childhood. In *Travels with Mae*, Julien asks a series of questions about the loss of her city, her neighborhood, her street, and her home, musing on the possible loss of the landscape of her childhood, the landscape where memories of her parents dwell: "Where to begin? Will the city come back? Will the levees hold? Will there ever again be life on this block, in this neighborhood? Will it be forever empty, unlit? Or a sparse frontier, prey to marauding youth?"[24]

White writer Eva Augustin Rumpf connected the loss of the city with reclamation of her girlhood. "I felt drawn back to see the devastation with my own eyes," she writes, "to grieve for my wounded city and to commiserate with relatives and friends who had lost their homes and possessions. It was a journey I had been anticipating with both dread and hope. It was a journey in search of my lost childhood. What would I find?"[25] For Rumpf, as well as for the black writers, this retelling is nostalgic. But for many black writers, this nostalgia was also tinged with reminders of segregation and its attendant traumas.

The return back and the devastated landscape also revealed the deep connection between geography and subjectivity. For Eileen Julien, rebuilding her home in the Seventh Ward meant rebuilding a piece of herself and her history—her mother had wanted the house badly; the men in her family had built it. Therefore the material space of the home is an affective geography, infused with emotions of love, grief, joy, and security. "It is not a rational decision," Julien explains. "It comes from the gut. I cannot forsake or sell this house. Not now. Not yet. Rebuild: this is what I must do. This is what I can do—for me and for the city."[26]

As is clear in Eileen Julien's Seventh Ward home, the material geographies devastated by Hurricane Katrina are also affective geographies— spaces invested with emotional meaning and associated with the past. In and through these geographies, black women make sense of themselves and their place in the city. The Sisters of the Holy Family faced massive devastation of their properties as a result of Hurricane Katrina: an all-girls high school, nursing home, apartment buildings, and the motherhouse all lay in ruin. These were more than simply buildings. They represented black geographical space—built by the black religious community to serve the black community in New Orleans, as the Sisters have done for nearly 175 years. As discussed in chapter 1, the Sisters of the Holy Family actively resisted geographic dislocation in the segregated city of New Orleans. Their school and motherhouse in the French Quarter during Jim Crow represented an important space of black women's achievement and self-sufficiency.

The Sisters moved from the French Quarter to the Plum Orchard neighborhood in New Orleans East in 1965, buying a large tract of land. Sister Claire of Assisi Pierre, the president of St. Mary's Academy, helped rebuild some of the property of the Sisters of the Holy Family after Hurricane Katrina. Her reflections on the space of New Orleans post-Katrina bring into view how black women's sense of self is bound up with affective geographies of past and present, for Sister Claire was a student at St. Mary's in the French Quarter during segregation.

Sister Claire began her narrative of surviving Katrina by noting place and marking material geographies: "See all those buildings over there—where those buildings are? There were oak trees over there and benches," she explained. She remembered the days just before the storm, sitting and reflecting on the Sisters of the Holy Family's land. Everything was quiet because the other Sisters in the community had evacuated; she and a few other Sisters finished up before leaving. "It was a beautiful sunshiny day, and so peaceful. You'd never think of the impending thing that was coming," Sister Claire recalled. "And I thought to myself, what a beautiful place it was."[27] Sister Claire emphasized the pre-Katrina geography of the motherhouse and the high school, defining that space in terms of legacy and emphasizing all of the work the Sisters had done during the years of segregation and then during the 1960s to obtain, build, grow, and nurture the space. On that day prior to the storm, she looked around and saw "the high school, the grass, the ducks, the squirrels, and then I thought, 'Gosh, we have inherited all of this. The older Sisters worked hard, and did without a lot, to be able to purchase this property.'" This sense of inheritance of black geographical space contrasts deeply with dislocation in geographies of racial-sexual domination. Instead, the motherhouse and associated properties were geographies controlled, constructed, and nurtured by black nuns for the black girls of St. Mary's Academy and for the black community. As such, the space functioned as a place of fulfillment and confidence building, away from the outside world. And so, as Sister Claire explained, "those were my last impressions when I left here. We have inherited all of this; how lucky we are." Sister Claire saw the material geography of the motherhouse and St. Mary's Academy in terms of past hard work and sacrifice. And she saw herself as a link in a chain, connected to those women who came before her, working to build the community up despite deeply ingrained histories of white supremacy and sexism.[28]

Sister Claire came back to New Orleans soon after the storm to assess and to begin the rebuilding process for the Mother Superior.[29] "Every single piece of property we owned was devastated," she recalled. Sister Claire remembered the feeling of entering the building for the first time; wrinkling her nose years later, "I can still smell the odor of fish." To rebuild the school and save the property inherited, Sister Claire looked to the past. Her ability to ignore the barriers and continue building came from her girlhood, when the Sisters of the Holy Family educated her. The Sisters taught her self-confidence, pride, and leadership and how to face problems with poise. In this way, the past mingled with the present in Sister Claire's own perception of her self, of her place on the New Orleans landscape, and of the material geography of the Sisters of the Holy Family.

Sister Claire's belief in geographic inheritance, which combined the past with the present, is another reminder that "black women think, write, and negotiate their surroundings" as "place-based critiques, or, respatializations."[30] The preceding chapters demonstrate that black women and girls have fought geographic dispossession through respatialization—by possessing spaces in the city where they could be safe, find pleasure, and make claims to the past. Indeed, Sister Claire conceptualized and inhabited space by opposing traditional geographies of domination. Her way of knowing space came from the oppositional histories of the Sisters of the Holy Family, black women who worked against white domination and found small spaces of freedom within complex histories of racial-sexual domination. Some of these spaces were the schools in which Sister Claire was educated and where she now works. This is the inheritance to which Sister Claire referred, an inheritance of a black geography.

There have been persistent patterns of segregation, state neglect, and denial of psychic interiority for women who came of age during Jim Crow. *Crescent City Girls* is a story about a generation of women who lived through a tumultuous time in New Orleans. The key themes of sexuality, geography, and affect demonstrate the ways in which segregation and intraracial tensions affected girls' notions of self. For black women of the generation who grew up during Jim Crow and lived through Hurricane Katrina, their lives have been defined, in part, by traumatic experiences. For many of them, being an American citizen has been full of contradiction. They have had to contend with multiple assaults on their dignity: daily insults from whites on the streets, pressure from family to remain "nice," expectations about who they *should be* as black Americans, and the varying costs of being forgotten by the state. Their inner worlds have also been full of pleasures—of pleasant memories of neighborhoods and of good friends and supportive families; those who were fortunate enough to attend school recall their educations

FIGURE E.1.
Onelia Sayas (left) and Onelia Bazenac, 1930
(Courtesy of Cherrie Family Papers)

with pride and happiness. Their stories must be told when reconstructing a history of Jim Crow, just as their stories must be included in any analysis of their generation.[31]

By focusing on the lives of black girls and young women, this book has uncovered the gendered violence of urban segregation. I have argued that black girls growing up during the Jim Crow era faced the extraordinarily difficult task of adhering to black middle-class expectations of purity and respectability even as they encountered the daily realities of Jim Crow violence, which included interracial sexual violence, street harassment, and presumptions of black girls' latent lasciviousness. Yet young black women responded to this dilemma in creative ways. For example, some girls reformed the imperatives of respectability into a central self-identity, while others constructed public pleasure cultures centered on romance and fanciful imagining.

BLACK GIRLS AND WOMEN's notions of self were deeply connected to their place in the urban geography. During segregation, black children developed complex mental maps that helped them navigate the city's social and political structure. But these mental maps also marked spaces of pleasure on the city's landscape. As I have shown, the site of memory/sight of memory highlights how the past haunts the geography of the present for these women.

Black girls of this generation also came to see themselves as subjects of certain types of sexuality. For many black girls, especially those who had to work, vulnerability to sexual violence and sexual harassment were some of the most intense ways that the Jim Crow state disciplined and defined "all black girls."[32] But *Crescent City Girls* also shows that black girls in various circumstances could understand themselves as "nice girls," just as Onelia Sayas Cherrie did when she chose to be a devout Catholic, collecting prayer cards and saving them for the rest of her life.[33]

These various categories offered black girls ways to construct notions of self through, around, and in the various constraints they faced as subjects of a segregated racial order. Fully examining these categories has allowed for a glimpse into black girls' elusive inner lives. After all, the emotional experience of growing up a second-class citizen in a segregated city contributed to how girls came to understand themselves and their place in New Orleans. In considering a wide range of archival sources, *Crescent City Girls* makes black female lives and suffering visible, engaging with the sight of memory. The links between sexuality, space, and the politics of segregation are thus made clear.

Notes

Introduction

1. "What to Do about It!" *Louisiana Weekly*, May 19, 1951.
2. Gilmore, *Gender and Jim Crow*; Hale, *Making Whiteness*.
3. J. Hall, *Revolt against Chivalry*; Hale, *Making Whiteness*.
4. Often, this trope overshadows the lynchings of black women and the other reasons for the lynchings of black men, such as economic intimidation.
5. Hodes, *Sex, Love, Race*, 1.
6. For examples of histories of Jim Crow violence, see Goodman, *Stories of Scottsboro*; Brundage, *Lynching in the New South*; Hahn, *Nation under Our Feet*; McMillen, *Dark Journey*; Oshinsky, *Worse Than Slavery*; Kelley, *Hammer and Hoe*; and Litwack, *Trouble in Mind*.
7. See J. Hall, "Mind That Burns in Each Body," 332; J. Hall, *Revolt against Chivalry*, introduction.
8. Carby, *Reconstructing Womanhood*, 39.
9. McGuire, *At the Dark End of the Street*.
10. "Rosa Parks Account Describes Attempted Rape."
11. Douglass, "Education of Negro Youth," 536. On Douglass, see Whinery, "Harl R. Douglass."
12. Quoted in Odem, *Delinquent Daughters*, 33.
13. Michele Mitchell, *Righteous Propagation*, xx.
14. Ibid. For the early Jim Crow period, Mitchell argues that "standard class labels" do not apply to African Americans—a group of Americans just out of slavery. She explains, "I use 'aspiring class,' then, as a means of differentiating African American strivers from contemporaneous middle-class, white Americans and to acknowledge the quickening of class stratification within African American communities" (xx).
15. Rogers, *Righteous Lives*, 7.
16. Quote from Grant and Rubens, "Interview with Jane Flax," 2. I have found useful Jane Flax's definition of subjectivity, which is influenced by poststructuralism and feminist reinterpretations of psychoanalysis. See Grant and Rubens and Flax, *Disputed Subjects*, 92–110. For other discussions of subjectivity, see Canning and Rose, "Gender, Citizenship and Subjectivity"; Butler, *Gender Trouble*; Hartman, *Scenes of Subjection*; and Reynolds, *Violence and Subjectivity*.
17. Friedman, *Mappings*, 19.
18. Hine, "Rape and the Inner Lives of Black Women," 912. For more on history and subjectivity, see Painter, *Southern History across the Color Line*.
19. More work needs to be done on intraracial sexual violence and domestic abuse, but for the past decade scholars have begun to probe the history of interracial sexual violence. For migration stories, see Orleck, *Storming Caesar's Palace*, 1. For histories of sexual violence, see Rosen, *Terror in the Heart of Freedom*; Warren, "'The Cause of Her Grief'"; Evans, *Silencing of Ruby McCollum*; Clinton, "Bloody Terrain"; Cardyn, "Sexual Terror in the Reconstruction South" and "Sexualized Racism/Gendered Violence"; Green, *Battling the Plantation Mentality*, 3; and Berry, *Pig Farmer's Daughter*, 7. On black reactions to interracial sexual violence and on intraracial conflict, see Michele Mitchell, *Righteous Propagation*, especially chapters 3–5 and 7–8.

20. Hine, "Rape and the Inner Lives of Black Women," 915–920. Hine continues to address the question of survival and interiority in her work. See, for example, Hine, "Corporeal and Ocular Veil."

21. According to the census, there were 11,835 black girls between the age of ten and nineteen in Orleans Parish in 1930. See the Social Explorer Dataset (SE), *Census 1930*, digitally transcribed by Inter-university Consortium for Political and Social Research; edited and verified by Michael Haines; compiled, edited, and verified by Social Explorer.

22. See Driscoll, *Girls*; DeLuzio, *Female Adolescence*.

23. DeLuzio, *Female Adolescence*, 3.

24. Driscoll, *Girls*, esp. 2–11; DeLuzio, *Female Adolescence*.

25. See, for example, the work of black scholars involved in the Negro Youth Study: C. S. Johnson, *Growing Up in the Black Belt*; Davis and Dollard, *Children of Bondage*; and Reid, *In a Minor Key*.

26. See the following articles from the *Louisiana Weekly*: Janover Davis, "Youth," March 4, 1939, Editorials and Opinions sec.; Janover Davis, "Youth versus Religion," March 4, 1939, Editorials and Opinions sec.; "Problems of Youth the Same," May 20, 1939, Editorials sec.; Nealy, "New Orleans Youth! Why Don't You Help Yourself?," January 21, 1939, Editorials and Opinions sec.; and "Youth, Crime, and Squalid Homes," March 6, 1937.

27. Frank et al., *Personality Development in Adolescent Girls*, 28.

28. Ibid., 29.

29. Ibid., 8.

30. Halberstam, *Female Masculinity*, 6.

31. This phrase refers to Stephanie Shaw's book by that name, *What a Woman Ought to Be and to Do*. Shaw takes the phrase from Zora Neale Hurston's *Their Eyes Were Watching God*.

32. Hawes and Hiner, "Hidden in Plain View," 47.

33. Stearns, "Challenges in the History of Childhood," 34.

34. Fass, "Cultural History/Social History," 45.

35. Borders interview, Behind the Veil: Documenting African-American Life in the Jim Crow South Records, John Hope Franklin Research Center, Duke University (hereafter BV).

36. McKittrick and Woods, *Black Geographies and the Politics of Place*, 4.

37. Ibid.

38. McMillen, *Dark Journey*, 11, 23. For other scholars taking up McMillen's insight, see Ritterhouse, *Growing Up Jim Crow*, 15.

39. T. Davis, *Southscapes*, 11.

40. Ritterhouse, *Growing Up Jim Crow*; Cahn, *Sexual Reckonings*.

41. Hirsch and Logsdon, *Creole New Orleans*.

42. Because I see this as an ethnic (not racial) difference, it is important to use two terms that work in tandem. In some ways the difference between black Creoles and American blacks could be described as Francophone culture versus Anglophone culture. But, the difference between black Creoles and American blacks is much more than linguistic; it is also ethnic, cultural and religious. Additionally, by the 1930s, both groups are English speaking. Hirsch and Logsdon use "black Americans" and "black Creoles" or "Afro-American" and "Afro-Creole"/ "Franco African" throughout their *Creole New Orleans*. An obvious limitation of these terms (as well as American black) is that both groups are considered "American"—even if second-class citizens— by the 1930s. Furthermore, both groups might be considered "African-American" by today's definition of the term. (Although some who identify as Creole do not identify as such.) Also, "black" has certain connotations as well. I use "black" in its broadest sense and in a diasporic context, including those who identify as "multiracial" in my definition of "black."

43. Blassingame, *Black New Orleans*, 155.

44. Hirsch and Logsdon, *Creole New Orleans*; T. Davis, *Southscapes*, 201–8; Blassingame, *Black New Orleans*; Williamson, *New People*; Kein, *Creole*; Desdunes, *Our People, Our History*.

45. JanMohamed, "Sexuality on/of the Racial Border," 94.

46. See Devlin, "Delinquents and Debutantes"; R. Alexander, *"Girl Problem"*; Odem, *Delinquent Daughters*; "Doing Something about Juvenile Delinquency," *Louisiana Weekly*, November 17, 1945, Editorials and Opinions sec.; "Juvenile Delinquency and Inadequate Recreational Facilities," *Louisiana Weekly*, July 2, 1947.

47. Higginbotham, *Righteous Discontent*, 196.

48. Michele Mitchell, *Righteous Propagation*.

49. See Higginbotham, *Righteous Discontent*; Michele Mitchell, *Righteous Propagation*; Gaines, *Uplifting the Race*; and Carby, *Reconstructing Womanhood*.

50. Peiss and Simmons, "Passion and Power," 4.

51. Simone, *Old Jim Crow Interview*.

52. Du Bois, *Souls of Black Folk*, 3.

53. Ibid., 4.

54. Painter, *Southern History across the Color Line*, 20.

55. See, for example, Painter, *Southern History across the Color Line*; Woolfork, *Embodying American Slavery in Contemporary Culture*; Tettenborn, "Melancholia as Resistance"; Berlant, "Subject of True Feeling" and *Queen of America Goes to Washington City*; Love, *Feeling Backward*; Cvetkovich, *Archive of Feelings*; Bouson, *Quiet as It's Kept*; Sedgwick, *Touching Feeling*; Terada, *Feeling in Theory*; and Ngai, *Ugly Feelings*.

56. Rumpf, *Reclamation*, xix.

57. Fussell, "Constructing New Orleans, Constructing Race," 847.

58. Julien, *Travels with Mae*, 83.

59. G. Hall, *Africans in Colonial Louisiana*.

60. Hirsch, "Creole New Orleans," 266, 318–19.

61. Estimated between 1.7 and 1.3, depending on the study and methods used. See Feibelman, "Social and Economic Study of the New Orleans Jewish Community," 6.

62. Ford and Stiefel, *Jews of New Orleans*, 86–87.

63. Fussell, "Constructing New Orleans, Constructing Race," 847.

64. Martinez and Lecorgne, *Uptown/Downtown*, xii.

65. Hyman and Stuart interview.

66. Ibid.

67. Joanne deLavigne Scott, "Uranus and I Are Pretty Good Friends," 7, May 1939, Federal Writers' Project Papers #3709, Southern Historical Collection, Wilson Library, University of North Carolina at Chapel Hill.

68. Wolcott, *Race, Riots, and Roller Coasters*, 200, 210; Fairclough, *Race and Democracy*, 152–53.

69. Fairclough, *Race and Democracy*, 85.

Chapter One

1. Borders interview, BV.

2. For a discussion of reading, racial signifiers, and Jim Crow signs, see Abel, "Bathroom Doors and Drinking Fountains."

3. Friedman, *Mappings*, 18–19.

4. This ideology did not extend as far as black nannies and nursemaids who were incorporated into the space of the white home. Hale, *Making Whiteness*; Hartman, *Scenes of Subjection*.

5. Quoted in Somers, "Black and White in New Orleans," 41.

6. Du Bois, *Souls of Black Folk*, vii.

7. Ginsburg, "Native Daughter," 128.

8. Ginsburg, "View from the Back Step," 198.

9. Holland's experience in Greenwood demonstrates the importance of geography in black girls' mental maps, just as it demonstrates the differences between New Orleans and other segregated cities. In New Orleans, racial spaces were more uneven because poor whites and blacks were closer together, their neighborhoods intermixed. Furthermore, blacks were forced to walk through white sections of the city because of the close proximity of each neighborhood, whereas Holland remembers that "black folks went into the white section of town cautiously, and only during the daylight" in Greenwood. Holland, *From the Mississippi Delta*, 22.

10. Cappie and Cappie interview, June 29, 1994, BV.

11. For example, Rumpf, *Reclamation*; Sancton and Sancton, *Song for My Fathers*.

12. McKittrick, *Demonic Grounds*, xi.

13. See ibid., xiv.

14. Walker, "Growing Out of Shadow," 4.

15. W. Johnson, "Southern City."

16. Boucree interview, BV.

17. Cardinal directions are not used in New Orleans, so when one uses "downtown" as a direction, it literally means toward the northeast. But "downtown" is also used to describe the section of the city northeast of Canal Street.

18. Martinez and Lecorgne, *Uptown/Downtown*, xii.

19. Hunter-Gault, *In My Place*, 7.

20. Holland, *From the Mississippi Delta*, 18.

21. Borders interview, BV.

22. Charles interview, BV.

23. Bouise interview, BV.

24. Bouise's phrasing also revealed the politics of the moment of her interview (the 1990s). Rather than use the term "colored," she paired "Creole" and "American" with "black," although at the outset of her interview she explained that she grew up "colored" and that "black," "African American," and "colored" do not have synonymous meanings. When asked to further explain, she could not quite articulate the different "connotations" of these words, perhaps because the changing nature of the words reflects the changing nature of race and identity over time. In her attempt she did call on history—on the black power movement as a significant moment in (re)defining the word "black," and also a moment that redefined black identity.

25. Allen and Dunbar interview, BV. In *Coming of Age in Mississippi*, Anne Moody writes about all of the rural Mississippians and Louisianans who moved to New Orleans looking (sometimes unsuccessfully) for better work during segregation. She, too, came to New Orleans over the summers looking for work while in high school. Moody, *Coming of Age in Mississippi*, 174.

26. Brown interview.

27. Pajeaud and Moutan interview, BV.

28. Braud and Cherrie interview.

29. I. M. Young, *On Female Body Experience*, 16.

30. Campanella, *Geographies of New Orleans*.

31. Aaron interview, BV.

32. Deggs, Gould, and Nolan, *No Cross, No Crown.*

33. Massaquoi, "St. Mary's Academy," 57.

34. Lucy Semmes Orrick, "Along the Color Line," *National Magazine,* October 1904, 172.

35. Quoted in Guillory, "Under One Roof," 75.

36. Orrick, "Along the Color Line," 172.

37. Early, *New Orleans Holiday,* 185.

38. Hyman and Stuart interview.

39. Early, *New Orleans Holiday,* 197–98.

40. Ibid., 196.

41. Hyman and Stuart interview.

42. Early, *New Orleans Holiday,* 186.

43. Ibid., 196.

44. McKittrick, *Demonic Grounds,* 5.

45. Massaquoi, "St. Mary's Academy," 57.

46. Hyman and Stuart interview.

47. Sister Claire of Assisi Pierre interview.

48. Ibid.; Hyman and Stuart interview.

49. Massaquoi, "St. Mary's Academy," 59.

50. Hyman and Stuart interview.

51. Sister Claire of Assisi Pierre interview.

52. Aaron interview, BV.

53. Ibid.

54. Ibid.

55. Hyman and Stuart interview.

56. Sister Claire of Assisi Pierre interview.

57. Hyman and Stuart interview.

58. The etymology of the name Tchoupitoulas is not precisely known, but folklorists and linguists alike believe it is a derivation of Choctaw meaning "those who live by the stream." Bright, "Native American Place Names"; Federal Writers' Project, *Louisiana,* 541.

59. "Sanborn Map: New Orleans, La.," Sanborn Map Company, 1940, Sanborn Fire Insurance Maps, Historic New Orleans Collection, Williams Research Center, New Orleans.

60. Campanella, *Geographies of New Orleans,* 305.

61. Fifteenth Census of the United States: 1930, April 2, 1930, Orleans Parish, Louisiana, New Orleans City, Ward 12, District 213, Ancestry.com, U.S. Federal Census; ibid., April 16, 1930, District 206.

62. All children's names from the Kingsley Project are pseudonyms. Carolyn Kolb, "Kingsley House: 1896–1996: A Brief History," ca. 1997, www.kingsleyhouse.org.

63. For discussions of "safe spaces" and childhood, see Gutman and Coninck-Smith, *Designing Modern Childhoods.*

64. According to one report, there were 1,700 white school-age children within a half-mile radius of the new project and 450 black children in the same area. Dorothy Spiker to Emeric Kurtagh, "Population Figures in Area of Textile Worker's Hall," January 28, 1946, Kingsley House Papers, Tulane Special Collections (hereafter KHP).

65. Constance Grigsby, "Grigsby Application," 1945, KHP.

66. The narrative of childhood unity is seen not only in my interviews with New Orleans residents but also in the Behind the Veil interviews with New Orleanians. Also

see Ritterhouse, *Growing Up Jim Crow*. This narrative of childhood unity might also be a consequence of the type of people who volunteer for oral history interviews or of the class of the particular people interviewed. In the New Orleans interviews, memories of neighborhood diversity and integration were often contrasted with the aggressive residential segregation associated with the white flight of the civil rights era and the increasing urban decline of the post–civil rights era. Interviewees also used neighborhood diversity to explain how New Orleans was distinct from other southern cities. Sardie interview; Brown interview; Braud and Cherrie interview.

67. Rumpf, *Reclamation*, 187–88.

68. Rumpf interview.

69. Constance Grigsby, "Program Report Kingsley House Extension Project," May 31, 1946, KHP.

70. Ibid.

71. "December 18th Report," December 1946, KHP.

72. Constance Grigsby, "Riverfront Update, June 30–July 6," n.d., KHP.

73. Ibid.

74. Constance Grigsby, "Kingsley House Project, July 15–20," July 20, 1946, KHP.

75. Ibid.

76. Ibid.

77. "Narrative on Negro Girls' Club at Riverfront for October 1946," October 16, 1946, KHP.

78. Ibid.

79. "Evaluation of Summer Program at Kingsley House Extension," August 15, 1947, KHP.

80. I. M. Young, *On Female Body Experience*, 30.

81. "Weekly Summary, Oct. 28–31," October 31, 1946, KHP.

82. "Daily Log, October 1–7," October 1946, KHP; "Riverfront Report, October 12," October 1946, ibid.; "Riverfront Report, 11th–16th," November 1946, ibid.

83. Grigsby, "Riverfront Update, June 30–July 6."

84. See for example, Kelley, "June 30–July 4, 1947," KHP.

85. Grigsby, "Kingsley House Project, July 15–20."

86. Ibid.

87. Kelley's first name is not noted in the Kingsley House documents.

88. Kelley, "June 30–July 4, 1947."

89. Ibid.

90. Ibid.

91. Coombs, "Negro Girls Club Fall [1946] Report," February 1, 1947, KHP.

92. Ibid.

93. For a discussion of childhood, race, and cognitive development of space, see Ginsburg, "View from the Back Step," 193.

94. Ibid., 198.

95. Braud and Cherrie interview; Brown interview; Borders interview, BV; Cappie and Cappie interview, June 29, 1994, BV.

96. "Picnic on Levee Report," November 1946, KHP.

97. Kelley, "Aug 4–8, Weekly Log," August 1947, KHP.

98. "Evaluation of Summer Program at Kingsley House Extension."

99. See McKittrick, *Demonic Grounds*, xiv.

100. "Claiborne Ave Birth's Negro City Park: Sweltering 'Citizens' Stranded on 4th of July," *Louisiana Weekly*, July 5, 1948; see also "More about Recreation for Negroes," *Louisiana Weekly*, July 12, 1948.

101. "NORD Program Report: 'Negro Division,'" 74–75, City of New Orleans, 1952, Commissioner Lionel G. Ott Papers, New Orleans Public Library, Louisiana Division (hereafter NOPL).

102. Ibid.; "America's Finest," *Life*, September 5, 1949.

Chapter Two

1. Reed interview, BV.

2. St. Julien interview, BV.

3. Merrick interview, BV.

4. Aaron interview, BV.

5. Audley (Queen Mother) Moore, interview by Cheryl Townsend Gilkes, June 6, 1978, Black Women's Oral History Project, Schlesinger Library, Radcliffe College.

6. Di Leonardo, "Political Economy of Street Harassment," quoted in Walkowitz, "Going Public," 2.

7. McKittrick, *Demonic Grounds*, 105.

8. My reading here of the unmapped and mapped, as well as of geographic displacements, is influenced by Katherine McKittrick's reading of Dionne Brand's *A Map to the Door of No Return*. In *Demonic Grounds*, McKittrick discusses Brand's work as a way to think through a black female sense of place. McKittrick's reading of Brand emphasizes "conflicting geographic patterns" and the ongoing tensions between "placelessness" *and* black places, between the mapped and the unmapped, and between the unspeakable and speakable. Ibid., 104–6.

9. Caitone interview, BV.

10. Julien, *Travels with Mae*, 7.

11. "Sets New Orleans Aglow," *New York Times*, February 25, 1930.

12. Ibid.

13. "Union Metal Manufacturing Ornamental Lamp Standards," *Saturday Evening Post*, date unknown. from H. George Friedman Collection. http://web.engr.illinois.edu/~friedman/album/Album.htm.

14. The paper and ad both played on words as "The Great Wide Way" (a Canal Street nickname), which became the "White Way."

15. Hunter, *To 'Joy My Freedom*, 98.

16. Merrick interview, BV.

17. "Report on Public Comfort Stations," June 9, 1931, New Orleans Association of Commerce Minutes, Louisiana and Special Collections, Earl K. Long Library, University of New Orleans, quoted in Stanonis, *Creating the Big Easy*, 134.

18. Sociologist Erving Goffman links these types of learning experiences with subjectivity. He argues that stigmatized individuals have "similar learning experiences" leading to "similar changes in conceptions of self." He marks this as a "socialization process" where "the stigmatized person . . . learns that he possesses a particular stigma and, this time in detail, the consequence of possessing it." See Goffman, *Stigma*, 45.

19. St. Julien interview, BV.

20. Brown, "Not Outside the Range," 109.

21. For discussions of memory and trauma, see Morrison, "Site of Memory"; Cvetkovich, *Archive of Feelings*; and Woolfork, *Embodying American Slavery in Contemporary Culture*.

22. Brown, "Not Outside the Range," 100–101.

23. Ibid., 107.

24. Braud and Cherrie interview.

25. Ibid.

26. Aaron interview, BV.

27. Mary Johnson was one of a handful of Behind the Veil interviewees who did not graduate from high school. In fact, most interviewees not only graduated from high school but also attended college. This was true in the interviews I conducted as well.

28. Johnson interview, BV.

29. "White Boys Hit Schoolgirl: Was on Her Way Home When Hit in the Face," *Louisiana Weekly*, April 29, 1939.

30. "Sanborn Map: New Orleans, La.," Sanborn Map Company, 1940, Sanborn Fire Insurance Maps, Historic New Orleans Collection, Williams Research Center, New Orleans.

31. At one time there was an interracial boardinghouse near the college for both black and white educators—presumably for Straight College professors and students. After the college closed its doors, the boardinghouse was converted into apartments occupied by whites.

32. Demographic information from Nellie Gaillard, Fifteenth Census of the United States: 1930 (see chapter 1, n. 61, for census information).

33. "The Lesson From the Clara Slush Case," *Louisiana Weekly*, March 31, 1951.

34. Germany, *New Orleans after the Promises*, 34; Rogers, *Righteous Lives*, 69.

35. Quoted in Laborde and Magill, *Canal Street*, 117.

36. Brown and Kimball, "Mapping the Terrain of Black Richmond," 81, 73.

37. Although there were black-owned businesses on Rampart, the majority were white-owned, an important point when thinking through the paradoxes of black geographic possession and dispossession. Marcus Christian, FWP writer, noted that "South Rampart Street is the 'leading Negro Street' only in the manner in which Negroes congregate there to spend their hard earned money in white-owned businesses." Christian and Federal Writers' Project, "A Black History of Louisiana," chapter 43, p. 7, ca. 1940s, Marcus Christian Papers, Louisiana and Special Collections, Earl K. Long Library, University of New Orleans; "prime black street" from Borders interview, BV.

38. Federal Writers' Project, *New Orleans City Guide*, 343.

39. For information on McKinney, his work with the FWP, and his interviews with black New Orleanians, see Vaz, *"Baby Dolls,"* 10–13.

40. See Federal Writers' Project, *New Orleans City Guide*; Tallant, *Romantic New Orleanians*; Tallant, *Voodoo Queen*; Tallant, *Voodoo in New Orleans*; and Saxon, Tallant, and Works Progress Administration, *Gumbo Ya-Ya*.

41. Vaz, *"Baby Dolls,"* 10–11.

42. McKinney's work for Tallant and Saxon seems much more "salacious" and "titillating" than the FWP work collected, edited, and prepared by black writer and educator Marcus Christian, working at Dillard University. See ibid., 10; and Christian and Federal Writers' Project, "Black History of Louisiana," 43.

43. McKinney, "Mary Davis," December 23, 1938, Robert Tallant Papers, NOPL.

44. Ibid.

45. In "Mapping the Terrain of Black Richmond," Elsa Barkley Brown and Greg Kimball suggest that investigating black geographies brings into view complex identities and self-fashionings (which I name shifting subjectivities). In exploring the "style and some flair" of the "fun-loving" Maggie Lena Walker, they note her complex use of space: "a second-story porch overhanging Leigh Street so she could still engage in street life even while maintaining a respectable distance from the street." Brown and Kimball, "Mapping the Terrain of Black Richmond," 88.

46. Dave interview, BV.

47. Later recordings replace "Colored" with "Creole." For lyrics, see Cox, *Blues for Rampart Street*; Cox, *Ida Cox: Vol. 1, 1923*.

48. Quoted in Rogers, *Righteous Lives*, 6.

49. Dave interview, BV.

50. Reed interview, BV.

51. Borders interview, BV.

52. Saxon, Tallant, and Works Progress Administration, *Gumbo Ya-Ya*, 459.

53. Borders interview, BV.

54. Braud and Cherrie interview.

55. In interview materials, Beverly Carter's aunt is referred to as "Mrs. Green." The 1940 census data show her full name as Pearl Green. Beverly Carter, interview by Thelma Shelby, August 11, 1938, St. Claire Drake Papers, Schomburg Center for Research in Black Culture, New York Public Library (hereafter SCDP); Pearl Green and Velma Green, interview by Thelma Shelby, August 10, 1938, ibid.

56. Charles interview, BV.

57. Ibid.

58. "New Orleans Ministers Condemn 'Juke' Boxes and Open Gambling," *Chicago Defender*, March 29, 1941, national ed.

59. Wilma Miller, "Anthropological Study of Mount Zion M.E. Church," 1936, SCDP.

60. "New Orleans Ministers Condemn 'Juke' Boxes and Open Gambling."

61. Merrick interview, BV.

62. McKittrick explains that paradoxical spaces are not passive spaces. Quoting Gillian Rose, she explains that such places "would be mutually exclusive if charted on a two dimensional map . . . [but are] occupied simultaneously." McKittrick, *Demonic Grounds*, 41.

63. Merrick interview, BV.

64. Ibid.

65. Cappie and Cappie interview, June 29, 1994, BV; Borders interview, BV; Aaron interview, BV.

66. Borders interview, BV.

67. Robertson interview, BV.

68. Long, *Great Southern Babylon*.

69. Pajeaud and Moutan interview.

70. "Rampart Street to Be Ghost of Days Gone," *Chicago Defender*, February 28, 1953.

71. "New Orleans Cleans Up after Betsy," *Baltimore Afro-American*, September 25, 1965.

72. On recent demolition on South Rampart, see Elie, "So Much for Satchmo." On the destruction of black neighborhoods in the name of progress, see Connolly, *World More Concrete*.

73. "13-Year-Old Girl Beaten by White Grocer," *Louisiana Weekly*, February 12, 1944; "Accuse Whites of Abusing Negroes in New Orleans," *Chicago Defender*, March 4, 1944, national ed.

Chapter Three

1. "Homicide Report: Charles Guerand," February 10, 1930, New Orleans Homicide Reports, NOPL.

2. Few scholars have been able to explore the sexual abuse of black girls and women by white men. Only recently have scholars begun to tackle this topic. For new work focused on incidents of sexual violence against women of color, see Rosen, *Terror in the Heart of Freedom*;

and McGuire, *At the Dark End of the Street*. For early foundational attempts to theorize sexual violence against women of color by historians, see Hine, "Rape and the Inner Lives of Black Women"; and J. Hall, "Mind That Burns in Each Body."

3. Amelda Betz, interview by Dorothy Schlessinger, November 26, 1984, Cabildo Oral History Project, NOPL. Kanton name is a pseudonym.

4. "School-Girl Seduced by White Man," *Louisiana Weekly*, March 18, 1933. For other discussions of black girls and sexual violence, see Ritterhouse, *Growing Up Jim Crow*, 198–99, 219–20; Orleck, *Storming Caesar's Palace*, 19–21, 24, 28; Chafe et al., *Remembering Jim Crow*, 8–15; and Shaw, *What a Woman Ought to Be and to Do*, 24–26. Susan Cahn writes about girls who were interviewed by the American Council of Education in the 1930s. These girls were silent about rape but vocal about harassment from white men. Cahn, *Sexual Reckonings*, 111.

5. Holland, *From the Mississippi Delta*, 90.

6. Ibid.

7. Ibid., 90–91.

8. Ibid., 91.

9. For histories of lynching that discuss the sexual and gendered dynamics of violence, see J. Hall, *Revolt against Chivalry*; S. Smith, *Photography on the Color Line*; Dorr, *White Women, Rape, and the Power of Race in Virginia*; Hodes, *White Women, Black Men*; and Hale, *Making Whiteness*.

10. Gilmore, *Gender and Jim Crow*, 91–119.

11. Thomas Dixon, *The Clansman: A Historical Romance of the Ku Klux Klan* (New York: Doubleday, 1905); Griffith, *Birth of a Nation*.

12. Gilmore, *Gender and Jim Crow*, 113.

13. J. Hall, *Revolt against Chivalry*, 156.

14. This type of language, sexualizing black girls, was not exclusive to white men only. William Hannibal Thomas, in *The American Negro*, suggested that incest was the result of poor black women and girls' degeneracy and immodesty within their own home. W. H. Thomas, *American Negro*, 173–207. Also see Michele Mitchell, *Righteous Propagation*, 83, 145–46.

15. Bernstein, *Racial Innocence*, 33.

16. White southerners often referred to grown women as "girls," and they likely would have not made any distinction between working preteens and teenagers and young women.

17. Dollard, *Caste and Class*, 140.

18. Evans, *Silencing of Ruby McCollum*, xxii.

19. JanMohamed, "Sexuality on/of the Racial Border," 103.

20. Ibid.

21. Wells-Barnett, "Southern Horrors," 12.

22. J. Hall, *Revolt against Chivalry*.

23. J. Hall, "Mind That Burns in Each Body," 339.

24. Evans, *Silencing of Ruby McCollum*, 5.

25. Hine, "Rape and the Inner Lives of Black Women."

26. See, for example, the oral history interviews and collected family histories in Judd, *African American Lives* and *African American Lives 2*.

27. See the following Behind the Veil interviews: Aaron; Borders; Cappie and Cappie, June 29, 1994; St. Julien.

28. For further discussion on historical method and black women, rape, and silence, see Hine, "Rape and the Inner Lives of Black Women."

29. Cappie and Cappie interview, July 2, 1994, BV.

30. Ibid.

31. Because I am discussing her request to turn the tape off and the silence that ensued, I have decided to use a pseudonym for this Behind the Veil interview. The initials are consistent. See Regan interview, BV. Like Regan, Anne Moody moved to New Orleans over the summer months during high school looking for better work opportunities. She, too, did not want to work as a domestic laborer, if possible. Initially, she found it difficult to find a decent job in the city. "I hadn't come to New Orleans to do housework. I'd go back home and work for [a family there] first." Moody, *Coming of Age in Mississippi*, 173.

32. Ibid.

33. Her insistence to turn the tape off continued later in the interview when she described the herbs that people used to help fight depression. Ibid.

34. Chafe et al., *Remembering Jim Crow*, 14.

35. Ibid.

36. Ibid. George repeated, "Like I said, she was about nine at the time" twice and gave his age twice, his brother's once, and their collective age as "all under ten" once in his short recounting of the event.

37. In another story, about his house burning down, this same insistence on his age and why he did not go in for his siblings is present. That there is still guilt associated with these memories speaks to the trauma of his childhood. Ibid., 13.

38. Ibid., 8.

39. Ibid., 9.

40. Canning, "Body as Method," 505.

41. Chafe et al., *Remembering Jim Crow*, 9.

42. In fact, Stine George told several stories in which he hid in the woods from whites, as his father had instructed him to do. Ibid., 13.

43. Holland, *From the Mississippi Delta*, 82.

44. JanMohamed, "Sexuality on/of the Racial Border," 101, quoting from Foucault, *History of Sexuality*, 84.

45. Chafe et al., *Remembering Jim Crow*, 9.

46. For an essay on sexual violence as terrorism, see Sheffield, "Sexual Terrorism."

47. "Homicide Report: Charles Guerand"; Matt Piacum, "Statement of Matt A. Piacum," February 10, 1930, New Orleans Homicide Reports, NOPL.

48. "Girl Refused Advances of White Beast," *Louisiana Weekly*, February 15, 1930.

49. The surnames of the jurors suggest some ethnic variation, including Spanish, but it is safe to say that all of these men were considered white in the local New Orleans community.

50. Hart appears in the class photo on the cover of this book; she is fourth from the right in the top row. In 2007, when I interviewed Marie Boyer Brown, a classmate of Hart's, I asked her about Hattie McCray and Charles Guerand. Brown did not recall Guerand's case. When I told her about it, she seemed surprised and disheartened. This strikes me as a purposeful or protective forgetting, given how well Brown remembered other details from her childhood, and, perhaps, speaks to the trauma of growing up Jim Crow. For Hart's letter, see Althea Hart to W. E. B. Du Bois, February 11, 1930, Papers of the NAACP, Part 12: Selected Branch Files, 1913–1939, Series A: The South, Microform Collections, Duke University.

51. Charles Guerand, "Statement of Charles Guerand," February 10, 1930, New Orleans Homicide Reports, NOPL.

52. "Homicide Report: Charles Guerand"; Guerand, "Statement of Charles Guerand"; Piacum, "Statement of Matt A. Piacum."

53. Fairclough, *Race and Democracy*, 5–20; Long, *Great Southern Babylon*, 11–13. For a discussion of color line crossing, see Guillory, "Under One Roof"; and Thompson, " 'Ah Toucoutou.' "

54. Hirsch and Logsdon, *Creole New Orleans*, 174–85, 250–51, 253–54.

55. Long, *Great Southern Babylon*, 10; Hirsch and Logsdon, *Creole New Orleans*, 183.

56. Quoted in Somerville, *Queering the Color Line*, 35; from "Editorial," *New Orleans Times Democrat*, July 9, 1890.

57. "Guerand Charity Hospital Record," n.d., State v. Guerand, NOPL; "Coroner's Report," n.d., State v. Guerand, ibid.

58. "Negro Girl, 14, Slain in Cafe by Patrolman," *New Orleans Times-Picayune*, February 11, 1930.

59. "Girl's Slayer Faces Charge," *New Orleans States*, February 11, 1930.

60. "Homicide Report: Charles Guerand."

61. Kristeva, *Powers of Horror*, 1–8.

62. See ibid., 2, 4.

63. Bernstein, *Racial Innocence*, 35.

64. For a discussion on the disavowal of pain, see Scarry, *Body in Pain*, 60.

65. "The Guerand Verdict," *New Orleans States*, April 15, 1930.

66. Ibid.

67. Afro-American papers throughout the South, as well as national papers, frequently discussed abuse against African Americans by police officers. In the *Louisiana Weekly*, see, for example, "Accused of Speeding, Is 'Beat Up,' " February 22, 1930; Schott, "Letter Sent White Press on Killings," March 29, 1930; and "All White Jury Frees Policeman for Raping Negro Girl," February 2, 1946. Also see "Two Colored Girls Assaulted by Texas Police," *Union*, August 14, 1920: "After raping and outraging these two young girls these two 'peace officers' carried the girls back to their escorts." The officers threatened to "kill them" if they told anyone.

68. Jessie Daniel Ames (1931), quoted in J. Hall, *Revolt against Chivalry*, xxvii.

69. "Girl Refused Advances of White Beast."

70. Ibid.

71. For a discussion of lynching scripts, see Hale, *Making Whiteness*, 199–240.

72. "Indict Cop for Murder of New Orleans Girl," *Chicago Defender*, March 8, 1930.

73. "Gallows for Girl's Slayer," *Pittsburgh Courier*, April 12, 1930, 8.

74. Bryan, "Marcus Christian's Treatment"; Fairclough, *Race and Democracy*, 18–19, 72–73; Hirsch, "Creole New Orleans," 266.

75. For example, see the following from the *Louisiana Weekly*: "Landry School Crowns Queen and King," January 7, 1939, Society: Of Interest to Women sec.; Norman Holmes, "Cause of Doubt and Despondency and Their Dissolution: Weekly Sermon," February 22, 1930; Nannie Burroughs, "Why Negroes Have 'Most Nigh Ruint' Their Dispositions," March 1, 1930.

76. Higginbotham, *Righteous Discontent*, 186.

77. Michele Mitchell, *Righteous Propagation*, 85. On "respectability" see also Higginbotham, *Righteous Discontent*; White, *Too Heavy a Load*; Gaines, *Uplifting the Race*; and Wolcott, *Remaking Respectability*.

78. Carby, "Policing the Black Woman's Body."

79. "Civic Bodies Raising Funds," *Louisiana Weekly*, February 22, 1930. In a 2009 article, "Justice Mocked," I argue for the need to understand the gendered dynamics of respectability as it relates to this case. For consideration of the political and civil rights ramifications of the

case, including the work of the Federation of Civic Leagues, see Coffey's 2013 article, "*State of Louisiana v. Charles Guerand.*"

80. "Service Men Seek Freedom for Girl in LA State Pen," *Louisiana Weekly*, February 24, 1945.

81. English, "W. E. B. Du Bois's Family Crisis."

82. Ibid., 300.

83. Ibid., 311.

84. Du Bois was editor of the *Crisis* until 1934. See covers of the *Crisis*, 1930–45.

85. Ivy Lenoir, "Defending Her Honor," *Louisiana Weekly*, February 22, 1930.

86. See "Ivy [misspelled in database as Inez] Lenoir" Year: 1940; Census Place: St. Ferdinand, St. Louis, Missouri; Roll: T627_2154; Page: 62A; Enumeration District: 95-307. Database: Ancestry.com; Ivy Anita LeNoir, *Sursum Corda (Lift Up Your Hearts)* (Gainesville, FL: Naylor Company, January 1, 1973); "Generous Donation," *Jet Magazine*, September 27, 1999; "Our Foundress: Elise Lenoir Morris," *The Drexel Society*. Accessed on November 12, 2014, http://drexelsociety.org/elise_lenoir_morris.htm.

87. Walkowitz, *City of Dreadful Delight*, 11.

88. "Cop to Die for Girl Slaying," *Chicago Defender*, April 12, 1930.

89. Ibid.

90. "Coroner's Report."

91. "Service Men Seek Freedom for Girl in LA State Pen."

92. For courtroom narrative see Coffey, "*State of Louisiana v. Charles Guerand,*" 74–90.

93. "Cop to Die for Girl Slaying."

94. Ibid.; "Indict Cop for Murder of New Orleans Girl." How long Hattie had been out of school is unclear, but Hattie McCray's mother, Moorelilli McCray, had only completed fourth grade. She had her first child at age nineteen in 1911. By 1920 Moorelilli was widowed with three daughters, Margell, Helen, and Hattie, the youngest. By 1930, Moorelilli had remarried, and she and her oldest daughter both worked in the homes of white families. But two months after Hattie McCray's death, when the census taker came to their home, Helen McCray was briefly back in school. Hattie and Helen's struggles to stay in school demonstrate just how difficult it was for black girls during segregation and the Depression to continue in school. The 1940 census shows Moorelilli using the last name McCray again and listed as head of household. She lived with one of her daughters, Helen, and a granddaughter. According to that census, Helen (McCray) Barton had completed eighth grade and had her daughter when she was nineteen years old. There are various spellings of Hattie McCray's mother's given name. For family information, see "Hattie McCray" 1920: Census Place: New Orleans Ward 3; Orleans, Louisiana; Roll: T625_619; Page: 1A; Enumeration District: 54; Image: 389. Database: Ancestry.com; "Helen McCray" 1930: Census Place: New Orleans Ward 3; Orleans, Louisiana; Roll: 801; Page: 8A; ED: 0029; Image: 721.0: FHl: microfilm: 2340563. Database: Ancestry.com; "Helen Barton" 1940; Census Place: New Orleans Ward 3; Orleans, Louisiana; Roll: T625_619; Page: 1A; Enumeration District: 54; Image: 389. Database: Ancestry.com; "Moorelilli McCray," United States Social Security Death Index. Number: 439-26-4024; Issue State: Louisiana; Issue Date: Before 1951.

95. The *Chicago Defender* article "Cop to Die for Girl Slaying" says, "According to the traditions of the South, a white man's life may not be taken in return for the life of one of our group. It is an unwritten law which is generally upheld by the people and one which has caused white men to kill with impunity, so long as their victims were of the darker races." For white reaction, see "Policeman Seeking Lunacy Board Aid," *New Orleans Times-Picayune*, April 22, 1930; "Begin Fight to Save Ex-cop from Noose," *New Orleans States*, n.d.

96. "Begin Fight to Save Ex-cop from Noose."

97. "Motion H-1," n.d., State v. Guerand, NOPL.

98. Quoted in Hunter, *To 'Joy My Freedom*, 215.

99. Michele Mitchell, *Righteous Propagation*, 81–83.

100. "Emile Guerand Death Certificate," n.d., NOPL; "Affidavit," n.d., State v. Guerand, ibid.

101. Holmes, "Will the Negro Survive in the North?," 560.

102. Dublin, "Health of the Negro," 79.

103. "Motion H-1."

104. "Petition #3," April 28, 1930, State v. Guerand, NOPL. Emphasis mine.

105. "August 27, 1935," State v. Guerand, NOPL.

106. Charles H. Houston to James Gayle, March 10, 1936, Papers of the NAACP, Part 12: Selected Branch Files, Series A: The South, Microform Collection, Duke University.

107. Fred Oser, "March 2, 1937," State v. Guerand, NOPL.

108. "Slayer of Colored Girl Escapes Noose," *Louisiana Weekly*, March 6, 1937.

109. "August 27, 1935."

110. Ibid. My emphasis. It should be noted that at this point a new judge was assigned to Guerand's case because Judge Henriques passed away before Guerand's trial could be heard again.

111. Young, "Abjection and Oppression," 208.

112. "Justice Mocked," *Louisiana Weekly*, March 1, 1937. For more on how this case relates to African Americans, race, and justice, see Simmons, " 'Justice Mocked.' "

113. Leon Lewis, "Slayer of Girl, 14, Wins Pardon after Escaping Electric Chair," *Atlanta Daily World*, April 25, 1938.

114. Ibid.

Chapter Four

1. Campanella, *Geographies of New Orleans*, 334, 373, 374, 376.

2. Jenkins interview, BV.

3. Bouise interview, BV.

4. Davis and Dollard, *Children of Bondage*, 173.

5. American Youth Commission, "A Proposal for a Study of Negro Youth," October 1936, 1, 3, American Council on Education, Hoover Institute, Stanford University (hereafter ACE).

6. American Youth Commission, "Activities of the American Youth Commission," October 12, 1936, 1, ACE.

7. Allison Davis, "Comments on Criticisms of Davis-Dollard Typoscript Transmitted by Dr. Sutherland," December 1939, ACE.

8. Robert Sutherland, "Revision of Prospects Worked Out at the Chicago Meeting of Negro Youth Study," n.d., ACE.

9. Other minor studies were also published, but the NYS led to "Four Principal Reports"; see Robert Sutherland, "Report of Progress on Negro Youth Study of the American Youth Commission," n.d., ACE. The other two published manuscripts were Frazier, *Negro Youth at the Crossways*; and Reid, *In a Minor Key*.

10. McKee, *Sociology and the Race Problem*, 182.

11. Lief, Thompson, and Thompson, *Eighth Generation Grows Up*.

12. Not all of the children's interviews have survived, but some can be found in the Allison Davis Papers, Special Collections Research Center, University of Chicago Library (hereafter ADP), and others in the SCDP.

13. These interviews are exceptional sources for both childhood history and African American gender history. Rarely are girls' daily concerns so carefully recorded and preserved in the archive.

14. Ellen Hill, interview by Elizabeth Davis, May 2, 1938, ADP.

15. For important works on the subject of black women's sexuality and respectability during the early twentieth century, see Michele Mitchell, *Righteous Propagation*; Higginbotham, *Righteous Discontent*; White, *Too Heavy a Load*; Gaines, *Uplifting the Race*; Wolcott, *Remaking Respectability*; Carby, "Policing the Black Woman's Body"; Carby, *Reconstructing Womanhood*; duCille, *Coupling Convention*; Gilmore, *Gender and Jim Crow*; and Hine, "Rape and the Inner Lives of Black Women."

16. Shaw, *What a Woman Ought to Be and to Do*, 24.

17. Michele Mitchell, *Righteous Propagation*, 85.

18. Beverly Carter, "I Have Always Been Influenced," ca. 1938, SCDP.

19. Beverly Carter, "What Would You Do," ca. 1938, SCDP.

20. Shaw, "Using the WPA Ex-slave Narratives," 637.

21. Smith and Watson, *Reading Autobiography*, 52.

22. Maynes, Pierce, and Laslett, *Telling Stories*, 4.

23. See Heap, "City as a Sexual Laboratory," 475.

24. On life history data presented in social worker case records, Regina Kunzel has warned that "case records often reveal as much, if not more, about those conducting the interview as they do about those interviewed." Kunzel, "Pulp Fictions," 1468. At the same time, Stephanie Shaw has pointed out the importance of listening to the voices of interviewees even in "flawed" conditions. On using WPA interviews, Shaw noted scholars' hesitance to use WPA life narratives because of "concerns about the power dynamics of the interview process, the competence of the interviewers, and the advanced age of the informants that led to . . . discomfort with the narratives as sources. And although most scholars of slavery writing during and since . . . chose to use the narratives, they did point out that the documents were, in some ways, flawed." Shaw, "Using the WPA Ex-slave Narratives," 625, 637. For further discussions of methodological approaches to reading life narratives, see Kunzel, "Pulp Fictions," 1468–73; Smith and Watson, *Reading Autobiography*; Hicks, " 'Bright and Good Looking Colored Girl' "; and R. Williams, "I'm a Keeper of Information."

25. For a discussion of the Chicago School methodology and life narratives, see Simmons, " 'To Lay Aside All Morals.' "

26. Hillis, "Allison Davis," 34; "Black Heritage Award for an African-American Educator."

27. Hillis, "Allison Davis," 34.

28. "Allison Davis, 1902–1983," *University of Chicago Centennial Catalogues*, accessed September 9, 2008. http://www.lib.uchicago.edu/e/spcl/centcat/fac/facch25_01.html.

29. "Guide to the Allison Davis Papers, 1932–1984: Biographical Note," n.d., ADP.

30. Davis and Dollard, *Children of Bondage*, xi.

31. "Allison Davis, 1902–1983"; Hillis, "Allison Davis," 34.

32. Ross, *Manning the Race*, 166–67; Lindstrom, Hardert, and Young, "Kimball Young on the Chicago School," 298; Simmons, " 'To Lay Aside All Morals' "; McKee, *Sociology and the Race Problem*.

33. McKee, *Sociology and the Race Problem*, 197.

34. Davis and Dollard, *Children of Bondage*, 7, 10, 263.

35. Dennis, "Review."

36. Adams and Gorton, "Southern Trauma," 335.

37. "Guide to John Dollard Research Papers," n.d., John Dollard Research Files for *Fear and Courage under Battle Conditions*, Tamiment Library and Robert F. Wagner Labor Archives, New York University.

38. Dollard's method of researching racial problems in the United States came directly from this psychological approach and is clear in articles such as "Culture, Society, Impulse, and Socialization."

39. Interview reprinted in Ferris and Dollard, "John Dollard," 7.

40. Ibid., 11.

41. Ibid., 17.

42. Quoted in McKee, *Sociology and the Race Problem*, 169.

43. Brewer, "Review," 114.

44. Ferris and Dollard, "John Dollard," 17.

45. Davis, "Comments on Criticisms," 1.

46. Ross, *Manning the Race*, 147.

47. Cottrell, "Review."

48. Ross, *Manning the Race*, 147.

49. Mordecai Johnson to Reeves, December 12, 1939, ACE.

50. C. S. Johnson, *Growing Up in the Black Belt*, 316.

51. Davis and Dollard, *Children of Bondage*, 122.

52. Ibid., 23–25.

53. Ibid., 23.

54. Ibid.

55. Ibid., 26–27, 38, 40.

56. Ibid., 40.

57. Ibid., 27, 40.

58. Ibid., 40.

59. Ibid., 27. They say, "There are even more puzzling aspects of Julia's behavior than her fear of accidents, sickness and sexual attack. . . . [She] displays behavior which is often childlike, almost infantile."

60. Jeanne Manuel, interview by Claude Haydel, August 2, 1938, ADP.

61. Ellen Hill, interview by Elizabeth Davis, June 7, 1938, ADP.

62. Davis and Dollard, *Children of Bondage*, 41.

63. Ibid., 43.

64. Ibid., 36.

65. Ibid., 24.

66. Bourke, "Fear and Anxiety."

67. Rosenwein, "Worrying about Emotions in History."

68. Elizabeth Davis, "Abstract of Interviews with Ellen Hill," 1938, ADP.

69. Ellen Hill, interview by Elizabeth Davis, June 15, 1938, ADP.

70. Ibid., May 12, 1938.

71. Hunter, *To 'Joy My Freedom*, 168. In fact whites were also concerned with what their girls were up to in their spare time. One letter to the editor in a Louisiana paper suggested that youth were drawn into vice by dancing and drinking at beer gardens. This letter was signed by an "anxious parent." See "Expressing the Public Mind: Letters to the Editor," *New Orleans Times Picayune*, August 4, 1936, Letters to the Editor sec. For an earlier discussion of white fears of dance halls, see also Peiss, *Cheap Amusements*.

72. "Problems of Youth the Same," *Louisiana Weekly*, May 20, 1939, Editorials sec.

73. Frumkin, "Expected versus Actual Social Behavior," 197–200.

74. Hill interview, May 2, 1938.

75. Ellen Hill, interview by Elizabeth Davis, March 28, 1938, ADP.

76. Davis and Dollard defined class in a complicated manner. They identified six social classes in black New Orleans society: lower-lower, upper-lower, lower-middle, middle-middle, upper-middle, and upper class. According to Davis and Dollard, "The sociologist identifies [the classes] and describes the forms of behavior which their members have in common. It is the community itself, however, not the sociologists, which classifies the inhabitants into social levels. . . . The people of any community ask only one question to determine an individual's class position, namely, '*Whom does he associate with?*'" See Davis and Dollard, *Children of Bondage*, 13, 256–62.

77. Ibid., 265.

78. Mrs. Hill, interview by Elizabeth Davis, May 30, 1938, ADP.

79. Ibid.

80. Davis and Dollard, *Children of Bondage*, 56.

81. Ibid., 54.

82. Ibid., 64.

83. Ibid.

84. Ibid.

85. Ibid.

86. Ellen Hill, interview by Elizabeth Davis, July 6, 1938, ADP.

87. Ibid., April 11, 1938.

88. Ibid., July 6, 1938.

89. Davis and Dollard, *Children of Bondage*, 52.

90. See Feldstein, *Motherhood in Black and White*, 40–61; and Mitchell, *Righteous Propagation*.

91. Feldstein, *Motherhood in Black and White*, "Racism as Un-American" chapter.

92. Ibid., 57.

93. Hill interview, May 2, 1938.

94. Ibid., March 28, 1938.

95. "Clinic Administration Record," May 20, 1939, ADP.

96. See Hill interview, July 6, 1938; Mrs. Greene, interview by Elizabeth Davis, May 17, 1938, ADP.

97. Hill interview, July 6, 1938.

98. Ibid.

99. Grandmother and mother's names are pseudonyms.

100. Mrs. Greene interview.

101. Mrs. Hill, interview by Elizabeth Davis, October 13, 1938, ADP.

102. Hill interview, March 28, 1938.

103. Ellen Hill, interview by Elizabeth Davis, May 18, 1938, ADP.

104. See Ritterhouse, *Growing Up Jim Crow*, 108–42.

105. Hill interview, March 28, 1938.

106. Ibid.

107. Ellen Hill, interview by Elizabeth Davis, August 4, 1938, ADP.

108. Lief, Thompson, and Thompson, *Eighth Generation Grows Up*, 296, 187.

109. Jeanne Manuel, interview by Claude Haydel, August 17, 1938, ADP.

110. Ibid.

111. Davis and Dollard, *Children of Bondage*, 153.

112. Ibid., 152.

113. Age calculated from C. Haydel, "New Orleans, Louisiana," Fifteenth Census of the United States, 1930 (Washington, D.C.: National Archives and Records Administration, 1930), http://search.ancestry.com/cgi-bin/sse.dll?indiv=1&db=1930usfedcen&recid=37552947.

114. B. Haydel, *Victor Haydel Creole Family*, 55; Emanuel and Tureaud, *More Noble Cause*, 77, 119.

115. Claude Haydel, "Jeanne Manuel Abstract," 1938, ADP.

116. Manuel interview, August 2, 1938.

117. Broyard, *One Drop*, 297–99.

118. Jeanne Manuel, interview by Claude Haydel, June 20, 1938, ADP.

119. Ibid.

120. Jeanne Manuel, interview by Elizabeth Davis, June 16, 1938, ADP.

121. Jeanne Manuel, interview by Claude Haydel, June 20, 1938, ADP.

122. Ibid.

123. Ibid.

124. Ibid., June 7, 1938.

125. Ibid., July 14, 1938.

126. Ibid., June 7, 1938.

127. Ibid., August 17, 1938.

128. Ellen Hill, interview by Elizabeth Davis, August 1, 1938, ADP.

129. Gaudin, "Autocrats and All Saints"; McPherson, "Creole Women of Color"; D. Smith, *New Orleans 7th Ward*; E. Alexander, *Lyrics of Sunshine and Shadow*.

130. Jeanne Manuel, interview by Claude Haydel, May 18, 1938, ADP.

131. Ibid., June 27, 1938.

132. Ibid., August 15, 1938.

133. Ibid., August 17, 1938.

134. Ibid.

135. Ibid., May 24, 1938.

136. Davis and Dollard, *Children of Bondage*, 153.

137. Connolly, *World More Concrete*.

138. Crutcher, *Tremé*, 60.

139. D. Smith, *New Orleans 7th Ward*, 1.

140. B. Anderson, *Cherished Memories*, xviii.

141. Trethewey, *Beyond Katrina*, 88.

142. Ibid.

Chapter Five

1. "Interpreters Give Intimate View of Chest Agencies," *New Orleans Times-Picayune*, August 29, 1937.

2. Addams interview.

3. D. Smith, *New Orleans 7th Ward*, 46.

4. Lilli Braud, conversation with LaKisha Simmons, November 16, 2008.

5. Solinger, *Wake Up Little Susie*, 104.

6. See Cahn, *Sexual Reckonings*, 68–70. Tennessee had biracial state reform homes, but the House of the Good Shepherd in Memphis was white only. See Trost, *Gateway to Justice*, 35, 136–37. In 1940 three House of the Good Shepherd locations served both black and white girls,

yet the New Orleans location was the only one in the segregated South (the other two were in Carthage, Ohio, and Peekskill, New York). Three other Houses of the Good Shepherd were colored only (in Baltimore, Maryland; Louisville, Kentucky; and Germantown, Pennsylvania). See Gillard, *Colored Catholics*, 227.

7. See Trost, *Gateway to Justice*, 35, 136–37; W. I. Thomas, "Unadjusted Girl," 108.

8. "Will Aid in Care of Delinquents," *New Orleans Times-Picayune*, March, 29, 1949; "School for Delinquents Crowded, Busy," *New Orleans Item*, May 6, 1951. Susan Cahn explores Afro-American struggles to obtain delinquency homes for black girls in the South; see Cahn, *Sexual Reckonings*, 68–97.

9. For numbers, see *Official Catholic Directory: Anno Domini 1930* and *Official Catholic Directory: Anno Domini 1954*. See also Sister Mary of St. Raymond to Most Reverend Jos. F. Rummel, December 21, 1950, House of the Good Shepherd Papers, Archdiocese of New Orleans (hereafter HGSP).

10. The story of the home provides a significant revision to the historiography of female moral reform, female delinquency, and the history of wayward (or fallen) young women. Understanding the historiography in relation to the House of the Good Shepherd highlights the importance of the struggles between the church and the professionalization of city officials. Typically, feminist scholars concerned with "delinquent" or "wayward" young women have focused on the historical shifts between four distinct periods in American history: moral reform movements of the mid- to late nineteenth-century, the Progressive Era and its aftermath, the era of the Great Depression, and post–World War II. For discussions of these periodizations, see Gordon, *Heroes of Their Own Lives*; Smith-Rosenberg, *Disorderly Conduct*; Ryan, *Women in Public*; Odem, *Delinquent Daughters*; Solinger, *Wake Up Little Susie*; Hicks, *Talk with You Like a Woman*; and Devlin, *Relative Intimacy*.

11. "The Good Shepherd," *Catholic Louisiana*, 1909; Roger Baudier, "Convent of the Good Shepherd, New Orleans, Louisiana," ca. 1924, Roger Baudier Historical Collection, Archdiocese of New Orleans.

12. Sister Mary of St. Terese, "At the Raffle, for the Benefit of the Convent of Good Shepherd," *New Orleans Times*, January 21, 1866.

13. Thomy Lafon, a black Creole businessman and philanthropist, left $20,000 to the institution after his death in 1893. The money was used to construct an additional brick building for the convent. "Lafon Home," *Daily States*, New Orleans, November 10, 1896; "Archdiocese of New Orleans Institutions Annual Report," 1942, HGSP.

14. During the Progressive Era, New Orleans established the most notorious vice district in 1897: Storyville. Storyville was closed during World War I. Long, *Great Southern Babylon*, 106–7.

15. Enstad, *Ladies of Labor*, 170, 179.

16. Odem, *Delinquent Daughters*, 14, 36–37.

17. Ibid., 14, 36.

18. Hicks, *Talk with You Like a Woman*; Chatelain, *South Side Girls*; Carby, "Policing the Black Woman's Body."

19. Reese, "A Study of the Social and Economic Factors."

20. "Memorandum of Conference Held at the Convent of the Good Shepherd," July 18, 1941, HGSP.

21. On female moral authority and "authoritarian domesticity," see Ryan, *Women in Public*, 101–2.

22. On "maternal justice" and female judges in the Progressive Era, see Odem, *Delinquent Daughters*, 128–56; and Trost, *Gateway to Justice*.

23. "Memorandum of Conference Held at the Convent of the Good Shepherd."

24. Sister Mary Bernard to Most Reverend Jos. F. Rummel, April 15, 1943, HGSP.

25. J. Jacobi, "Summary of Cases and Action Taken by Judge Levy in Juvenile Court, April 1942."

26. Levy, *Other People's Children*, 278.

27. "Memorandum of Conference Held at the Convent of the Good Shepherd."

28. The shifts in the Sisters' methods over this period do not fit neatly with the trajectory of reform schools and maternity homes familiar to the historiography. For example, see Odem, *Delinquent Daughters*; and Solinger, *Wake Up Little Susie*.

29. Homer and Abbott, *Juvenile Court Laws in the United States*, 43. "Fallen" was the popular term in the nineteenth century. But as early as the 1890s, the Sisters of the Good Shepherd were beginning to use the term "wayward." "Wayward" was often used in the local paper through the 1930s but was sometimes used even in the 1940s. "Delinquent" was commonly used in the popular press in the 1940s and 1950s. John Delaney, "Catholic Reformatory Agencies," 1897, National Conference on Social Welfare Proceedings Papers, University of Michigan Digital Library Text Collection; "Interpreters Give Intimate View of Chest Agencies"; "Juvenile Delinquency and Inadequate Recreational Facilities," *Louisiana Weekly*, July 2, 1947.

30. Goffman, *Stigma*, 16–17. To be a stigmatized individual means to have "an attribute that is deeply discrediting." See ibid., 19.

31. For a discussion of the southern "girl problem" see Cahn, *Sexual Reckonings*, 4–5. For a discussion of early twentieth-century youth problems, see, for example, Odem, *Delinquent Daughters*; R. Alexander, *"Girl Problem"*; and Fass, *Damned and the Beautiful*.

32. Goffman, *Stigma*, 58–64.

33. A. Davis, "Socialization of the American Negro Child and Adolescent," 266–67.

34. "Youth, Crime, and Squalid Homes," *Louisiana Weekly*, March 6, 1937.

35. For a sensationalized novel (written by a white male writer) that explores the supposed links between slums, aberrant sexuality, delinquency, and race, see I. S. Young, *Jadie Greenway*.

36. Jackson, "Community Organization Activities," 66.

37. See Michele Mitchell, *Righteous Propagation*, 141–72.

38. "Indifference Aids Delinquency Rate," *New York Amsterdam News*, July 8, 1944.

39. "Youngsters in Droves Are Straying from 'Straight and Narrow' Path, Officers Find," *Louisiana Weekly*, March 17, 1951.

40. Goffman, *Stigma*, 58–64.

41. For example, Mason, "Community Organization Activities among Negroes," 71.

42. "House of the Good Shepherd Building Fund," ca. 1955, HGSP. For examples of crimes, see "Arrest, Fine, 64 at Mixed Youth Party in New Orleans," *Chicago Defender*, February 19, 1949; and "Camp St. Yields Child B-Drinker," *New Orleans Item*, October 29, 1949.

43. This is true for the period of my study. However, the policy may have been different in the nineteenth century. A. Miller, "Study of the Convent of the Good Shepherd in New Orleans," 86.

44. I can deduce the youths' race if they were later sent to a segregated institution. These estimates are calculated based on a small sample of cases seen in juvenile court in April 1942 and July 1940–July 1941. See J. Jacobi, "Summary of Cases and Action Taken by Judge Levy in Juvenile Court, April 1942"; J. Jacobi, "Cases Heard in Juvenile Court from July 1, 1940–July 1, 1941: Judge Nix"; and J. Jacobi, "Cases Heard in Juvenile Court from July 1, 1940–July 1, 1941: Judge Wingrave," all in HGSP.

45. See, for example, J. Jacobi, "Cases Heard in Juvenile Court from July 1, 1940–July 1, 1941: Judge Wingrave."

46. J. Jacobi, "Cases Heard in Juvenile Court from July 1, 1940–July 1, 1941: Judge Nix"; J. Jacobi, "Cases Heard in Juvenile Court from July 1, 1940–July 1, 1941: Judge Wingrave."

47. Washington, *Medical Apartheid*, 161; Brandt, "AIDS in Historical Perspective," 426–34.

48. Leslie, "Delinquent," 1300–1301; Weldon, "Psychiatric Studies of Delinquents"; V. Anderson, "Immoral Woman as Seen in Court."

49. J. Jacobi, "Cases Heard in Juvenile Court from July 1, 1940–July 1, 1941: Judge Wingrave."

50. Washington, *Medical Apartheid*, 157–215.

51. Spitzer, "What of the Negro Future?," 282.

52. All girls' names associated with House of the Good Shepherd are pseudonyms, unless otherwise noted. Here, Dorothy Jackson and Vivian Thomas are actual names.

53. Names and father's location changed. Reese, "Study of the Social and Economic Factors," 35–36.

54. "What's Become of Arnold Jackson and Trial for Attempted Murder?," *Louisiana Weekly*, July 5, 1947; "Daughter Still Missing, Police Continue Search," ibid., July 6, 1946.

55. "What's Become of Arnold Jackson and Trial for Attempted Murder?"

56. Ibid.

57. Ibid.

58. "Man Kills Wife, Tries to Cremate Four Children," *New Orleans States*, June 5, 1951; "Confesses on Death Bed," *Louisiana Weekly*, June 9, 1957.

59. H. Jos. Jacobi to Most Reverend Jos. F. Rummel, June 25, 1942; J. Jacobi, "Cases Heard in Juvenile Court from July 1, 1940–July 1, 1941: Judge Nix"; J. Jacobi, "Cases Heard in Juvenile Court from July 1, 1940–July 1, 1941: Judge Wingrave."

60. H. Jacobi to Rummel, June 25, 1942.

61. J. Jacobi, "Cases Heard in Juvenile Court from July 1, 1940–July 1, 1941: Judge Wingrave."

62. Ibid.

63. "School-Girl Seduced by White Man," *Louisiana Weekly*, March 18, 1933.

64. Michael DeHart to A. P. Tureaud, February 28, 1949, A. P. Tureaud Papers, Amistad Research Center, Tulane University.

65. Campanella, *Geographies of New Orleans*, 311.

66. DeHart to Tureaud, February 28, 1949.

67. Robert S. Browne, "62 to Appeal 'Interracial Party' Verdict: Judge Metes Out $5 Fine or 5 Days in 'Midnight-to-Dawn' Court Trial," *Louisiana Weekly*, February 12, 1949.

68. Diamond, *Compromised Campus*, 32, 61; Beveridge, *Domestic Diversity*, 72–74; L. Moore, *Carl B. Stokes and the Rise of Black Political Power*, 15; Ides, "Cruising for Community," 178–79; Horne, *Black and Red*, 13.

69. "Raided Inter-Racial Party Leads to $5 Fines for 64," *New Orleans Times-Picayune*, February 8, 1949.

70. "Record of Arrest," February 6, 1949, New Orleans Police Department: Arrest Records, 1881–1966, microfilm, NOPL.

71. Mohr and Gordon, *Tulane*, 80.

72. DeHart to Tureaud, February 28, 1949.

73. Ibid.

74. Browne, "62 to Appeal 'Interracial Party' Verdict."

75. DeHart to Tureaud, February 28, 1949; "64 Arrested, Fined $5 After Mixed Party Raid," *Baltimore Afro-American*, February 26, 1949.

76. Browne, "62 to Appeal 'Interracial Party' Verdict."

77. Dailey, "Sex, Segregation, and the Sacred after Brown."

78. Browne, "62 to Appeal 'Interracial Party' Verdict."

79. Although the records are not clear on this point, it appears that the Sisters detained black girls for short periods of time for the juvenile court. If there were enough rooms, it is likely that they were housed separately from other wards. See "House of the Good Shepherd Building Fund."

80. Gwendolyn Midlo Hall to Jari Honora, "Re: Creole Research," January 31, 2009.

81. Here, I am working with Julia Kristeva's notion of a religious subject. Kristeva, when sketching out a religious subjectivity, variously calls it a "Christian consciousness," "Christic subjectivity," and "evangelical attitude." See Kristeva, *Powers of Horror*, 113, 118.

82. Gillard, *Colored Catholics*, 20, 140; Fussell, "Constructing New Orleans, Constructing Race."

83. Tardy, *Light Will Rise in Darkness*, 65.

84. On the other hand, the mother figures, such as Mother Delille and the Virgin Mary, reinforced lessons specific to chastity and right conduct.

85. The Orleans Parish did not have any black priests until the 1950s. Fairclough, *Race and Democracy*, 7.

86. Tardy, *Light Will Rise in Darkness*, 87–88.

87. Charles interview, BV; see also Borders interview, BV.

88. Charles interview, BV; Borders interview, BV.

89. "The Good Shepherd."

90. This model of secrecy and silence harkens back to turn-of-the-century female moral reform movements and was held up in the House of the Good Shepherd from that time into the 1950s. See "Interpreters Give Intimate View of Chest Agencies"; "House of the Good Shepherd Building Fund." As Joan Jacobs Brumberg has noted, the Florence Crittenton maternity home also renamed the girls in their care. Dr. Kate Waller Barrett wrote, "We try to impress upon our girls the fact that they must not discuss their fall with anyone; that if someone should ask them anything in regard to their past life they should say with quiet dignity: 'I have had a great deal of trouble in my life and it only brings up painful memories to discuss the subject.'" See Brumberg, "'Ruined' Girls," 251.

91. Roger Baudier, "Convent of the Good Shepherd," Roger Baudier Historical Collection, Archdiocese of New Orleans.

92. The Convent of the Good Shepherd was not the only delinquency home, particularly in post–World War II America, that worked to reconstruct identities. The methods of maternity homes and delinquency homes across the nation used a postwar notion of "fluidity of personal identity" to give worthy girls a chance to obtain a new life through the adoption of middle-class mores. Rickie Solinger argues that white girls in particular were given the opportunity to reconstruct themselves. I would argue that there were certainly spaces where this was true for black girls as well—particularly in Catholic Louisiana, where the black community had long been divided by class (and ethnicity). Besides the House of the Good Shepherd, an important space of self-refashioning according to notions of class was the black schools—both Catholic and public. See Solinger, *Wake Up Little Susie*, 105.

93. Roger Baudier, "Convent of the Good Shepherd, New Orleans, Louisiana."

94. For example, Mary Niall Mitchell argues that "the perceived purity, innocence, and vulnerability of young white children made them powerful disciplinary agents of reform." M. N. Mitchell, *Raising Freedom's Child*, 68. For the root of the idea that children were pure and innocent, see, for example, Sanchez-Eppler, *Dependent States*; and Gorham, *Victorian Girl*.

95. Kristeva, *Powers of Horror*, 113.

96. "The Good Shepherd."

97. "Memorandum of Conference Held at the Convent of the Good Shepherd."

98. Coogan, "Religion a Preventive of Delinquency," 32–33.

99. See J. Jacobi, "Cases Heard in Juvenile Court from July 1, 1940–July 1, 1941: Judge Wingrave"; J. Jacobi, "Cases Heard in Juvenile Court from July 1, 1940–July 1, 1941: Judge Nix."

100. Bernard to Rummel, April 15, 1943.

101. "House of the Good Shepherd Building Fund."

102. Coogan, "Religion a Preventive of Delinquency," 30–31.

103. Kristeva, *Powers of Horror*, 129.

104. According to his oral history interviews with people who grew up in New Orleans, Father R. Bentley Anderson found that "a young man or woman was expected to remain sexually pure until marriage, and any sexual activity outside of marriage was considered a serious matter for confession." See R. Anderson, *Black, White, and Catholic*, 8.

105. St. Julien interview, BV.

106. Julien, *Travels with Mae*, 19.

107. Ibid.

108. Coogan, "Religion a Preventive of Delinquency," 31.

109. "House of the Good Shepherd Building Fund."

110. Sister Mary of St. Raymond to Rummel, December 21, 1950.

111. "Interpreters Give Intimate View of Chest Agencies."

112. Emphasis mine. Baudier, "Convent of the Good Shepherd, New Orleans, Louisiana."

113. A. Miller, "Study of the Convent of the Good Shepherd in New Orleans," 78.

114. Holland, Spence, and Watney, *Photography/Politics*, 2.

115. Wexler, *Tender Violence: Domestic Visions in an Age of U.S. Imperialism*, 5.

116. S. Smith, *Photography on the Color Line*, 7.

117. "House of the Good Shepherd Building Fund."

118. Ibid.

119. Baudier, "Convent of the Good Shepherd."

120. "The Good Shepherd."

Chapter Six

1. "White Boys Hit Schoolgirl: Was on Her Way Home When Hit in the Face," *Louisiana Weekly*, April 29, 1939.

2. "Annual Meeting Young Women's Christian Association," May 11, 1948, Fannie C. Williams Papers, Amistad Research Center, Tulane University.

3. They noted that 40 percent of black New Orleanians were Catholic and that "religious animosity keeps the groups separate." "1931 YWCA Report," YWCA Papers, Tulane Special Collections, Tulane University.

4. Often, when feminist scholars have discussed sexual pleasure in women's lives, they have had to distinguish it from sexual danger. In the 1980s, feminist debates over sexuality were polarized between two camps: those who understood sexuality as primarily dangerous for all women and those who saw pleasurable sexuality as a domain of radical liberation. Mariana Valverde explains that those who saw sexuality as dangerous defined "sexuality as uniformly oppressive, a picture of relentless male violence" (242). In black women and girls' lives the stark dichotomy between pleasure/danger is artificial. A long history of sexual vulnerability

and exploitation makes ignoring sexual danger impossible and the project of identifying and naming pleasure even more important, especially in regard to black girls and women's subjectivities. Quotidian sexual harassment, such as that described in Ferdie Walker's oral history interview, proved to be "bad for all black girls"; and more, sexual danger could well mean death, as it did for Hattie McCray. For discussions of and texts that constitute the pleasure/danger debate, see Valverde, "Beyond Gender Dangers and Private Pleasures"; Rich, "Feminism and Sexuality in the 1980s"; Snitow, Stansell, and Thompson, *Powers of Desire*; and Vance, *Pleasure and Danger*. On black women and sexual danger, see chapter 3, "Defending Her Honor: Interracial Sexual Violence, Silences, and Respectability" in this text and Chafe et al., *Remembering Jim Crow*, 9.

5. Spillers, "Interstices," 74.

6. For a discussion of this overdetermined silence, see Hammonds, "Black (W)holes"; and Blair, "African American Women's Sexuality."

7. We see this dynamic at work in chapter 3, "Defending Her Honor: Interracial Sexual Violence, Silences, and Respectability."

8. Hine, "Rape and the Inner Lives of Black Women."

9. For a discussion of "nice girls," see chapter 4.

10. Hammonds, "Black (W)holes," 130.

11. Spillers, "Interstices," 74.

12. Ibid., 79.

13. Trouillot, *Silencing the Past*, especially chapter 1. Finding texts on white women's pleasure is also difficult, although white women had greater access to publishing and presses.

14. As I began this project, I wanted to build an extensive archive of photographs, diaries, letters, and personal documents. This was Joan Jacobs Brumberg's archival approach in *The Body Project*. Brumberg, rather than turning to traditional archives, sought out the personal documents of women stored in chests and attics and forgotten in storage facilities—some even recovered from the trash. But shortly after I contemplated this approach, Hurricane Katrina devastated New Orleans. The photographs, diaries, letters, and personal documents of thousands of women were some of the many things lost to the storm. Therefore, the archive available for "finding" pleasure is limited. Still, this is a project I am committed to because without it black girls remain constituted by moments of trauma.

15. Hammonds, "Black (W)holes," 134.

16. Cvetkovich, *Archive of Feelings*, 241.

17. On "respatialization," see McKittrick, *Demonic Grounds*, xix.

18. Cvetkovich, *Archive of Feelings*, 7.

19. Ibid., introduction, especially 9–11.

20. Flamming, *Bound for Freedom*; Chatelain, *South Side Girls*; Grossman, *Land of Hope*.

21. Ages calculated from 1940 census. Census place: New Orleans, Orleans, Louisiana; roll: T627_1435; page: 61A; enumeration district: 36–439. For Doris Daniels's age, see 1930 census. Census place: New Orleans, Orleans, Louisiana; roll: 808; page: 15B; enumeration district: 176; image: 1022.0; FHL microfilm: 2340543.

22. Doris Daniels and Georgetta Green, interview by Thelma Gertrude Bryant, March 19, 1936, SCDP.

23. Beverly Carter, interview by Thelma Shelby, August 11, 1938, SCDP.

24. Michael Warner defines "public" as "the kind of public that comes into being only in relation to texts and their circulation." A counterpublic lacks the power of the dominant worldview of a "public." Meanwhile Joanna Brooks argues that "a black counterpublic emerges

through black-founded, black-governed institutional venues that permit black collectives to establish a more secure, self-possessed, self-determined presence in a generally hostile and dangerous public sphere dominated by white property owners." For discussions of the meaning of "counterpublic," see Warner, "Publics and Counterpublics"; Fraser, "Rethinking the Public Sphere"; and Brooks, "Early American Public Sphere."

25. duCille, *Coupling Convention*, especially chapter 5. See also Curwood, *Stormy Weather*.

26. Regina Kunzel's study of calls for help to the Children's Bureau from readers of *True Confessions* provides an important look at young girls' and women's reading culture and sexuality. For information on *True Confessions* and pulp magazines, see Kunzel, "Pulp Fictions"; Fabian, "Making a Commodity of Truth"; McClellan, "Review"; Lazarsfeld and Wyant, "Magazines in 90 Cities"; Walraven, "Magazines in the High-School Library"; and Berelson and Salter, "Majority and Minority Americans."

27. On tone and voice in oral history see R. Williams, "I'm a Keeper of Information."

28. Brown interview.

29. Ibid.

30. Ibid.

31. Ibid.

32. Ibid.

33. Beverly Carter, interview with Thelma Shelby, June 30, 1938, SCDP.

34. Mary Willie Johnson, "The Beauty Shop and the Beautician in an Urban Negro Community," 1950, p. 12, Hylan G. Lewis Papers, Atlanta University.

35. Edelman, *Measure of Our Success*, 61.

36. Marie Boyer Brown lived on the second floor of the Sisters of the Holy Family nursing home when Hurricane Katrina hit. Although she lost her home (the center closed as a result of the storm) and many of her friends passed away due to the storm, Marie Boyer Brown's scrapbook survived. We read parts of the scrapbook during our interview. Brown interview.

37. Ibid.

38. Ibid.

39. Lorde, *Sister Outsider*, 56.

40. Ibid., 58.

41. The normal school was a public school for African Americans that gave certificates in education to black teachers. It took two years to complete the program in the 1930s. The school also functioned as an elementary school where the normal school students would receive part of their training.

42. E. Alexander, *Lyrics of Sunshine and Shadow*, 74.

43. Inez Jolivette, "When Fate Takes a Turn," *The Moving Finger*, 1938, Fanny C. Williams Papers, Amistad Research Center, Tulane University.

44. Ibid.

45. Ibid.

46. See Cahn, *Sexual Reckonings*, 211–40; Fass, *Damned and the Beautiful*, 260–91; Bailey, *From Front Porch to Back Seat*; and Schrum, *Some Wore Bobby Sox*, 129–69.

47. Peiss, *Cheap Amusements*, 51.

48. Lois Williams, "Triolets," in "Sequel," 1949, Oakley Johnson Papers, Schomburg Center for Research in Black Culture, New York Public Library.

49. Helen Hagin, "Explanation," 1935, Lillian Welch Voorhees Papers, Amistad Research Center, Tulane University.

50. duCille, *Coupling Convention*, 86–87.

51. Beulah Jones, "Absence," 1939, Lillian Welch Voorhees Papers, Amistad Research Center, Tulane University.

52. Twitty, "Loneliness."

53. Countess Twitty, preface to *Debut*, 1948, Oakley Johnson Papers, Schomburg Center for Research in Black Culture, New York Public Library.

54. Sardie interview.

55. Wilbur, "I Had a Heart," ca. 1931, Onelia Sayas Cherrie Autograph Book, Cherrie Family Papers.

56. This writing culture may have extended to working-class girls as well, although finding writings authored by working-class girls is difficult.

57. For more on Ellen Hill, see chapter 4, "The Geography of Niceness."

58. Ellen Hill, interview by Elizabeth Davis, October 14, 1938, ADP.

59. Cuthbert, "Negro Youth and the Educational Program of the Y.M.C.A.," 363.

60. Heathcott, "Black Archipelago"; Weisenfeld, *African American Women and Christian Activism*; Lewis, *In Their Own Interests*.

61. For a discussion of ideology and the public sphere, see Berlant, *Queen of America Goes to Washington City*, especially the introduction, "The Intimate Public Sphere."

62. Borders interview, BV; L. Thomas, "Kissing Ass," 137.

63. Height, "Adult Education Program," 391.

64. Ibid., 393.

65. The posed photographs appear alongside another photograph depicting a "Ranch Party," for example.

66. Sartain, *Invisible Activists*, 63.

67. Ibid.

68. May, *Homeward Bound*.

69. Taylor, *Archive and the Repertoire*, 16–20.

70. Ibid., 20; Bernstein, *Racial Innocence*, 12.

71. Martinez and Lecorgne, *Uptown/Downtown*, 156.

72. Mary Johnson, interview by Wilma Miller, February 27, 1936, SCDP.

73. Martinez and Lecorgne, *Uptown/Downtown*, 146.

74. Rumpf interview.

75. Early, *New Orleans Holiday*, 257.

76. "Welcome! Welcome! Carnival Visitors," *Louisiana Weekly*, March 1, 1930.

77. Lipsitz, "Mardi Gras Indians"; Vaz, *"Baby Dolls."*

78. Early, *New Orleans Holiday*, 275–76.

79. See, for example, ibid., 185.

80. Taylor, *Archive and the Repertoire*, 28.

81. Ibid., 29.

82. "Beautiful Pageant Staged by Wicker High," *Louisiana Weekly*, March 4, 1939.

83. "Little Miss Eldridge Duvigneaud," *Louisiana Weekly*, February 13, 1932; "Girl Reserves Entertain," *Louisiana Weekly*, March 7, 1931.

84. Rumpf interview.

85. Hamilton, *Beacon Lights of the Race*, 537.

86. Ibid., 538.

87. "What Colored New Orleans Has Been Awaiting," *Louisiana Weekly*, June 6, 1927.

88. According to the census, Clyde is indeed her first name. She was named after her mother, also named Clyde. In the 1920s census, Clyde Angle's family is listed as white, pointing to

the way color, ethnicity, and privilege interacted in some of New Orleans' pleasure clubs. I calculated Angle's age using the U.S. Census. "Young Men's Illinois in Sixth Annual Ball," *Louisiana Weekly*, February 13, 1932; "Year 1930," census place: New Orleans, Orleans, Louisiana; roll 802; page 21A; enumeration district: 57; image: 955.0; FHL microfilm: 2340537, n.d.

89. McKittrick, *Demonic Grounds*, chapter 2, "The Last Place They Thought Of: Black Women's Geographies."

90. This analysis pushes Diana Taylor's work on performance and Katherine McKittrick's work on respatialization by thinking about the geography of performance in light of the Jim Crow cityscape. Taylor, *Archive and the Repertoire*; McKittrick, *Demonic Grounds*.

91. McKittrick, *Demonic Grounds*, xix.

92. Early, *New Orleans Holiday*, 275.

93. Vaz, *"Baby Dolls."*

94. Johnson interview, February 27, 1936.

95. Rumpf interview.

96. Johnson interview, February 27, 1936.

97. "Killings and Cuttings Are Sore Spots," *Louisiana Weekly*, March 8, 1930.

98. Carter, "On the Morning of Wednesday," June 23, 1938, SCDP.

99. Julien, *Travels with Mae*, 119.

100. Taylor, *Archive and the Repertoire*, 82.

101. McKittrick, *Demonic Grounds*, 54.

102. Rumpf, *Reclamation*, 188–89.

103. Ibid., 189.

104. Bernstein, *Racial Innocence*, 72.

105. Martinez and Lecorgne, *Uptown/Downtown*, 147–48.

106. "Debutantes Entertain Illinois," *Louisiana Weekly*, February 13, 1932.

107. "Carnival Season," *Louisiana Weekly*. March 1, 1930.

108. For scholars of African American gender history, productive dialogue might also be gained by grappling with the distinctions between talking about "pleasure" and studying "desire." What would it mean for historians of African American history to center black female desire? What sources would allow us to grapple with black women as subjects of desire? Such a discussion would necessarily have to take into account the multiplicities of sexual desire while also detailing if and how compulsory heterosexuality worked among the middle and aspiring classes of Afro-Americans. See Richardson, "No More Secrets."

109. Kelley, *Race Rebels*, 1–13.

110. Ibid., 36.

111. Hunter, *To 'Joy My Freedom*; Lewis, *In Their Own Interests*; Camp, "Pleasures of Resistance."

112. Literary scholars Ann duCille and Eleanor Alexander seek to do this in their important scholarship on black writers. They are able to use the work of black writers and thus have more sources to work from than a typical social historian. However, their discussions are crucial in helping to contextualize the love-culture in black communities. See duCille, *Coupling Convention*; and Alexander, *Lyrics of Sunshine and Shadow*.

Epilogue

1. Nina Simone, "Old Jim Crow"; Feldstein, *How it Feels to Be Free*, 84–113.

2. Eddie Cherrie to Vicki Smith, November 8, 2005, Cherrie Family Papers.

3. No last name is noted on the autograph. The author is either Mildred De Sargant or Mildred Fauria. Mildred, "Tis the Sad, Sad Fate," June 1931, Onelia Sayas Cherrie Autograph Book, Cherrie Family Papers.

4. Lipsitz, "Learning from New Orleans," 460.

5. Douglass, "Education of Negro Youth for Modern America," 536.

6. My thinking has been influenced by Enstad, "On Grief and Complicity."

7. Painter, *Southern History across the Color Line*, 39.

8. McKittrick, *Demonic Grounds*, xviii.

9. Hyman and Stuart interview.

10. Ibid.

11. McKittrick, *Demonic Grounds*, 5.

12. Hyman and Stuart interview.

13. Campanella, "An Ethnic Geography of New Orleans."

14. Morrison, "Site of Memory"; McKittrick, *Demonic Grounds*, 32–34.

15. McKittrick, *Demonic Grounds*, 33.

16. Hyman and Stuart interview.

17. Ibid.

18. McKittrick, *Demonic Grounds*, 33.

19. B. Anderson, *Cherished Memories*; Julien, *Travels with Mae*; Rumpf, *Reclamation*; Gervais, *Black-Eyed Susan*. See also memoirs by men: Wolf, *My New Orleans*; Battiste and Celestan, *Unfinished Blues*; Fertel, *Gorilla Man*.

20. B. Anderson, *Cherished Memories*, xv.

21. Ibid., xvi.

22. Trethewey, *Beyond Katrina*, 2.

23. Julien, *Travels with Mae*, 123.

24. Ibid., 124.

25. Rumpf, *Reclamation*, xiii.

26. Julien, *Travels with Mae*, 125.

27. Sister Claire of Assisi Pierre interview.

28. Indeed, the Sisters of the Holy Family were founded in the antebellum period and so contended with the institution of slavery.

29. The Sisters of the Holy Family evacuated to Shreveport, Louisiana. Evacuation and rebuilding from Shreveport was not easy. Sister Claire remembered that "we didn't know how long we would be away; we didn't know when we would come back to New Orleans; we didn't see how we could rebuild in New Orleans." The emotional cost of this uncertainty and displacement was the loss of many elderly Sisters. In those first few years after the storm, the Sisters of the Holy Family lost nearly twenty Sisters from a community of about eighty.

30. McKittrick, *Demonic Grounds*, xix.

31. For discussion of the "Greatest Generation" see Brokaw, *Greatest Generation*; Lindenmeyer, *Greatest Generation Grows Up*; Zinn, "Greatest Generation?"

32. Chafe et al., *Remembering Jim Crow*, 9.

33. Lolita Cherrie, conversation with author, October 22, 2008.

Bibliography

Primary Sources

Libraries, Archives, and Collections

Archdiocese of New Orleans
  Roger Baudier Historical Collection
  House of the Good Shepherd Papers
Cherrie Family Papers, personal collection in possession of Lolita Villavasso Cherrie
  Onelia Sayas Cherrie Autograph Book
Duke University
  Behind the Veil: Documenting African-American Life in the Jim Crow South Records,
    John Hope Franklin Research Center
    Aaron, Dolores. Interview by Michele Mitchell. Tape, June 30, 1994.
    Allen, Philomene Guillory and Dunbar, Viola Guillory. Interview by Kate Ellis and
      Michele Mitchell. Tape, July 4, 1994.
    Borders, Florence. Interview by Kate Ellis and Michele Mitchell. Tape,
      June 20, 1994.
    Boucree, John Harold. Interview by Kate Ellis. Digital, July 5, 1994.
    Bouise, Louise. Interview by Kate Ellis. Tape, June 20, 1994.
    Caitone, Beverly. Interview by Michele Mitchell. Tape, July 8, 1994.
    Cappie, Herbert, and Ruth Irene Cappie. Interview by Michele Mitchell. Tape,
      June 29 and July 2, 1994.
    Charles, Millie McClellan. Interview by Felix Armfield. Tape, July 12, 1994.
    Dave, Peter E., Jr. Interview by Michele Mitchell. Tape, June 23, 1994.
    Jenkins, Julius. Interview by Felix Armfield. Tape, June 27, 1994.
    Johnson, Mary. Interview by Michele Mitchell. Tape, June 27, 1994.
    Merrick, Olga. Interview by Michele Mitchell. Tape, July 2, 1994.
    Pajeaud, Marjorie Bellsina, and Moutan, Jessie Larence. Interview by Felix Armfield.
      Tape, June 23, 1994.
    Reed, Clarita. Interview by Michele Mitchell. Tape, June 24, 1994.
    Regan, Wanda Dell [pseudonym]. Interview by Michele Mitchell. Tape,
      June 28, 1994.
    Robertson, Audrey Carr. Interview by Kate Ellis. Tape, June 24, 1994.
    St. Julien, Aline. Interview by Michele Mitchell. Tape, July 1, 1994.
Historic New Orleans Collection, Williams Research Center, New Orleans
  Sanborn Fire Insurance Maps
Hoover Institute, Stanford University American Youth Commission
Louisiana and Special Collections, Earl K. Long Library, University of New Orleans
  Marcus Christian Papers

New Orleans Association of Commerce Minutes
New Orleans Public Library, Louisiana Division
    Cabildo Oral History Project
    New Orleans Arrest Records
    New Orleans Homicide Reports
    Commissioner Lionel G. Ott Papers
    State v. Guerand, Docket C., Case No. 52554
    Robert Tallant Papers
Schlesinger Library, Radcliffe College
    Black Women's Oral History Project
Schomburg Center for Research in Black Culture, New York Public Library
    St. Claire Drake Papers
    Oakley Johnson Papers
Southern Historical Collection, Wilson Library, University of North Carolina at Chapel Hill
    Jessie Daniel Ames Papers
    Federal Writers' Project Papers
    Arthur F. Raper Papers
Special Collections Research Center, University of Chicago Library
    Allison Davis Papers
Tamiment Library and Robert F. Wagner Labor Archives, New York University
    John Dollard Research Files for *Fear and Courage under Battle Conditions*
Tulane University
    Amistad Research Center
        A. P. Tureaud Papers
        Hylan G. Lewis Papers
        Lillian Welch Voorhees Papers
        Fannie C. Williams Papers
    Tulane Special Collections
        Kingsley House Papers
        YWCA Papers
University of Michigan Digital Library Text Collection
    National Conference on Social Welfare Proceedings Papers

Interviews

Addams, Eugenia. Interview by LaKisha Simmons. Digital, March 2007. In possession of author.
Braud, Lilli, and Lolita Villavasso Cherrie. Interview by LaKisha Simmons. Digital, March 2007. In possession of author.
Brown, Marie Boyer. Interview by LaKisha Simmons and Lolita Villavasso Cherrie. Digital, March 2007. In possession of author.
Hyman, Joycelyn, and Ann Stuart. Interview by LaKisha Simmons and Lolita Villavasso Cherrie. Digital, April 1, 2012. In possession of author.
Rumpf, Eva Augustin. Interview by LaKisha Simmons. Digital, March 18, 2013. In possession of author.
Sardie, Jacqueline. Interview by LaKisha Simmons. Digital, November 18, 2008. In possession of author.
Sister Claire of Assisi Pierre. Interview by LaKisha Simmons and Lolita Villavasso Cherrie. Digital, April 2, 2012. In possession of author.

Books, Articles, and Other Media

Anderson, Beverly Jacques. *Cherished Memories: Snapshots of Life and Lessons from a 1950s New Orleans Creole Village*. Bloomington, Ind.: iUniverse Inc., 2011.

Anderson, R. Bentley. *Black, White, and Catholic: New Orleans Interracialism, 1947–1956*. Nashville: Vanderbilt University Press, 2005.

Anderson, V. V. "The Immoral Woman as Seen in Court: A Preliminary Report." *Journal of the American Institute of Criminal Law and Criminology* 8, no. 6 (March 1918): 902–10.

Battiste, Harold, and Karen Celestan. *Unfinished Blues: Memories of a New Orleans Music Man*. New Orleans: Historic New Orleans Collection, 2010.

Berelson, Bernard, and Patricia Salter. "Majority and Minority Americans: An Analysis of Magazine Fiction." *Public Opinion Quarterly* 10, no. 2 (1946): 168–90.

Brewer, W. M. "Review: [untitled]." *Journal of Negro History* 26, no. 1 (January 1941): 113–15.

Chafe, William Henry, Raymond Gavins, Robert Rodgers Korstad, and Behind the Veil Project. *Remembering Jim Crow: African Americans Tell about Life in the Segregated South*. New York: New Press distributed by W. W. Norton, 2001.

Coogan, Reverend John Edward. "Religion a Preventive of Delinquency." *Federal Probation* 18, no. 4 (1954): 29–35.

Cottrell, Leonard S. "Review: [untitled]." *American Journal of Sociology* 47, no. 1 (July 1941): 111–15.

Cox, Ida. *Blues for Rampart Street*. Prestige, 2006.

_____. *Ida Cox: Vol. 1, 1923*. Document Records, 2005.

Cuthbert, Marion. "Negro Youth and the Educational Program of the Y.M.C.A." *Journal of Negro Education* 9, no. 3 (July 1940): 363–71.

Davis, Allison, and John Dollard. *Children of Bondage: The Personality Development of Negro Youth in the Urban South*. Washington, D.C.: American Council on Education/Oryx Press, 1940.

Delaney, John J. "Catholic Reformatory Agencies," 1897. National Conference on Social Welfare Proceedings Papers. University of Michigan Digital Library Text Collection.

Dennis, Wayne. "Review: [untitled]." *American Journal of Psychology* 55, no. 1 (January 1942): 149.

Dollard, John. *Caste and Class in a Southern Town*. 2nd ed. Madison: University of Wisconsin Press, 1989.

_____. "Culture, Society, Impulse, and Socialization." *American Journal of Sociology* 45, no. 1 (July 1939): 50–63.

Douglass, Harl. "The Education of Negro Youth for Modern America: A Critical Summary." *Journal of Negro Education* 9, no. 3 (July 1940): 534–46.

Dublin, Louis I. "The Health of the Negro." *Annals of the American Academy of Political and Social Science* 140 (November 1928): 77–85.

Early, Eleanor. *New Orleans Holiday*. New York: Dodo Press, 2007.

Edelman, Marian Wright. *The Measure of Our Success: A Letter to My Children and Yours*. Boston: Harper Paperbacks, 1993.

Elie, Lolis Eric. "So Much for Satchmo: How about Another Downtown Parking Lot?" *The Lens: Focused on New Orleans and the Gulf Coast*, September 21, 2012.

Federal Writers' Project. *Louisiana: A Guide to the State*. American Guide Series. New York: Hastings House, 1941.

_____. *New Orleans City Guide*. Boston: Houghton Mifflin, 1938.

Ferris, William R., and John Dollard. "John Dollard: Caste and Class Revisited." *Southern Cultures* 10, no. 2 (2004): 7–18.

Fertel, Randy. *The Gorilla Man and the Empress of Steak: A New Orleans Family Memoir.* Jackson: University Press of Mississippi, 2011.

Frank, Lawrence Kelso, Ross Harrison, Elisabeth Hellersberg, Karen Machover, and Meta Steiner. *Personality Development in Adolescent Girls.* Vol. 16. Monographs of the Society for Research in Child Development, 53. New Orleans: Child Development Publications, 1953.

Frazier, E. Franklin. *Negro Youth at the Crossways: Their Personality Development in the Middle States.* Washington, D.C.: American Council on Education/Oryx Press, 1944.

Frumkin, Robert M. "Expected Versus Actual Social Behavior of Negro Adolescent Girls." *Journal of Negro Education* 23, no. 2 (Spring 1954): 197–200.

Gervais, Fran. *Black-Eyed Susan among the Roses: A New Orleans Memoir.* Charleston: CreateSpace Independent Publishing Platform, 2010.

Gillard, John Thomas. *Colored Catholics in the United States: An Investigation of Catholic Activity in Behalf of the Negroes in the United States and Survey of the Present Condition of the Colored Missions.* Baltimore: The Josephite Press, 1941.

Griffith, D. W., dir. *Birth of a Nation.* DVD. Reel Enterprises, 2006.

Height, Dorothy I. "The Adult Education Program of the YWCA among Negroes." *Journal of Negro Education* 14, no. 3 (Summer 1945): 390–95.

Holland, Endesha Ida Mae. *From the Mississippi Delta: A Memoir.* Chicago: Lawrence Hill Books, 1999.

Holmes, S. J. "Will the Negro Survive in the North?" *Scientific Monthly* 27, no. 6 (December 1928): 557–61.

Homer, Thomas Johnston, and Grace Abbott. *Juvenile Court Laws in the United States: A Summary by States.* New York: Russell Sage Foundation, 1918.

Hunter-Gault, Charlayne. *In My Place.* 7th ed. New York: Vintage, 1993.

Jackson, Nelson. "Community Organization Activities among Negroes for Venereal Disease Control." *Social Forces* 23, no. 1 (October 1944): 65–70.

Johnson, Charles S. *Growing Up in the Black Belt: Negro Youth in the Rural South.* Washington, D.C.: American Council on Education/Oryx Press, 1941.

Johnson, Willietta. "Southern City: Reflections." *African Methodist Episcopal Church Review,* July 1893.

Julien, Eileen M. *Travels with Mae: Scenes from a New Orleans Girlhood.* Bloomington: Indiana University Press, 2009.

Lazarsfeld, Paul F., and Rowena Wyant. "Magazines in 90 Cities—Who Reads What?" *Public Opinion Quarterly* 1, no. 4 (October 1937): 29–41.

Leslie, Frank E. "The Delinquent." *Public Health Reports (1896–1970)* 37, no. 22 (June 2, 1922): 1297–1307.

Levy, Anna Judge Veters. *Other People's Children.* New York: Ronald Press, 1956.

Lief, Harold, Daniel Thompson, and William Thompson. *The Eighth Generation Grows Up: Cultures and Personalities of New Orleans Negroes.* Edited by John Rohrer and Munro Edmonson. New York: Harper and Row, 1960.

Martinez, Elsie, and Margaret Lecorgne. *Uptown/Downtown: Growing Up in New Orleans.* Lafayette: University of Southwestern Louisiana Press, 1986.

Mason, W. A. "Community Organization Activities among Negroes for Venereal Disease Control: Discussion." *Social Forces* 23, no. 1 (October 1944): 70–73.

Massaquoi, Hans. "St. Mary's Academy—A Living Legend: Girls School Thrives on Historic Quadroon Ball Site in French Quarter of New Orleans." *Ebony,* December 1961.

McClellan, George H. "Review: [untitled]." *Educational Research Bulletin* 18, no. 2 (February 1, 1939): 57–58. doi:10.2307/1472453.

Miller, Agnes. "A Study of the Convent of the Good Shepherd in New Orleans." Master's thesis, Tulane University, 1941.

Moody, Anne. *Coming of Age in Mississippi.* New York: Delta Trade Paperbacks, 2004.

The Official Catholic Directory: Anno Domini 1930. New York: Kenedy and Sons, Publishers, 1931.

The Official Catholic Directory: Anno Domini 1954. New York: Kenedy and Sons, Publishers, 1955.

Reese, Mildred Lyons. "A Study of the Social and Economic Factors in Twenty Selected Cases of Neglected and Delinquent Children under Care of the Associated Catholic Charities, New Orleans, Louisiana, 1948–1949." Master's thesis, Atlanta University, 1950.

Reid, Ira DeA. *In a Minor Key: Negro Youth in Story and Fact.* Washington, D.C.: American Council on Education/Oryx Press, 1941.

Rumpf, Eva Augustin. *Reclamation: Memories from a New Orleans Girlhood.* Booklocker.com, 2009.

Sancton, Tom, and Tommy Sancton. *Song for My Fathers: A New Orleans Story in Black and White.* New York: Other Press, 2006.

Saxon, Lyle, Robert Tallant, and Works Progress Administration. *Gumbo Ya-Ya: A Collection of Louisiana Folk Tales.* Boston: Houghton Mifflin, 1945.

Simone, Nina. "Old Jim Crow," in *Nina Simone in Concert.* New York City: Phillips, 1964. MP3.
———. "Old Jim Crow Interview," in *Protest Anthology.* New York City: Artwork Media, 2008. MP3.

Smith, Darrlyn A. *The New Orleans 7th Ward: Nostalgia Dictionary, 1938–1965.* 2nd rev. ed. Seattle: Jada, 1996.

Spitzer, Murray. "What of the Negro Future?" *Journal of Educational Sociology* 5, no. 5 (January 1930): 275–87.

Tallant, Robert. *The Romantic New Orleanians.* New York: Dutton, 1950.
———. *Voodoo in New Orleans.* New York: Macmillan, 1946.
———. *The Voodoo Queen; a Novel.* New York: Putnam, 1956.

Tardy, Jo Anne. *A Light Will Rise in Darkness: Growing Up Black and Catholic in New Orleans.* Chicago: ACTA Publications, 2006.

Thomas, William Hannibal. *The American Negro.* New York: Macmillan, 1901.

Thomas, William I. "The Unadjusted Girl: With Cases and Standpoint for Behavior Analysis." *Criminal Science Monographs*, no. 4 (1923): 1–257.

Trethewey, Natasha D. *Beyond Katrina: A Meditation on the Mississippi Gulf Coast.* Athens: University of Georgia Press, 2012.

Twitty, Countess. "Loneliness." In *"America Sings": Anthology of College Poetry*, 48. Los Angeles: National Poetry Association, 1947.

Walker, Margaret. "Growing Out of Shadow." In *How I Wrote* Jubilee: *And Other Essays on Life and Literature*, edited by Maryemma Graham, 3–9. New York: Feminist Press at City University of New York, 1990.

Walraven, Margaret Kessler. "Magazines in the High-School Library." *English Journal* 24, no. 2 (February 1935): 134–36.

Weldon, L. O. "Psychiatric Studies of Delinquents: Part II. A Study of Physical and Mental Conditions of 100 Delinquent White Women in Louisville, Ky." *Public Health Reports (1896–1970)* 35, no. 22 (May 28, 1920): 1247–69.

Wells-Barnett, Ida. "Southern Horrors: Lynch Law in All Its Phases." In *On Lynchings*, 25–54. Salem: Aver Company, 1987.

Wolf, Peter M. *My New Orleans, Gone Away: A Memoir of Loss and Renewal*. Harrison, N.Y.: Delphinium Books, 2013.

Young, I. S. *Jadie Greenway: A Novel*. New York: Crown, 1947.

Secondary Sources

Abel, Elizabeth. "Bathroom Doors and Drinking Fountains: Jim Crow's Racial Symbolic." *Critical Inquiry* 25, no. 3 (Spring 1999): 435–81.

Adams, Jane, and D. Gorton. "Southern Trauma: Revisiting Caste and Class in the Mississippi Delta." *American Anthropologist*, n.s., 106, no. 2 (June 2004): 334–45.

Alexander, Eleanor. *Lyrics of Sunshine and Shadow: The Tragic Courtship and Marriage of Paul Laurence Dunbar and Alice Ruth Moore, a History of Love and Violence among the African American Elite*. New York: NYU Press, 2001.

Alexander, Ruth M. *The "Girl Problem": Female Sexual Delinquency in New York, 1900–1930*. Ithaca: Cornell University Press, 1998.

Anderson, Beverly Jacques. *Cherished Memories: Snapshots of Life and Lessons from a 1950s New Orleans Creole Village*. Bloomington, Ind.: iUniverse, 2011.

Anderson, R. Bentley. *Black, White, and Catholic: New Orleans Interracialism, 1947–1956*. Nashville: Vanderbilt University Press, 2005.

Bailey, Beth L. *From Front Porch to Back Seat: Courtship in Twentieth-Century America*. Baltimore: Johns Hopkins University Press, 1989.

Battiste, Harold, and Karen Celestan. *Unfinished Blues: Memories of a New Orleans Music Man*. New Orleans: Historic New Orleans Collection, 2010.

Berkes, Howard. "Study: Many Katrina Victims Were Elderly, Black." Podcast. National Public Radio, October 24, 2005.

Berlant, Lauren. *The Queen of America Goes to Washington City: Essays on Sex and Citizenship*. Durham: Duke University Press, 1997.

———. "The Subject of True Feeling." In *Feminist Consequences: Theory for the New Century*, edited by Elisabeth Bronfen and Misha Kavka, 126–60. New York: Columbia University Press, 2001.

Bernstein, Robin. *Racial Innocence: Performing American Childhood and Race from Slavery to Civil Rights*. New York: NYU Press, 2011.

Berry, Mary Frances. *The Pig Farmer's Daughter and Other Tales of American Justice: Episodes of Racism and Sexism in the Courts from 1865 to the Present*. New York: Knopf, 1999.

Beveridge, Lowell P. *Domestic Diversity: And Other Subversive Activities*. Minneapolis: Hillcrest, 2010.

"Black Heritage Award for an African-American Educator." *Journal of Blacks in Higher Education*, no. 3 (Spring 1994): 23.

Blair, Cynthia. "African American Women's Sexuality." *Frontiers: A Journal of Women Studies* 35, no. 1 (January 2014): 4–10.

Blassingame, John. *Black New Orleans, 1860–1880*. Chicago: University of Chicago Press, 2008.

Bourke, Joanna. "Fear and Anxiety: Writing about Emotion in Modern History." *History Workshop Journal* 55, no. 1 (2003): 111–33.

Bouson, J. Brooks. *Quiet as It's Kept: Shame, Trauma, and Race in the Novels of Toni Morrison*. Albany: State University of New York Press, 1999.

Brandt, Allan M. "AIDS in Historical Perspective: Four Lessons from the History of Sexually Transmitted Diseases." In *Sickness and Health in America: Readings in the History of Medicine*

and *Public Health*, edited by Judith Walzer Leavitt and Ronald L. Numbers, 426–34. 3rd rev.
ed. Madison: University of Wisconsin Press, 1997.

Bright, William. "Native American Place Names in the Louisiana Purchase." *American Speech*
78, no. 4 (2003): 353–62.

Brokaw, Tom. *The Greatest Generation*. New York: Delta, 2001.

Brooks, Joanna. "The Early American Public Sphere and the Emergence of a Black Print
Counterpublic." *William and Mary Quarterly* 62, no. 1 (January 2005): 67–92.

Brown, Elsa Barkley, and Greg Kimball. "Mapping the Terrain of Black Richmond." In *The New
African American Urban History*, edited by Kenneth W. Goings and Raymond Mohl, 66–115.
Thousand Oaks, Calif.: Sage, 1996.

Brown, Laura S. "Not Outside the Range: One Feminist Perspective on Psychic Trauma."
In *Trauma: Explorations in Memory*, edited by Cathy Caruth, 100–112. Baltimore: Johns
Hopkins University Press, 1995.

Broyard, Bliss. *One Drop: My Father's Hidden Life—A Story of Race and Family Secrets*. New
York: Back Bay Books, 2008.

Brumberg, Joan Jacobs. *The Body Project: An Intimate History of American Girls*. New York:
Random House, 1998.

———. " 'Ruined' Girls: Changing Community Responses to Illegitimacy in Upstate New York,
1890–1920." *Journal of Social History* 18, no. 2 (Winter 1984): 247–72.

Brundage, W. Fitzhugh. *Lynching in the New South: Georgia and Virginia, 1880–1930*. Chicago:
University of Illinois Press, 1993.

Bryan, Violet Harrington. "Marcus Christian's Treatment of Les Gens de Couleur Libre." In
Creole: The History and Legacy of Free People of Color, edited by Sybil Kein, 42–56. Baton
Rouge: Louisiana State University Press, 2000.

Butler, Judith. *Gender Trouble: Feminism and the Subversion of Identity*. New York: Routledge,
2006.

Cahn, Susan K. *Sexual Reckonings: Southern Girls in a Troubling Age*. Cambridge, Mass.:
Harvard University Press, 2007.

Camp, Stephanie M. H. "The Pleasures of Resistance: Enslaved Women and Body Politics in
the Plantation South, 1830–1861." *Journal of Southern History* 68, no. 3 (August 2002): 533–72.
doi:10.2307/3070158.

Campanella, Richard. "An Ethnic Geography of New Orleans." *The Journal of American History*
94, no. 3 (December 2007): 704–15.

———. *Geographies of New Orleans: Urban Fabrics before the Storm*. Lafayette: Center for
Louisiana Studies, 2006.

Canning, Kathleen. "The Body as Method? Reflections on the Place of the Body in Gender
History." *Gender and History* 11, no. 3 (November 1999): 499–513.

Canning, Kathleen, and Sonya Rose. "Gender, Citizenship and Subjectivity: Some Historical
and Theoretical Considerations." *Gender and History* 13, no. 3 (November 2001): 427–43.

Carby, Hazel. "Policing the Black Woman's Body in an Urban Context." *Critical Inquiry* 18, no. 4
(Summer 1992): 738–55.

———. *Reconstructing Womanhood: The Emergence of the Afro-American Woman Novelist*. New
York: Oxford University Press, 1989.

Cardyn, Lisa. "Sexualized Racism/Gendered Violence: Outraging the Body Politic in the
Reconstruction South." *Michigan Law Review* 100 (February 2002): 675–867.

_____. "Sexual Terror in the Reconstruction South." In *Battle Scars: Gender and Sexuality in the American Civil War*, edited by Catherine Clinton and Nina Silber, 140–67. New York: Oxford University Press, 2006.

Chafe, William Henry, Raymond Gavins, Robert Rodgers Korstad, and Behind the Veil Project. *Remembering Jim Crow: African Americans Tell about Life in the Segregated South*. New York: New Press distributed by W. W. Norton, 2001.

Chatelain, Marcia. *South Side Girls: Growing Up in the Great Migration*. Durham: Duke University Press, 2015.

Clinton, Catherine. "Bloody Terrain: Freedwomen, Sexuality, and Violence during Reconstruction." *Georgia Historical Quarterly* 76 (Summer 1992): 313–32.

Coffey, Michele Grigsby. "*The State of Louisiana v. Charles Guerand*: Interracial Sexual Mores, Rape Rhetoric, and Respectability in 1930s New Orleans." *Louisiana History* 54, no. 1 (Winter 2013): 47–93.

Connolly, Nathan. *A World More Concrete: Real Estate and the Remaking of Jim Crow South Florida*. Chicago: University of Chicago Press, 2014.

Crutcher, Michael Eugene. *Tremé: Race and Place in a New Orleans Neighborhood*. Athens: University of Georgia Press, 2010.

Curwood, Anastasia C. *Stormy Weather: Middle-Class African American Marriages between the Two World Wars*. Chapel Hill: University of North Carolina Press, 2010.

Cvetkovich, Ann. *An Archive of Feelings: Trauma, Sexuality, and Lesbian Public Cultures*. Durham: Duke University Press, 2003.

Dailey, Jane. "Sex, Segregation, and the Sacred after Brown." *Journal of American History* 91, no. 1 (June 2004): 119–44.

Davis, Thadious. *Southscapes: Geographies of Race, Region, and Literature*. Chapel Hill: University of North Carolina Press, 2011.

Deggs, Mary Bernard, Virginia Meacham Gould, and Charles E. Nolan. *No Cross, No Crown: Black Nuns in Nineteenth-Century New Orleans*. Bloomington: Indiana University Press, 2002.

DeLuzio, Crista. *Female Adolescence in American Scientific Thought, 1830–1930*. Baltimore: Johns Hopkins University Press, 2007.

Desdunes, Rodolphe. *Our People, Our History: Fifty Creole Portraits*. Translated by Sister Dorothea Olga McCants. Baton Rouge: Louisiana State University Press, 2001.

Devlin, Rachel. "Female Juvenile Delinquency and the Problem of Sexual Authority in America, 1945–1965." In *Delinquents and Debutantes: Twentieth-Century American Girls' Cultures*, Edited by Sherrie Inness, 83–107. Illustrated ed. New York: NYU Press, 1998.

_____. *Relative Intimacy: Fathers, Adolescent Daughters, and Postwar American Culture*. Chapel Hill: University of North Carolina Press, 2005.

Diamond, Sigmund. *Compromised Campus: The Collaboration of Universities with the Intelligence Community, 1945–1955*. New York: Oxford University Press, 1992.

Di Leonardo, Micaela. "Political Economy of Street Harassment." *Aegis: Magazine on Ending Violence Against Women* (Summer 1981): 51–52.

Dorr, Lisa Lindquist. *White Women, Rape, and the Power of Race in Virginia, 1900–1960*. Chapel Hill: University of North Carolina Press, 2004.

Driscoll, Catherine. *Girls: Feminine Adolescence in Popular Culture and Cultural Theory*. New York: Columbia University Press, 2002.

Du Bois, W. E. B. *The Souls of Black Folk*. Cambridge, Mass.: John Wilson and Son, 1903.

duCille, Ann. *The Coupling Convention: Sex, Text, and Tradition in Black Women's Fiction*. New York: Oxford University Press, 1993.

Edelman, Marian Wright. *The Measure of Our Success: A Letter to My Children and Yours.* Boston: Harper Paperbacks, 1993.

Emanuel, Rachel L., and Alexander P. Tureaud. *A More Noble Cause: A. P. Tureaud and the Struggle for Civil Rights in Louisiana: A Personal Biography.* Baton Rouge: Louisiana State University Press, 2011.

English, Daylanne. "W. E. B. Du Bois's Family Crisis." *American Literature* 72, no. 2 (June 2000): 291–319.

Enstad, Nan. *Ladies of Labor, Girls of Adventure.* New York: Columbia University Press, 1999.

_____. "On Grief and Complicity: Notes toward a Visionary Cultural History." In *The Cultural Turn in U.S. History,* edited by James Cook, Lawrence Glickman, and Michael O'Malley, 319–42. Chicago: University of Chicago Press, 2009.

Evans, Tammy D. *The Silencing of Ruby McCollum: Race, Class, and Gender in the South.* Gainesville: University Press of Florida, 2006.

Fabian, Ann. "Making a Commodity of Truth: Speculations on the Career of Bernard Macfadden." *American Literary History* 5, no. 1 (Spring 1993): 51–76.

Fairclough, Adam. *Race and Democracy: The Civil Rights Struggle in Louisiana, 1915–1972.* 2nd ed. Athens: University of Georgia Press, 2008.

Fass, Paula S. "Cultural History/Social History: Some Reflections on a Continuing Dialogue." *Journal of Social History* 37, no. 1 (2003): 39–46.

_____. *The Damned and the Beautiful: American Youth in the 1920s.* New York: Oxford University Press, 1979.

Feibelman, Julian Beck. "A Social and Economic Study of the New Orleans Jewish Community." Diss., University of Pennsylvania, 1941.

Feldstein, Ruth. *How it Feels to be Free: Black Women Entertainers and the Civil Rights Movement.* New York: Oxford University Press, 2013.

_____. *Motherhood in Black and White: Race and Sex in American Liberalism, 1930–1965.* Ithaca: Cornell University Press, 2000.

Fertel, Randy. *The Gorilla Man and the Empress of Steak: A New Orleans Family Memoir.* Jackson: University Press of Mississippi, 2011.

Flamming, Douglas. *Bound for Freedom: Black Los Angeles in Jim Crow America.* Berkeley: University of California Press, 2005.

Flax, Jane. *Disputed Subjects: Essays on Psychoanalysis, Politics, and Philosophy.* New York: Routledge, 1993.

Ford, Emily, and Barry Stiefel. *The Jews of New Orleans and the Mississippi Delta: A History of Life and Community along the Bayou.* Charleston: History Press, 2012.

Foucault, Michel. *The History of Sexuality: An Introduction.* Vol. 1. New York: Vintage Books, 1990.

Fraser, Nancy. "Rethinking the Public Sphere: A Contribution to the Critique of Actually Existing Democracy." In *Habermas and the Public Sphere,* edited by Craig Calhoun, 122–23. Cambridge: MIT Press, 1992.

Friedman, Susan Stanford. *Mappings: Feminism and the Cultural Geographies of Encounter.* Princeton: Princeton University Press, 1998.

Fussell, Elizabeth. "Constructing New Orleans, Constructing Race: A Population History of New Orleans." *Journal of American History* 94 (December 2007): 846–55.

Gaines, Kevin K. *Uplifting the Race: Black Leadership, Politics, and Culture in the Twentieth Century.* Chapel Hill: University of North Carolina Press, 1996.

Gaudin, Wendy. "Autocrats and All Saints: Migration, Memory, and Modern Creole Identities." Diss., New York University, 2005.

Germany, Kent B. *New Orleans after the Promises: Poverty, Citizenship, and the Search for the Great Society*. Athens: University of Georgia Press, 2007.

Gervais, Fran. *Black-Eyed Susan among the Roses: A New Orleans Memoir*. Charleston: CreateSpace Independent Publishing Platform, 2010.

Gilmore, Glenda Elizabeth. *Gender and Jim Crow: Women and the Politics of White Supremacy in North Carolina, 1896–1920*. Chapel Hill: University of North Carolina Press, 1996.

Ginsburg, Rebecca. "Native Daughter: Home, Segregation, and Mental Maps." *Home Cultures* 1, no. 2 (July 2004): 127–45.

———. "The View from the Back Step: White Children Learn about Race in Johannesburg's Suburban Homes." In *Designing Modern Childhoods: History, Space, and the Material Culture of Children*, edited by Marta Gutman and Ning De Coninck-Smith, 193–212. New Brunswick: Rutgers University Press, 2008.

Goffman, Erving. *Stigma: Notes on the Management of Spoiled Identity*. New York: Penguin Books, 1990.

Goodman, James E. *Stories of Scottsboro*. New York: Pantheon Books, 1994.

Gordon, Linda. *Heroes of Their Own Lives: The Politics and History of Family Violence*. Chicago: University of Illinois Press, 2002.

Gorham, Deborah. *The Victorian Girl and the Feminine Ideal*. Bloomington: Indiana University Press, 1982.

Grant, Megan, and Amanda Rubens. "Interview with Jane Flax." *Melbourne Journal of Politics* 24 (1997): 1–25.

Green, Laurie B. *Battling the Plantation Mentality: Memphis and the Black Freedom Struggle*. Chapel Hill: University of North Carolina Press, 2007.

Grossman, James R. *Land of Hope: Chicago, Black Southerners, and the Great Migration*. Chicago: University of Chicago Press, 1991.

Guillory, Monique. "Under One Roof: The Sins and Sanctity of the New Orleans Quadroon Balls." In *Race Consciousness: African American Studies for the New Century*, edited by Judith Jackson Fossett and Jeffrey Tucker, 67–92. New York: New York University Press, 1997.

Gutman, Marta, and Ning De Coninck-Smith, eds. *Designing Modern Childhoods: History, Space, and the Material Culture of Children*. New Brunswick: Rutgers University Press, 2008.

Hahn, Steven. *A Nation under Our Feet: Black Political Struggles in the Rural South from Slavery to the Great Migration*. Cambridge: Belknap Press, 2005.

Halberstam, Judith. *Female Masculinity*. Durham: Duke University Press, 1998.

Hale, Grace Elizabeth. *Making Whiteness: The Culture of Segregation in the South, 1890–1940*. New York: Pantheon Books, 1998.

Hall, Gwendolyn Midlo. *Africans in Colonial Louisiana: The Development of Afro-Creole Culture in the Eighteenth Century*. Baton Rouge: Louisiana State University Press, 1995.

Hall, Jacquelyn Dowd. "The Mind That Burns in Each Body: Women, Rape and Racial Violence." In *Powers of Desire: The Politics of Sexuality*, edited by Ann Snitow and Christine Stansell, 328–49. New York: Monthly Press Review, 1983.

———. *Revolt against Chivalry: Jessie Daniel Ames and the Women's Campaign against Lynching*. Rev. ed. New York: Columbia University Press, 1993.

Hamilton, Green Polonius. *Beacon Lights of the Race*. Memphis: P. H. Clarke & Brother: E. H. Clarke & Brother, 1911.

Hammonds, Evelynn. "Black (W)holes and the Geometry of Black Female Sexuality: (More Gender Trouble: Feminism Meets Queer Theory)." *Differences: A Journal of Feminist Cultural Studies* 6, no. 2–3 (Summer/Fall 1994): 126–46.

Hartman, Saidiya V. *Scenes of Subjection: Terror, Slavery, and Self-Making in Nineteenth-Century America*. New York: Oxford University Press, 1997.

Hawes, Joseph M., and N. Ray Hiner. "Hidden in Plain View: The History of Children (and Childhood) in the Twenty-First Century." *Journal of the History of Childhood and Youth* 1, no. 1 (2007): 43–49.

Haydel, Belmont F. *The Victor Haydel Creole Family*. Warminster, Pa.: Cooke, 2009.

Heap, Chad. "The City as a Sexual Laboratory: The Queer Heritage of the Chicago School." *Qualitative Sociology* 26, no. 4 (December 2003): 457–87.

Heathcott, Joseph. "Black Archipelago: Politics and Civic Life in the Jim Crow City." *Journal of Social History* 38, no. 3 (Spring 2005): 705–37.

Hicks, Cheryl D. " 'Bright and Good Looking Colored Girl': Black Women's Sexuality and 'Harmful Intimacy' in Early-Twentieth-Century New York." *Journal of the History of Sexuality* 18, no. 3 (2009): 418–56.

_____. *Talk with You Like a Woman*. Chapel Hill: University of North Carolina Press, 2010.

Higginbotham, Evelyn Brooks. *Righteous Discontent: The Women's Movement in the Black Baptist Church, 1880–1920*. Cambridge, Mass.: Harvard University Press, 1993.

Hillis, Michael R. "Allison Davis and the Study of Race, Social Class, and Schooling." *Journal of Negro Education* 64, no. 1 (Winter 1995): 33–41.

Hine, Darlene Clark. "The Corporeal and Ocular Veil: Dr. Matilda A. Evens (1872–1935) and the Complexity of Southern History." *Journal of Southern History* 70, no. 1 (February 2004): 3–34.

_____. "Rape and the Inner Lives of Black Women in the Middle West: Preliminary Thoughts on the Culture of Dissemblance." *Signs* 14, no. 4 (1989): 912–20.

Hirsch, Arnold R. "Simply a Matter of Black and White: The Transformation of Race and Politics in Twentieth-Century New Orleans." In *Creole New Orleans: Race and Americanization*, edited by Arnold R. Hirsch and Joseph Logsdon, 262–320. Baton Rouge: Louisiana State University Press, 1992.

Hirsch, Arnold R., and Joseph Logsdon. *Creole New Orleans: Race and Americanization*. Baton Rouge: Louisiana State University Press, 1992.

Hodes, Martha Elizabeth. *Sex, Love, Race: Crossing Boundaries in North American History*. New York: New York University Press, 1999.

_____. *White Women, Black Men: Illicit Sex in the Nineteenth-Century South*. New Haven: Yale University Press, 1997.

Holland, Endesha Ida Mae. *From the Mississippi Delta: A Memoir*. Chicago: Lawrence Hill, 1999.

Holland, Patricia, Jo Spence, and Simon Watney. *Photography/Politics: Two*. London: Comedia Publishing Group, 1987.

Horne, Gerald. *Black and Red: W. E. B. Du Bois and the Afro-American Response to the Cold War, 1944–1963*. Albany: SUNY Press, 1986.

Hunter, Tera W. *To 'Joy My Freedom: Southern Black Women's Lives and Labors after the Civil War*. Cambridge, Mass.: Harvard University Press, 1997.

Hunter-Gault, Charlayne. *In My Place*. 7th ed. New York: Vintage, 1993.

Ides, Matthew Allan. "Cruising for Community: Youth Culture and Politics in Los Angeles, 1910–1970." Diss., University of Michigan, 2009.

JanMohamed, Abdul. "Sexuality on/of the Racial Border: Foucault, Wright, and the Articulation of 'Racialized Sexuality.' " In *Discourses of Sexuality*, edited by Domna Stanton, 94–116. Ann Arbor: University of Michigan Press, 1992.

Jenkins, Henry. " 'People from That Part of the World': The Politics of Dislocation." *Cultural Anthropology* 21, no. 3 (August 2006): 469–86.

Judd, Graham. *African American Lives*. DVD. PBS Paramount, 2006.

———. *African American Lives 2*. DVD. PBS Paramount, 2008.

Julien, Eileen M. *Travels with Mae: Scenes from a New Orleans Girlhood*. Bloomington: Indiana University Press, 2009.

Kein, Sybil, ed. *Creole: The History and Legacy of Louisiana's Free People of Color*. Baton Rouge: Louisiana State University Press, 2000.

Kelley, Robin D. G. *Hammer and Hoe: Alabama Communists during the Great Depression*. Chapel Hill: University of North Carolina Press, 1990.

———. *Race Rebels: Culture, Politics, and the Black Working Class*. New York: Free Press, 1994.

Kristeva, Julia. *Powers of Horror: An Essay on Abjection*. Translated by Leon S. Roudiez. New York: Columbia University Press, 1982.

Kunzel, Regina. "Pulp Fictions and Problem Girls: Reading and Rewriting Single Pregnancy in the Postwar United States." *American Historical Review* 100, no. 5 (December 1995): 1465–87.

Laborde, Peggy Scott, and John Magill. *Canal Street: New Orleans' Great Wide Way*. Gretna, La.: Pelican, 2006.

Lewis, Earl. *In Their Own Interests: Race, Class and Power in Twentieth-Century Norfolk, Virginia*. Berkeley: University of California Press, 1993.

Lindenmeyer, Kriste. *The Greatest Generation Grows Up: American Childhood in the 1930s*. Chicago: Ivan R. Dee, 2007.

Lipsitz, George. "Learning from New Orleans: The Social Warrant of Hostile Privatism and Competitive Consumer Citizenship." *Cultural Anthropology* 21, no. 3 (August 2006): 451–68.

———. "Mardi Gras Indians: Carnival and Counter-Narrative in Black New Orleans." *Cultural Critique*, no. 10 (October 1, 1988): 99–121. doi:10.2307/1354109.

Litwack, Leon F. *Trouble in Mind: Black Southerners in the Age of Jim Crow*. New York: Knopf, 1998.

Long, Alecia P. *The Great Southern Babylon: Sex, Race, and Respectability in New Orleans, 1865–1920*. Baton Rouge: Louisiana State University Press, 2004.

Lorde, Audre. *Sister Outsider: Essays and Speeches*. Berkeley: Crossing Press, 2007.

Love, Heather. *Feeling Backward: Loss and the Politics of Queer History*. Cambridge, Mass.: Harvard University Press, 2007.

Martinez, Elsie, and Margaret Lecorgne. *Uptown/Downtown: Growing Up in New Orleans*. Lafayette: University of Southwestern Louisiana, 1986.

May, Elaine Tyler. *Homeward Bound: American Families in the Cold War Era*. 2nd rev. and updated ed. New York: Basic, 2008.

Maynes, Mary Jo, Jennifer L. Pierce, and Barbara Laslett. *Telling Stories: The Use of Personal Narratives in the Social Sciences and History*. Ithaca: Cornell University Press, 2008.

McGuire, Danielle L. *At the Dark End of the Street: Black Women, Rape, and Resistance; A New History of the Civil Rights Movement from Rosa Parks to the Rise of Black Power*. New York: Random House, 2010.

McKee, James B. *Sociology and the Race Problem: The Failure of a Perspective*. Urbana: University of Illinois Press, 1993.

McKittrick, Katherine. *Demonic Grounds: Black Women and the Cartographies of Struggle*. Minneapolis: University of Minnesota Press, 2006.

McKittrick, Katherine, and Clyde Woods. *Black Geographies and the Politics of Place*. Cambridge, Mass.: South End, 2007.

McMillen, Neil R. *Dark Journey: Black Mississippians in the Age of Jim Crow*. Urbana: University of Illinois Press, 1990.

McPherson, Natasha. "Creole Women of Color and the Making of a Community in 19th-Century New Orleans." Diss., Emory University, forthcoming.

Mitchell, Mary Niall. *Raising Freedom's Child: Black Children and Visions of the Future after Slavery*. New York: New York University Press, 2008.

Mitchell, Michele. *Righteous Propagation: African Americans and the Politics of Racial Destiny after Reconstruction*. Chapel Hill: University of North Carolina Press, 2004.

Mohr, Clarence L., and Joseph E. Gordon. *Tulane: The Emergence of a Modern University, 1945–1980*. Baton Rouge: Louisiana State University Press, 2001.

Moore, Leonard N. *Carl B. Stokes and the Rise of Black Political Power*. Champaign: University of Illinois Press, 2003.

Morrison, Toni. "The Site of Memory." In *Out There: Marginalization and Contemporary Cultures*, edited by Russell Ferguson, Marath Gever, Trinh T. Minh-ha, and Cornel West, 299–306. Cambridge, Mass.: MIT Press, 1990.

Ngai, Sianne. *Ugly Feelings*. Cambridge, Mass.: Harvard University Press, 2005.

Odem, Mary. *Delinquent Daughters: Protecting and Policing Adolescent Female Sexuality in the United States, 1885–1920*. Chapel Hill: University of North Carolina Press, 1995.

Orleck, Annelise. *Storming Caesar's Palace: How Black Mothers Fought Their Own War on Poverty*. Boston: Beacon Press, 2005.

Oshinsky, David M. *Worse Than Slavery: Parchman Farm and the Ordeal of Jim Crow Justice*. New York: Free Press, 1997.

Painter, Nell Irvin. *Southern History across the Color Line*. Chapel Hill: University of North Carolina Press, 2002.

Peiss, Kathy. *Cheap Amusements: Working Women and Leisure in Turn-of-the-Century New York*. Philadelphia: Temple University Press, 1986.

Peiss, Kathy, and Christina Simmons. "Passion and Power: An Introduction." In *Passion and Power: Sexuality in History*, edited by Kathy Peiss, Christina Simmons, and Robert A. Padgug, 3–31. Philadelphia: Temple University Press, 1989.

Reynolds, Pamela. *Violence and Subjectivity*. Edited by Veena Das, Arthur Kleinman, and Mamphela Ramphele. Oakland: University of California Press, 2000.

Riccardi, Nicholas, and David Zucchino. "Families Lose Loved Ones Again—in a Bureaucratic Mire." *Los Angeles Times*, October 2, 2005.

Rich, B. Ruby. "Feminism and Sexuality in the 1980s," *Feminist Studies* 12, no. 3 (Autumn 1996): 525–61.

Richardson, Mattie Udora. "No More Secrets, No More Lies: African American History and Compulsory Heterosexuality." *Journal of Women's History* 15, no. 3 (2003): 63–76.

Ritterhouse, Jennifer Lynn. *Growing Up Jim Crow: How Black and White Southern Children Learned Race*. Chapel Hill: University of North Carolina Press, 2006.

Rogers, Kim Lacy. *Righteous Lives: Narratives of the New Orleans Civil Rights Movement*. New York: New York University Press, 1994.

"Rosa Parks Account Describes Attempted Rape." *All Things Considered*. National Public Radio, August 1, 2011.

Rosen, Hannah. *Terror in the Heart of Freedom: Citizenship, Sexual Violence, and the Meaning of Race in the Postemancipation South*. Chapel Hill: University of North Carolina Press, 2009.

Rosenwein, Barbara. "Worrying about Emotions in History." *American Historical Review* 107, no. 3 (June 2002): 821–45.

Ross, Marlon Bryan. *Manning the Race: Reforming Black Men in the Jim Crow Era*. New York: New York University Press, 2004.

Rumpf, Eva Augustin. *Reclamation: Memories from a New Orleans Girlhood*. Booklocker.com, 2009.

Ryan, Mary P. *Women in Public: Between Banners and Ballots, 1825–1880*. Baltimore: Johns Hopkins University Press, 1992.

Sanchez-Eppler, Karen. *Dependent States: The Child's Part in Nineteenth-Century American Culture*. Chicago: University of Chicago Press, 2005.

Sancton, Tom, and Tommy Sancton. *Song for My Fathers: A New Orleans Story in Black and White*. New York: Other Press, 2006.

Sartain, Lee. *Invisible Activists: Women of the Louisiana NAACP and the Struggle for Civil Rights, 1915–1945*. Baton Rouge: Louisiana State University Press, 2007.

Scarry, Elaine. *The Body in Pain: The Making and Unmaking of the World*. New York: Oxford University Press, 1985.

Schrum, Kelly. *Some Wore Bobby Sox: The Emergence of Teenage Girls' Culture, 1920–1945*. New York: Palgrave Macmillan, 2004.

Sedgwick, Eve. *Touching Feeling: Affect, Pedagogy, Performativity*. Durham: Duke University Press, 2003.

Shaw, Stephanie. "Using the WPA Ex-slave Narratives to Study the Impact of the Great Depression." *Journal of Southern History* 69, no. 3 (2003): 623–58.

———. *What a Woman Ought to Be and to Do*. Chicago: University of Chicago Press, 1996.

Sheffield, Carole. "Sexual Terrorism." In *Sexualities: Identities, Behaviors and Society*, edited by Michael Kimmel and Rebecca F. Plante, 409–23. New York: Oxford University Press, 2004.

Simmons, LaKisha Michelle. "'Justice Mocked': Violence and Accountability in New Orleans." *American Quarterly* 61, no. 3 (2009): 477–98.

———. "'To Lay Aside All Morals': Respectability, Sexuality, and Black College Students in the 1930s." *Gender and History* 24, no. 2 (2012): 431–55.

Smith, Shawn Michelle. *Photography on the Color Line : W. E. B. Du Bois, Race, and Visual Culture*. Durham: Duke University Press, 2004.

Smith, Sidonie, and Julia Watson. *Reading Autobiography: A Guide for Interpreting Life Narratives*. Minneapolis: University of Minnesota Press, 2001.

Smith-Rosenberg, Carroll. *Disorderly Conduct: Visions of Gender in Victorian America*. New York: Oxford University Press, 1986.

Snitow, Ann, Christine Stansell, and Sharon Thompson, eds. *Powers of Desire: The Politics of Sexuality*. New York: Monthly Press Review, 1983.

Solinger, Rickie. *Wake Up Little Susie: Single Pregnancy and Race before* Roe v. Wade. 2nd ed. New York: Routledge, 2000.

Somers, Dale. "Black and White in New Orleans: A Study in Urban Race Relations, 1865–1900." *Journal of Southern History* 40, no. 1 (February 1974): 19–42.

Somerville, Siobhan B. *Queering the Color Line: Race and the Invention of Homosexuality in American Culture*. Series Q. Durham: Duke University Press, 2000.

Spillers, Hortense. "Interstices: A Small Drama of Words." In *Pleasure and Danger: Exploring Female Sexuality*, edited by Carole S. Vance, 73–100. Boston: Routledge and Kegan Paul, 1984.

Stanonis, Anthony J. *Creating the Big Easy: New Orleans and the Emergence of Modern Tourism, 1918–1945*. Athens: University of Georgia Press, 2006.

Stearns, Peter N. "Challenges in the History of Childhood." *Journal of the History of Childhood and Youth* 1, no. 1 (2007): 34–42.

Tardy, Jo Anne. *A Light Will Rise in Darkness: Growing Up Black and Catholic in New Orleans*. Chicago: ACTA Publications, 2006.

Taylor, Diana. *The Archive and the Repertoire: Performing Cultural Memory in the Americas.* Durham: Duke University Press, 2003.

Terada, Rei. *Feeling in Theory: Emotion after the "Death of the Subject."* Cambridge, Mass.: Harvard University Press, 2003.

Tettenborn, Éva. "Melancholia as Resistance in Contemporary African American Literature." *MELUS* 31, no. 3 (Fall 2006): 101–21. doi:10.2307/30029653.

Thomas, Lynnell. "Kissing Ass and Other Performative Acts of Resistance: Austin, Fanon, and New Orleans Tourism." *Performance Research* 12, no. 3 (September 2007): 137–45.

Thompson, Shirley. "'Ah Toucoutou, Ye Conin Vous': History and Memory in Creole New Orleans." *American Quarterly* 53, no. 2 (2001): 232–66.

Trethewey, Natasha D. *Beyond Katrina: A Meditation on the Mississippi Gulf Coast.* Athens: University of Georgia Press, 2012.

Trost, Jennifer. *Gateway to Justice: The Juvenile Court and Progressive Child Welfare in a Southern City.* Athens: University of Georgia Press, 2005.

Trouillot, Michel-Rolph. *Silencing the Past.* Boston: Beacon Press, 1997.

Valverde, Mariana. "Beyond Gender Dangers and Private Pleasures: Theory and Ethics in the Sex Debates." *Feminist Studies* 15, no. 2 (Summer 1989): 237–54. doi:10.2307/3177786.

Vance, Carole S., ed. *Pleasure and Danger: Exploring Female Sexuality.* Boston: Routledge and Kegan Paul, 1984.

Vaz, Kim Marie. *The "Baby Dolls": Breaking the Race and Gender Barriers of the New Orleans Mardi Gras Tradition.* Baton Rouge: Louisiana State University Press, 2013.

Walker, Margaret. "Growing Out of Shadow." In *How I Wrote* Jubilee: *And Other Essays on Life and Literature,* edited by Maryemma Graham, 3–9. New York: Feminist Press at City University of New York, 1990.

Walkowitz, Judith. *City of Dreadful Delight: Narratives of Sexual Danger in Late-Victorian London.* Chicago: University of Chicago Press, 1992.

_____. "Going Public: Shopping, Street Harassment, and Streetwalking in Late Victorian London." *Representations* 62 (Spring 1998): 1–30.

Warner, Michael. "Publics and Counterpublics." *Public Culture* 14, no. 1 (2002): 49–90.

Warren, Wendy Anne. "'The Cause of Her Grief': The Rape of a Slave in Early New England." *Journal of American History* 93, no. 4 (March 2007): 1031–49.

Washington, Harriet A. *Medical Apartheid: The Dark History of Medical Experimentation on Black Americans from Colonial Times to the Present.* New York: Doubleday, 2007.

Weisenfeld, Judith. *African American Women and Christian Activism: New York's Black YWCA, 1905–1945.* Cambridge, Mass.: Harvard University Press, 1998.

Wexler, Laura. *Tender Violence: Domestic Visions in an Age of U.S. Imperialism.* Chapel Hill: University of North Carolina Press, 2000.

Whinery, Barbara. "Harl R. Douglass." In *The Encyclopedia of Middle Grades Education,* edited by Vincent A. Anfara, Gayle Andrews, and Steven B. Mertens. 108. Greenwich: Information Age Publishing, 2005.

White, Deborah Gray. *Too Heavy a Load: Black Women in Defense of Themselves, 1894–1994.* New York: W. W. Norton, 1999.

Williams, Rhonda. "I'm a Keeper of Information: History-Telling and Voice." *Oral History Review* 28, no. 1 (Winter/Spring 2001): 41–63.

Williamson, Joel. *New People: Miscegenation and Mulattoes in the United States.* Baton Rouge: Louisiana State University Press, 1995.

Wolcott, Victoria W. *Race, Riots, and Roller Coasters: The Struggle over Segregated Recreation in America*. Philadelphia: University of Pennsylvania Press, 2012.

_____. *Remaking Respectability: African American Women in Interwar Detroit*. Chapel Hill: University of North Carolina Press, 2001.

Wolf, Peter M. *My New Orleans, Gone Away: A Memoir of Loss and Renewal*. Harrison, N.Y.: Delphinium, 2013.

Woods, Clyde Adrian. "Do You Know What It Means to Miss New Orleans? Katrina, Trap Economics, and the Rebirth of the Blues." *American Quarterly* 57, no. 4 (2005): 1005–18.

Woolfork, Lisa. *Embodying American Slavery in Contemporary Culture*. Chicago: University of Illinois Press, 2008.

Young, Iris Marion. "Abjection and Oppression: Dynamics of Unconscious Racism, Sexism, and Homophobia." In *Crises in Continental Philosophy*, edited by Arleen Dallery, Charles Scott, and Holley Roberts, 201–14. Albany: State University of New York Press, 1990.

_____. *On Female Body Experience: "Throwing Like a Girl" and Other Essays*. New York: Oxford University Press, 2005.

Zinn, Howard. "The Greatest Generation?" *Progressive* 65, no. 10 (October 2001): 12.

Index

McKinney, Robert, 69, 70

Mead, Margaret, 7

Mental maps: childhood learning, 27, 52, 215; and race, 28, 34, 41, 54, 59, 68; and home, 30, 47, 220 (n. 9); and safety or danger, 42, 51, 55, 57–58, 78, 80, 81

Merrick, Olga, 57, 61, 77, 78

Million Dollar Baby Dolls, 196, 200

Mississippi, 1, 32, 83, 140, 211, 227 (n. 31); Greenwood, 26, 30; Indianola, 85, 115–16; Natchez, 114

Mississippi River, 34, 41

Mitchell, Michele, 90,

Moore, Audley, 57

Motherhood, 5, 57, 101, 125, 127–29, 151

Mount Zion Methodist, 76

Moutan, Jesse Lawrence, 79

National Association for the Advancement of Colored People (NAACP), 21, 68, 93, 100, 105, 106

Negro Girls Club, 47, 48, 51

Negro Youth Study (NYS), 110–14, 116–19, 122, 124, 132

New Deal, 22, 110

New Orleans: population distribution, 7, 14, 19–21, 28; uptown/downtown distinctions, 11, 29–33; antebellum history, 14, 19. See also Geography

New Orleans Recreation Department (NORD), 54, 55

New Orleans States, 97

New Orleans Times-Picayune, 96, 141, 166

New Orleans Young Progressives, 157–59

Oral history method, 15, 112, 113

Original Illinois Club, 203

Orleans Ballroom, 34–38

Pain, 81, 90, 96, 102, 157, 188, 208

Painter, Nell, 18, 208

Pajeaud, Marjoire, 32

Paradoxical space. See Geography

Passing, racial, 62–63

Peete's Pharmacy, 108

Peiss, Kathy, 185

Peters, Mercadel Renette, 211

Piacum, Matt, 82, 94

Pierre, Sister Claire of Assisi, 38, 40, 41, 213, 214

Pittsburgh Courier, 69, 98

Plaçage, 35

Place. See Geography

Play, 42, 46, 49, 108, 203; clubs, 47, 190, 191; sports, 48, 83, 184; parties, 48, 190, 192–93, 198, 199, 203; playgrounds, 51, 52, 71. See also New Orleans Recreation Department

Pleasure, 15, 16, 18, 23, 190, 214, 239 (n. 4); on Rampart Street, 70, 80; and sex, 136–38, 153, 156–57, 176; and make-believe, 175, 187, 192–94; pleasure cultures, 178–80, 189, 191, 194, 195, 198, 199, 202–5, 215; and writing, 183–84, 186; and romance, 185, 189; and intimacy, 188

Plessy v. Ferguson, 29, 94

Plum Orchard, 139, 213

Poetry, 101, 102, 180, 182, 183, 186–89, 207, 211

Police, 67, 76, 132, 149, 153–56; brutality, 14, 56, 82, 88, 93–107, 118; and sexual harassment, 57, 67, 91–92, 112, 157–60, 228 (n. 67)

Powdermaker, Hortense, 116

Progressive Era, 104, 143, 144

Protestantism: ministers, 76, 77, 182; baptismal, 126, 176; churches, 127, 179

Psychoanalysis, 113, 115, 117

Pythian Temple, 198, 199, 204

Quadroon Balls. See Orleans Ballroom

Racial slurs, incidents of, 21, 46, 49, 57, 93, 159, 201

Rampart Street, 22, 32, 68–80, 108, 179, 224 (n. 37)

Rape: black men accused of, 1–2, 56, 86, 98; of black girls, 1, 4, 15, 82–84, 86–94, 97–8, 100, 102–3, 150, 156; of black women, 2–3, 85, 86–87. See also Sexual harassment

Reconstruction, 27

Reed, Calrita, 56–58, 71, 72, 75, 78

Religion. See Catholicism; Protestantism

Respatialization. See Geography

Respectability, 38, 40, 107, 118, 123, 127, 130, 199, 215; class status, 4–5, 14, 22, 72, 100, 116, 124–25, 134, 146; sexual respectability, 15, 57,

White, E. Frances, 177
Whiteness, 20, 34, 50, 95, 105, 106, 194, 203
Wicker Junior High School, 67, 122, 123, 134, 197, 198
William, Hattie Louise, 81
Williams, Lois, 186
Williams Chapel Methodist Church, 179
Wilson, Julia, 118–20, 138
Wingrave, John, 163,
Work, 166; domestic work, 5, 42, 66, 82, 83, 90, 110, 123, 126, 129, 152, 166, 172, 179, 227 (n. 31); unemployment, 22; father's job, 41–42, 71, 108; cook, 69; waitressing, 90, 93; seamstress, 90, 108

Work Progress Administration (WPA), 68, 69, 112
World War II, 19, 21

Xavier University, 101, 137, 157–58, 160
Xavier University Prep, 30, 32, 207

Young, Iris Marion, 33, 106
Young Men's Illinois Club, 198, 199
Young Progressives of America. *See* New Orleans Young Progressives
Youth problem, 4, 7, 146

Zulu King, 195–97